Emily Elizabeth Constance Jones

Elements of Logic as a Science of Propositions

Emily Elizabeth Constance Jones
Elements of Logic as a Science of Propositions
ISBN/EAN: 9783337034801
Printed in Europe, USA, Canada, Australia, Japan
Cover: Foto ©Thomas Meinert / pixelio.de

More available books at **www.hansebooks.com**

ELEMENTS OF LOGIC AS A SCIENCE
OF PROPOSITIONS.

PRINTED BY MORRISON AND GIBB,
FOR
T. & T. CLARK, EDINBURGH,

LONDON,	HAMILTON, ADAMS, AND CO.
DUBLIN,	GEORGE HERBERT.
NEW YORK,	SCRIBNER AND WELFORD.

ELEMENTS OF LOGIC

AS A

SCIENCE OF PROPOSITIONS.

BY

E. E. CONSTANCE JONES,

LECTURER IN MORAL SCIENCES, GIRTON COLLEGE, CAMBRIDGE;
JOINT-TRANSLATOR AND EDITOR OF LOTZE'S "MICROCOSMUS."

EDINBURGH:
T. & T. CLARK, 38 GEORGE STREET.
1890.

PREFACE.

The following pages have grown out of an attempt to reach, point by point, some solution of various questions in Logic, which, both in learning and in teaching, I have felt to be special sources of difficulty. The continued use of Jevons's *Elementary Lessons in Logic* with beginners, has particularly contributed to keep these problems before my mind; for Jevons's little book, though full of interest and suggestion, is not free from inconsistencies and confusions in connection with the questions referred to.

Having reached apparent solutions of some difficulties, and finding that these solutions are, as it seems to me, consistent among themselves, and in harmony with a certain general view of Logic which I take, I am desirous to submit what I have written to the test of publication.

I at first intended to call this collection of chapters "Notes"; but as objections to this name, which I could not gainsay, were put before me, I have adopted the present title; meaning to convey by it, not that the following pages are intended for beginners, but that they present what is necessary for indicating the outlines of the Science of Logic as I conceive it. What I most strongly feel the need of, and what I should have preferred to attempt to write, is an elementary handbook, corresponding in some respects to Jevons's; but I think that certain divergences of my view from current views require an amount of explanation and justification which would be out of place in a book intended for beginners.

The very large number of references introduced is due to two causes. First, to the wish to confirm my opinion by that of accepted authorities when the two seem to accord; and secondly, to the desire to indicate as precisely as possible, in cases of difference, the doctrines which I am combating.

I am greatly indebted to the kindness of Mr. W. E. Johnson, of King's College, who read through most of my sections as they originally stood in manuscript, and whose judicious and penetrating criticism has enabled me to work out some points in my own view more fully and clearly, to avoid several inconsistencies, and to correct some serious mistakes. It would take too long to specify in detail all the cases referred to; but I ought to mention that Mr. Johnson's views differ from mine on some points of fundamental importance.[1]

I am also under very great obligations to Mr. J. N. Keynes, of Pembroke College, who has been so kind as to read the proofs of this book, and whose criticisms have been most valuable to me, though I have not, in every case, been able to accept them. This has (in part) necessarily resulted from a general difference of view—a difference which is clearly seen by reference to Mr. Keynes's work on *Formal Logic*, the name of which occurs so often in the following pages.

I should like to say that I trace the distinction which I have drawn between Independent and Dependent Categorical Propositions, and, indeed, I believe my whole view of the Import of Categoricals, to a suggestion received from some strictures on Locke's treatment of propositions, in a lecture (heard several years ago) of Professor Sidgwick's. And it was some remarks of Professor Sidgwick's, indicating the confusion between logical and psychological points of view in Mill, that first made me feel the necessity of treating Logic as a non-psychological Science.

I must also mention that I am indebted to Mr. Alfred Sidgwick for criticisms that have helped me to put several points more clearly.

Girton College, Cambridge,
November 30, 1889.

---

[1] The Import of Hypothetical and Disjunctive Propositions, and some questions connected with Predication and Existence, should perhaps be specially indicated.

CONTENTS.

PART I.—IMPORT OF PROPOSITIONS.

(I.)—OF TERMS AS ELEMENTS OF PROPOSITIONS.

SECTION I. (INTRODUCTORY).

DEFINITION OF LOGIC.

Logic may be defined as the Science of the Import and Relations of Propositions, or more briefly, as the Science of Propositions. Logic is not psychological,[1] both because it is not subjective and because it is of universal application. It starts from the standpoint of ordinary thought, and assumes reason in man and trustworthiness in language, ... pp. 1–3

SECTION II.

NAMES AND TERMS.

Names are to be distinguished from *Terms*. In All R is P, the Terms are All R, and P. All R, the Subject-term, consists of Term-name (or Term-sign) (R)+Term-indicator (All). A *Name* is a word or group of words applying to a thing, or things. A *Thing* is whatever has Existence (Quantitiveness) and Character (Qualitiveness). A *Term* is any word or combination of words occurring in a Categorical Proposition, and applying to that of which something is asserted (S), or that which is asserted of it (P). *Denomination* of a Name or Term corresponds to Quantitiveness of a Thing; and *Attribution* of a Name or Term corresponds to Qualitiveness of a Thing. All Names have both Denomination and Attribution. *Determination* is Attribution in as far as *explicitly* signified. *Implication* is Attribution in as far as only implied. The Determination of any Name includes the Attribute of being called by that Name. By *Import* of a Name or Term is signified its Denomination together with its Attribution. Things are either (1) Subjects of Attributes, or (2) Attributes. The names which apply to (1) are *Substantival Names;* those which apply to (2) are *Attribute Names*. The Characterization of Attributes, as well as of Subjects, is largely effected by (3) *Adjectival Names*, which can never occur as Subject, but only as Predicate, of a Cate-

[1] For the distinction of Psychology from other Sciences, cf. *Encyclopædia Britannica*, 9th edition, part 77, p. 3ª, article *Psychology*.

gorical Proposition. Substantival Names are subdivided into (a) Common, (b) Special, (c) Unique Names, ... pp. 3-15

Tables I. II. (Adjectival Terms), ... pp. 16, 17

Table III. (Names), ... p. 18

SECTION III.

TERMS.

The characteristics of terms often cannot be settled without reference to the propositions of which they are terms. Still, many of the most important distinctions in *propositions* depend upon differences in the *terms*, especially in the Subject Terms. The widest distinction between terms is that between Uni-terminal or Adjectival Terms—terms which can only be used as Predicates of propositions; and Bi-terminal Terms—terms which may be used both as Subjects and as Predicates. The principal division of these is into Attribute Terms and Substantive Terms. Among the further subdivisions of terms a specially important one is that into Dependent or Systemic (implying a dependence or relation of subjects of attributes connected in some system, which may be of any degree of complexity, from the simplicity of a class or of any two related subjects to the intricacy of a genealogical tree, or even of the universe itself) and Independent. From a proposition containing a Systemic Term — *e.g.* E is equal-to-F — a number of Immediate Inferences can be drawn in addition to those which can be drawn from other propositions, ... pp. 19-25

Tables IV.-XVI. (Terms), ... pp. 25-34

SECTION IV.

NOTE ON DEFINITION AND CONNOTATION.

The definition of a name sets forth its meaning, and the meaning of a name is said to be its *Connotation*. Connotation has been understood in various senses; but the best view seems to be that what a name connotes is *those attributes on account of which we apply the name, and in the absence of any of which we should not apply it*, ... pp. 35-37

SECTION V.

THE MEANING OF *ABSTRACT* AND *CONCRETE*, AND OF *CONCEPT*.

An examination of the definitions and use of the terms Abstract and Concrete by different logical writers reveals an inconsistency between the various statements of the same writer and a divergence between different writers, that indicate considerable difficulty in the distinction which is had in view. It will not do to say that an Abstract Term, as opposed to a Concrete Term, means a term the application of which presupposes a process of abstraction—for this is true of every significant term. And we do not escape difficulty by saying that a Concrete Name is the name of a Subject of Attributes, while an Abstract Name is the name of an Attribute of Subjects. Nor is it satisfactory to restrict the application of Abstract Term to *Concepts*, whether Concept means *something complete in itself and isolated from all else*, or *the mental equivalent of a general name*, ... pp. 37-44

(II.)—OF PROPOSITIONS AS WHOLES.

(A.)—CATEGORICAL PROPOSITIONS.

SECTION VI.

IMPORT AND CLASSIFICATION OF CATEGORICAL PROPOSITIONS.

Formal (most General) Import of Categoricals.

Having treated Terms, the elements of Categorical Propositions, as applying to *things*, and not to the mental process of apprehending things, it would be incongruous to define a Categorical Proposition as *the expression of a Judgment;* and, moreover, this would leave us still asking for the definition of Judgment. A Categorical Proposition may be defined as—A Proposition which affirms, or negates (= absolutely denies), Identity of Denomination in Diversity of Determination. Or it might be defined more briefly as—A Proposition which asserts Identity (or Non-Identity) in Diversity (cf. Section XXVII. By *Non-Identity* I mean *Complete absence of Identity*), pp. 44–54

Classification of Categorical Propositions.

The primary division of Categorical Propositions is into Adjectival and Coincidental (cf. p. 21). Most of the further subdivisions of Categoricals are summed up in Table XVII. p. 62, and the whole are given in detail in the Tables, pp. 62–76. Important differences in use, depending on differences of relation to other propositions, are connected with the differences of form exhibited in the Tables, ... pp. 54–61

Tables XVII.–XXXI. (Categorical Propositions), . pp. 62–76

SECTION VII.

NOTE ON THE PREDICABLES.

In the doctrine of Predicables we are concerned with the *matter* of propositions. In the accounts of Predicables we find confusion of points of view and of the elements concerned; and, in particular, confusion between Denomination and Determination, ... pp. 76–78

SECTION VIII.

MILL'S VIEW OF THE IMPORT OF PROPOSITIONS.

Any general differences in ordinary Categorical Propositions, beyond those already noticed, depend upon either—I. Relations of Determination between S-name and P-name, and under this head comes Mill's distinction between Real and Verbal Propositions. Or II. Determination of S-name, or of P-name, or of both. Under this head comes Mill's division of propositions into Propositions of Existence, Co-existence, Sequence, Causation, and Resemblance. Mill's application of these Categories to the Import of Categorical Propositions is strained, and he confuses Formal and Material (Non-Formal) points of view, ... pp. 79–81

SECTION IX.

SYSTEMIC OR DEPENDENT PROPOSITIONS.

The characteristic which distinguishes Systemic or Dependent Propositions from Independent Propositions is this:—In Systemic Propositions—such as, D is equal to F, A is like B—of the two terms (S and P) one applies to some thing or group of things, and the other expresses *the relation of that thing or group to a second thing or group.* Hence it is possible for a person knowing the system referred to, to draw more inferences from Dependent Propositions than from Independent Propositions. A *fortiori* arguments, and other arguments containing Dependent Propositions, can, with the help of Immediate Inferences, always be expressed in strict syllogistic form, pp. 82–84

SECTION X.

NOTE ON MATHEMATICAL PROPOSITIONS.

The copula = in Mathematical Propositions is to be understood as meaning *is equal to* (i.e. *is exactly similar quantitatively*); and since a thing cannot be said to be *equal* to *itself*, the terms of Mathematical Propositions (taking = as the copula) must have different denominations, *i.e.* they must apply to different things. Hence the terms of Mathematical Propositions can be quantified with *any*, only when they have the most abstract application possible, *i.e.* when they apply to numbers generally, and are not understood to refer to some assigned unit (cf. Sections IX. and XXVII.), . pp. 84–86

SECTION XI.

PREDICATION AND EXISTENCE.

The view that Universal Categoricals *do not* (while Particulars *do*) imply the "existence" of what is referred to by S and P, and the interpretation of All S is P, No S is P, to mean $Sp = 0$, $SP = 0$, respectively, are not to be accepted. For *first*, if we take "existence" in the widest possible sense, to deny that our terms *do apply* and *are meant to apply* to what has a minimum of existence of some kind, implies the view that our terms do not apply, or are not meant to apply, to *things* at all. It also cuts off all possibility of positing or implying existence in general (except in what appears to me to be a wholly arbitrary, and therefore inadmissible, way). But *second*, "existence" may be taken to mean "membership of the Universe of Discourse." On such a view, our Universe of Discourse may be (1) all-embracing, or (2) restricted. Let X represent the Universe of Discourse. Then if (1), it follows that Everything is X. But this by Obversion gives us Nothing is x. Here we have transcended our Universe, so it was not all-embracing. And similarly with restricted Universes, whenever we *mention* our Universe, we can transcend it. And in interpreting All S is P, as $Sp = 0$, we do transcend it; for since O is not X, it must be x. And when we transcend X, and talk of what is x, there seems no reason why we should call X rather than x, or than X $+$ x, our Universe of Discourse. And $Sp = 0$ must mean either $SpX = 0$ ($= SpX = x$)—in which case we have a contradiction in terms—or $Spx = x$, in which case both our terms refer to the region x and not to X. Among the inconveniences involved by the view which this Section attempts to refute are the following:—Universals and Particulars are to be differently interpreted, and no interpretation can be given to S is P, S is-not P; Subversions and Conversions of A are not valid inferences;[1] All S is P and No S is P may be asserted together, ... pp. 86-102

SECTION XII.

(B.) INFERENTIAL PROPOSITIONS.

An Inferential Proposition is a Proposition expressing a relation between Antecedent and Consequent, such that an identity (or identities) *expressed or indicated* by the Consequent is an inference from an identity (or identities) *expressed or indicated* by the Antecedent. Inferential Propositions may be (1) Hypothetical, or (2) Conditional. A Hypothetical Proposition is one in which two (expressed or indicated) Categoricals (or combinations of Categoricals) are combined in such a way as to express that one (Consequent) is an inference from the other (Antecedent). A Conditional Proposition is one which asserts that any object which is indicated by a given class-name and distinguished in some particular way, may be inferred to have also some further distinction. The import of an Inferential may be expressed in a Categorical of the form, *C is an inference from A*. Hypotheticals are either Self-contained or Referential. Conditionals are either Divisional or Quasi-Divisional. Conditionals (but not all Hypotheticals) are reducible to Categoricals of the form, Any E that is F, is H; and it is only Categoricals of this form that are reducible to Conditionals, ... pp. 103-113

Tables XXXII., XXXIII. (Hypothetical and Conditional Propositions),
pp. 114, 115

SECTION XIII.

(C.) ALTERNATIVE PROPOSITIONS.

Alternatives may have some element of unexclusiveness, but must also have some element of exclusiveness, otherwise there is no alternation. In as far as "alternatives" are absolutely unexclusive, they are of the form *A or A*. Where the Alternatives are Propositions, there must be some difference of meaning in the Propositions, or there is no Alternation, and so far there is exclusiveness; but Alternatives may be true together, and so far there is unexclusiveness. Where the Alternatives are Terms, there may be unexclusiveness of denomination, but there must be some exclusiveness of determination. An Alternative Proposition may be defined as—A Proposition in which a plurality of differing elements (connected by *or*, and called the Alternatives) are so related that *not all* of them can be denied, because the denial of some justifies the assertion of the rest. Alternative Propositions may be divided into Classificatory, Quasi-Divisional, and Contingent (cf. Section XXVII.), ... pp. 115-121

Table XXXIV. (Alternative Propositions), . . . p. 122

SECTION XIV.

NOTE ON CLASSIFICATION AND DIVISION.

Division and Classification are the same thing looked at from different points of view: any table presenting a Division presents also a Classification. It is

[1] The Quantification of A would also, I presume, be illegitimate.

CONTENTS.

desirable to distinguish Classification from Classing, and from Systematization, ... pp. 123, 124

SECTION XV.
QUANTIFICATION AND CONVERSION.

Quantification is a necessary stage in the Conversion of Categorical Propositions. It is only Coincidentals that can be quantificated and converted. From the view of the Import of Categoricals advocated in Section VI. it follows that the Quantification of Common Categoricals is always possible, but is only to be admitted as a transformation-stage. This view of Quantification is confirmed by a consideration of the traditional logical treatment of O propositions, ... pp. 124–130

SECTION XVI.
THE MEANING OF *SOME*.

The special force and meaning of propositions in the stage of Quantification depends principally upon the meaning given to *Some*. To define *Some* as meaning "Some but not all," or "Some at least, it may be all," or "Not none," is not satisfactory. It seems best to say that *Some R* means *an indefinite quantity or number of R*. Taking this meaning of Some, Quantification by Some merely makes our terms *explicitly* indeterminate, and the function of Quantification, on the whole, seems to be simply to *bring into prominence the quantitive* (*denominational*) *aspect* of the Predicate, . pp. 130-132

PART II.—RELATIONS OF PROPOSITIONS.

SECTION XVII.
GENERAL REMARKS ON THE RELATIONS OF PROPOSITIONS.

Two Propositions may be related to each other as Incompatible, or Unattached, or Correlative, or Premissal. To any two Promissal Propositions a third proposition may be related, either as inferrible, or as non-inferrible, pp. 133–135

Table XXXV. (Relations of Propositions), ... p. 136

SECTION XVIII.
INFERENCE.

One Proposition is an Inference from another or others, when the assertion of the former is justified by the latter, and the latter is, in some respect, different from the former. An "Inductive" Inference must be allowed to be formal, as well as the Inferences commonly distinguished as "Deductive," and a "Mediate" Inference only differs from an "Immediate" Inference in being more complex, ... pp. 137–141

Table XXXVI. (Inferences), ... p. 142

SECTION XIX.

IMMEDIATE INFERENCES (EDUCTIONS).

When we pass from one proposition to another, and the latter is justified by the former, and differs from it in some respect, the latter is an Immediate Inference (Eduction) from the former. Eductions may have—I. Categoricals (*a*), or Inferentials (*b*), or Alternatives (*c*), for both educt and educend : these may be called Pure Eductions, or Eversions. Or, II. they may have a Categorical with an Inferential (*a*), or a Categorical with an Alternative (*b*), or an Inferential with an Alternative (*c*). These may be called Mixed Eductions or Transversions. There are eight principal kinds of Categorical Eversions (cf. Table, p. 150). The only Inferential Eversion may be most appropriately called Contraversion. There seems to be only one strictly formal Alternative Eversion, which may be called a Converse. In Transversion the most interesting points are that all Inferentials and Alternatives may have their meaning expressed in Categorical form; that Conditionals and Categoricals (of which S and P in the one correspond to A and C in the other) are reciprocally educible; that Inferentials are educible from Alternatives, and Alternatives from Inferentials, and thus the Alternative answering to any Inferential has a corresponding Categorical, educible from the Categorical which answers to the Inferential, ... pp. 143-149

Table XXXVII. (Immediate Inferences or Eductions), . . p. 150

SECTION XX.

INCOMPATIBLE PROPOSITIONS.

Propositions are Incompatible when they cannot both be true. Two Propositions are *Contrary* when they cannot both be true, but may both be false; they are *Contradictory* when they cannot both be true and cannot both be false, ... pp. 151-156

MEDIATE INFERENCES (SYLLOGISMS).

SECTION XXI.

(A.) CATEGORICAL SYLLOGISMS.

The *Dictum de omni et nullo* is merely a formulation of the truth that if any object or objects belong to a class, what can be said about the class (distributively) can be said about it or them. It applies only in cases in which we are dealing with A, E, I, or O propositions. And Jevons's Rule of Inference is not satisfactory. If Syllogism means Formal Mediate Inference, Categorical Syllogism may be defined as—A combination of three categorical propositions, one of which (the Conclusion) is inferred from the other two taken together—these two being called the Premisses, and having in common one term-name which does not occur in the conclusion. The conclusion has its S-name in common with one premiss, and its P-name in common with the other premiss.—And of such Categorical Syllogisms the following may be accepted as Canon :—If the denomination of two terms is identical (or non-identical),[1] any third term which has a different term-name and is denominationally identical with the whole (or a part) of one of those two, is also identical (or non-identical), in whole or part, with the denomination of the other.—The traditional rules of Categorical Syllogism may be condensed, and amended in correspondence with the above Canon, . pp. 156-163

SECTION XXII.

(B.) INFERENTIAL SYLLOGISMS.

Inferential Syllogisms are Syllogisms which have an Inferential Premiss. A Pure Inferential Syllogism (1) is—A Syllogism of which the conclusion and both the premisses are Inferential Propositions. A Mixed Inferential Syllogism (2) is—A Syllogism of which the major premiss is an Inferential Proposition, the minor premiss and the conclusion being Categorical Propositions. (1) May be Hypothetical (a), or Conditional (b); (2) may be Hypothetico-Categorical (c), or Conditio-Categorical (d). There are separate Canons for (a), (b), (c), (d), ... pp. 163-165

Table XXXVIII. (Inferential Syllogisms), ... p. 166

SECTION XXIII.

(C.) ALTERNATIVE SYLLOGISMS.

An Alternative Syllogism is—A Syllogism of which *one* premiss is always an Alternative Proposition or a combination of Alternative Propositions, and of which one premiss and the conclusion, or both premisses, or both premisses and the conclusion, *may be* alternative. Alternative Syllogisms may be Pure (a) or Mixed, and Mixed subdivide into Categorico-Alternative (b), Hypothetico-Alternative (c), and Conditio-Alternative (d). The four classes, (a), (b), (c), (d), have distinct Canons, ... pp. 167, 168

Tables XXXIX., XL. (Alternative Syllogisms), . . pp. 169, 170

SECTION XXIV.

NOTE ON THE GROUND OF INDUCTION.

Cause, as defined by Mill, is a contradictory notion, and all Inductive Inference is based upon the assumption of a certain constant coinherence of attributes in the subjects concerned. In Induction we proceed upon the principle that any subject of attributes that is like another in one respect is like it in a plurality of respects (or that any attribute is one of a set recurring uniformly). With this are connected the further principles, that no subject of attributes is unlike another (or its former self) in one respect only, that no two objects or classes are alike in all respects, and that no two objects or classes are unlike in all respects (cf. Section XXVII.), . . . pp. 171-175

SECTION XXV.

NOTE ON THE LAWS OF THOUGHT.

The Law of Identity is an expression of the permanence of things, of their *identity in diversity*, and is better conveyed by the formula *Every A is B*

---

[1] I take *identical* to mean *completely coincident*, and *non-identical* to mean *altogether uncoincident*.

[or *not B*] than by the strictly unmeaning *A is A*. *If A is B, A is-not non-B*, or *Two contradictory propositions cannot both be affirmed;* and *A is either B or not-B*, or *Two contradictory propositions cannot both be denied*, seem the best formulæ for the Laws of Contradiction and Excluded Middle respectively. These three Laws may be called the Axioms of Logic, and express the three principles (1) of the possibility of significant assertion, (2) of consistency, (3) of inter-relation or reciprocity (cf. p. 206),   pp. 175-178

SECTION XXVI.

FALLACIES.

Confusion should be regarded not as itself Fallacy, but as a *source* of Fallacy. All Fallacy consists (1) in identifying what is different, or (2) in differencing what is identical; thus we get a primary subdivision of Fallacies into those of (1) professed Identification or Discontinuity, (2) professed Difference or Tautology. Fallacy may be defined as—The assertion or assumption of some relation between (i.) Terms, or (ii.) Propositions, which does not hold between them. Or taking the word in a narrower sense, there is Fallacy whenever we conclude from one or more propositions to another, the conclusion not being justified by the premiss or premisses. All Fallacies are reducible to Formal Fallacies—Elemental, or Eductive, or Syllogistic, or Circular (cf. Tables XLI., XLII.), ...   pp. 178-193

Tables XLI., XLII. (Fallacies), ...   pp. 194, 195

SUPPLEMENT.

SECTION XXVII.

RECAPITULATORY.

This Section is, for the most part, a recapitulation, .   .   .   pp. 196-208

PART I.
IMPORT OF PROPOSITIONS.

(I.)—*OF TERMS AS ELEMENTS OF PROPOSITIONS.*

SECTION I. (INTRODUCTORY).

DEFINITION OF LOGIC.

To provide a satisfactory definition of Logic is admittedly difficult. The definitions which have actually been given differ among themselves; and in many cases an author's definition does not seem to apply directly and naturally to the topics of which he subsequently treats. For instance, Jevons says that Logic is the Science of Reasoning, or the Science of the Laws of Thought (*Elementary Lessons in Logic*, Less. I.), and then proceeds to consider Terms, Propositions, Immediate Inference, Fallacies, Method, Induction, Abstraction, etc., to some of which subjects, certainly, the definition does not obviously and without straining apply.

He suggests, however, another and, I think, a more satisfactory definition when, in the *Elementary Lessons* (p. 69, 7th edition; cf. also *op. cit.*, Preface, p. vi.), he speaks of Logic as treating of "the relations of the different propositions and the inferences which can be drawn from them" (*inferences*, of course, come under the head of relations).[1] In accordance with this suggestion, I propose to define Logic as the *Science of the Import and Relations of Propositions*, or more briefly, as the *Science of Propositions*.

[1] Cf. also Mill, *Logic*, Bk. i. ch. i. § 2, and Boole, *Laws of Thought*, p. 7.

All the subjects usually treated in handbooks of Logic come simply and naturally under the above definition, and are conveniently classifiable. We may, I think, without any violence include a consideration of Names and Terms, which are elements of propositions; a consideration of Predicables and Categories, of Definition, of the meaning of Categorical and other propositions, and of Quantification, comes under the head of "Import of Propositions;" Opposition and Immediate Inference, Syllogism, Analogy, Induction, Scientific Explanation, Fallacy, etc., would be included in "Relations of Propositions."

Logic is *objective*, for it relates to *objects* of thought; *universal*, for it applies to *all* objects. As concerned with objects known, it implies a knower. But all sciences imply a knower, all deal with objects. It is because of an unique characteristic—pervading explicit reference of *known Object* to *knowing Subject*—that Psychology is called "subjective": the knower *quâ* knower is not *the known* even in Psychology. Logic, I think, just as much *applies to* and just as little *is* Psychology, as it applies to or is any other science; and I do not see why, if we are studying the *mental processes* concerned in Inference, etc., we should call our study Logic and not Psychology. We can only tell in any case of reasoning whether our *processes* have been right—*i.e.* logical—by comparing the proposition which states our result with the propositions which state our data. If we regard Logic as concerned with the elements, import, and relations of assertions expressed in language, we have assigned to it a sphere coextensive with knowledge itself, and in accordance with the general recognition of it as *fundamental* and *of universal application*, and with its old name *Science of Sciences*. The burden of proof lies with those who narrow this sphere, and call it *psychological*, or *metaphysical*, or *physical*, or anything else except *logical*.

Since, however, Logic is admittedly concerned with Truth, —with *what we ought to think*—and propositions are valuable only as a means of arriving at and expressing Truth, it might be asked, Why not define it at once as the Science of Truth?

To this, I think, a twofold answer might be made; for first, the use of the word *Propositions* instead of *Truth* in the definition seems to simplify both the application and the articulation of the science; and second, there is no way of expressing truth except in propositions, and no way of testing any truth which is called in question except by comparing the proposition which expresses it with other propositions.

If Logic is the Science of Propositions, it must start from the standpoint of ordinary thought, ascertained by reflexion on ordinary language. Two assumptions which appear to be involved in ordinary thought are, that (1) the meaning and application of terms is uniform, and (2) that which is self-evident ought to be believed. That is to say, ordinary thought assumes reason in man, and trustworthiness in language. These assumptions may in any given case turn out to be unwarranted; but in order to prove that they are so in that particular case, in order even to doubt or to examine that case, we are *bound* to assume them to some extent—at least provisionally. Thus it seems that a comparatively general and permanent faith in the validity of these assumptions is an indispensable condition of intelligent scepticism in any particular instance.

The following pages are chiefly concerned with Formal Logic—*Formal* being taken to mean *most general* (cf. Professor Sidgwick's *History of Ethics*, ch. iii. § 1, p. 108, first edition).

SECTION II.

NAMES AND TERMS.

Although we frequently see *Names* and *Terms* used synonymously, it seems desirable to distinguish Names which are Terms from Names which are not Terms, and even to emphasize the distinction, since the failure to keep this distinction in view tends, I think, to confusion (cf. *post*, Section on Categorical Syllogisms). For instance, it is very unsatisfactory to find, in a treatise on Logic, in which a Categorical Proposition is analysed into "two terms and the copula," that S and P are referred to as the *terms* of such a proposition as All S is P, while such syllogisms as—

All P is M,
All M is S,
Some S is P ;

All men are animals,
All animals are mortals,
Some mortals are men ;

are spoken of as having "three and only three terms."[1]

If a proposition contain nothing but *two terms* and a *copula*, it is clear that the *terms* in the above propositions are All S (Some) P, All P, (Some) M, All men, (Some) animals, and so on.[2] Again, if in All birds are feathered, Tully is Cicero, the *terms* are *birds, feathered, Tully, Cicero*, what are we to call *All birds?* Supposing we get out of the difficulty by saying

---

[1] Cf. *e.g.* Jevons' *Elementary Lessons in Logic*, 7th edition, p. 183 foot, p. 124 ("whatever is predicated of a *term* distributed "), p. 127 (*e.g.* "Every syllogism has three and only three *terms*"), etc.

[2] When Mill (*Logic*, ii. 383, 9th edition) says that Fallacies of Ratiocination "generally resolve themselves into having more than three terms to the syllogism, either avowedly, *or in the covert mode of an undistributed middle term, or an illicit process of one of the two extremes*," he implicitly allows the meaning of *term* advocated in this Section. And if the *Subject* and the *Predicate* of a proposition are its *terms*, then this meaning which I wish to assign to *term* is countenanced by Mill in the following passage (*Logic*, Bk. i. ch. i. § 2, vol. i. p. 19, 9th edition) :—"In the proposition, the earth is round, the Predicate is the word *round*, which denotes the quality affirmed, or (as the phrase is) predicated : *the earth*, words denoting the object which that quality is affirmed of, compose the Subject." (Mill also uses *Name* in the sense in which I wish to use *Term* (a sense which is frequently assigned to it); cf. *Logic, loc. cit.*, "The first glance at a proposition shows that it is formed by putting together two *names*." "Every proposition consists of three parts : the Subject, the Predicate, and the Copula. The Predicate is *the name*, denoting that which is affirmed or denied. The Subject is *the name*, denoting the person or thing which something is affirmed or denied of.") The distinction which I draw between *term* and *term-name* is also taken by Mr. W. E. Johnson, but with different terminology.—Cf. Keynes, *Formal Logic*, p. 54, § 35.

that *All birds* consists of *term* + *indicator*, there remains the objection that in *one* case the *term* applies to the *whole* of the Subject, while in another case it applies to only a part of it. And in such propositions as, Snowdon is the highest mountain in Wales, These men are sailors, are we to say that *highest mountain in Wales* or *the highest mountain in Wales*, that *men* or *these men* are *terms?* If *S is P* is a form representative of all affirmative Categoricals, and if, in it, S and P are *terms*, I do not see how inconsistency of terminology can be escaped if in such a proposition as, *e.g.*, All birds are feathered, we call *birds* a *term*. And the circumstance that in my opinion an essential point in Categorical Propositions is the quantitive identity of certain elements, is to me a further reason for wishing to attach the appellation of *term* to those elements rather than to what is very frequently only a constituent of them. We might call M, P, S, Men, Animals, Mortals, the *Term-names*—or perhaps it might be better to use the expression *Term-signs* when we make letters stand for significant words, reserving the expression *Term-names* for cases where significant words are used. Thus in the above instances Men, Animals, Mortals would be *Term-names*, M, P, S *Term-signs*. We can, in this way, mark a distinction of *Names as part of Terms*, both from the *terms of propositions* and from *names* in the ordinary wide sense of that word, which allows us to use it of isolated words or groups of words that apply to objects, *e.g.* the nouns, etc., occurring in alphabetical order in dictionaries and indexes. Many substantival words are commonly or always modified when they occur as Subject-names of propositions, by some characterization (expressed or implied) that need not attach to them when they are in isolation; *e.g.* by the words all, some, one, certain, this, those. This constituent of the Term may perhaps be called the *Term-indicator*, or more briefly, the *Indicator*. In some cases Term and Term $\left\{ \begin{array}{l} \text{-sign} \\ \text{-name} \end{array} \right\}$ are the same, *e.g.* in S is P, Tully is Cicero.

Name may be defined as *any word or group of words* applying to or indicating *a Thing, or Things*. By *thing* I mean whatever has Existence and Character.[1] *Existence* and *Character* have a certain correspondence with Quantity and Quality as sometimes used; but since *Quantity*, *Quality*, and their derivatives have in ordinary logical use also narrower and somewhat different meanings, I should propose to use *Quantitiveness* and *Qualitiveness* (with the corresponding adverbs and adjectives). These words seem to me convenient because they mark both a distinction from and a likeness to Quantity and Quality as ordinarily used, and they are preferable to That-ness and What-ness (which are more unequivocal in meaning), because they have corresponding adjectives and adverbs. By *Quantitiveness* I mean that in virtue of which anything is *something*, that which is involved in calling it *something* or *anything*—*just the bare minimum of existence of some kind* which justifies the application of a name (that is, of *any name at all*). To attribute *Quantitiveness* to anything would be simply to say *that* it is. Thus Quantitiveness would have a meaning nearly allied to that of *Quantity* in the phrase *Quantity of Propositions*, meaning the Universality or Particularity of their Subject-term, *i.e.* the application of that Term to *all* or *some* of the things indicated by the Term-name. But when we say that mathematical, as distinguished from logical, propositions deal with Quantity, or are quantitative, *Quantity* means *Quality which is increased or decreased (but not altered in intensity) by addition or subtraction of homogeneous parts.* I think it would be convenient to call this *Extensive Quality* as contrasted with Quality in which increase or decrease of amount involves alteration of intensity. This latter may perhaps be called *Intensive Quality*. The peculiarity of mathematical propositions is, that the whole characterization of their Terms is concerned with what I venture to call *Extensive Quality*.

[1] Cf. Mr. Bradley's *Principles of Logic*, p. 3, "In all that is we can distinguish two sides—(1) existence, and (2) content." (It is, of course, only *as thought of* that things have names applied to them.) Cf. also Professor W. James, *The Psychology of Belief* (*Mind*, lv. 331), "In the strict and ultimate sense of the word existence, everything which can be thought of at all exists as *some* sort of object, whether mythical object, individual thinker's object, or object in outer space and for intelligence at large."

By *Qualitiveness* I mean that in virtue of which anything is *what* it is. The Qualitiveness of a Thing includes *all* its attributes, thus completely characterizing the *kind* of its Quantitiveness; and whatever we predicate of a thing expresses *some* attribute of it. Quality is commonly used both in this sense and also in a narrower sense, as, *e.g.*, when we speak of the Quality of Propositions, meaning their character as affirmative or negative. And when we distinguish between (1) Quantity and (2) Quality in an object, referring all the while to its attributes—as, *e.g.*, between (1) the weight and (2) the nutritive, etc., attributes of a loaf of bread—Quantity means Extensive Quality, and Quality means Intensive Quality (in the sense indicated above). The use of Quality as meaning the affirmative or negative character of propositions would perhaps be justified by the consideration that this affirmativeness or negativeness is such an important characteristic as to merit being called Quality κατ' ἐξοχήν. But no confusion need result if we add the qualification *of propositions* when using *Quality* in this sense.

A *Term* is any combination of words occurring in a Categorical Proposition, and applying to that of which something is asserted (S), or that which is asserted of it (P).

Attributes may be (1) Intrinsic or Essential, (2) Extrinsic or Accidental. Either of these again may be Extensive, Intensive, or Simple. An Intrinsic Attribute of anything named is some attribute included in the meaning of its name; all other Attributes are Extrinsic. *E.g.* Carnivorousness, four-footedness, are Intrinsic Attributes of a lion; being of a particular shade of colour, being born in Africa, having a tufted tail, are Extrinsic Attributes.

Again, Intrinsic and Extrinsic Attributes may be either Dependent (or Systemic)—that is, attributes in which explicit reference is made to something other than that which has the attributes—or Independent—that is, not making such reference. These differences come to be of consequence when Adjectival Names are used in propositions, that is, when they become Terms (Predicates). They are of consequence partly with reference to the most general (or formal), and partly with reference to the less general (or material), distinctions between terms and propositions. We may therefore classify Adjectival Terms (in accordance with the distinctions above taken) as in Tables I. and II. It would seem that whatever is indicated by a name is *thought* as having what I have called quantitiveness and qualitiveness. And unless it *has* quantitiveness and qualitiveness—some continuity of existence[1] and some distinguishing attributes—it must be wholly characterless or a nonentity.

I propose to use the word *Denomination* (of a Name or Term) as corresponding to *Quantitiveness* (of a Thing); and *Attribution* (of a Name or Term) as corresponding to *Qualitiveness* (of a Thing). Denomination of a Name or Term will therefore refer to the continued identical existence of the things, whether Subjects or Attributes, which are indicated; and Attribution of a Name or Term will mean the distinctive character of the things named. The Attribution of a Name or Term in as far as *explicitly* signified may be called the Determination; in as far as it is only *implied*, it may be called the *Implication*: thus *Attribution* will mean *Determination + Implication*.[2] I agree with those logicians[3] who maintain that *every* name or term has what I have called Denomination and Determination (if we may admit as part of the Determination of a name the attribute of being called by that name). Indeed it seems to me that Denomination and Attribution (of which Determination is always a part) are mutually implicated in terms, as inevitably as quantitiveness and qualitiveness in the things indicated, or as lines and angles, or likeness and difference.

In as far as a term is *denominative*, it applies (as I understand *denominative*) to the quantitiveness, the mere undeter-

[1] Cf. *post*, Section on the Laws of Thought.
[2] I have avoided the words Denotation and Connotation, because they have, as Fowler says, been "already employed with so much uncertainty" that it is difficult to use them without some risk of confusion; and indeed no use of those terms that I am acquainted with corresponds to the distinction which I have in view here.
[3] Cf. *e.g.* Bradley, *Principles of Logic*, p. 156.

mined existence,' of the thing of which it is the name—that identity which enables us to speak of a thing as *one*, under whatever change of attributes. In as far as it is *determinative*, it applies to the qualitiveness of the thing—including in qualitiveness the *kind* of its existence (material, fictitious, ideational, etc.).

This difference of aspect in terms is possibly what Jevons is thinking of when in the *Elementary Lessons in Logic* (Lesson V.) he emphasizes the distinction between Intension and Extension. The importance which he attributes to this, saying that when it is once grasped there is little further difficulty to be encountered in Logic, is hardly borne out by his further treatment; but if what he had in view corresponds to what I have called Attribution and Denomination, the importance he assigns to it is, I think, not exaggerated.

The following passages from Dr. Bain, Dr. Venn, and Mill, seem to me confirmatory of that view of Existence and Character in Things, and Denomination and Determination in Names or Terms, which I have here taken.—Dr. Bain says (*Logic*, 2nd ed. i. 59), " Existence has no real opposite;" (p. 107), " With regard to the predicate *Existence*, occurring in certain propositions, we may remark no science, or department of logical method, springs out of it. Indeed, all such propositions are more or less abbreviated or elliptical, etc."

Dr. Venn (*Empirical Logic*, p. 232) says, " Though mere *logical* existence cannot be intelligibly predicated, inasmuch as it is presupposed necessary by the use of the term, yet the *special kind*[1] of existence which we call objective or experiential can be so predicated. *It*[1] is not implied by the use of the term; *it*[1] is not conveyed by the ordinary copula; *it is a real restriction upon anything thus indicated, and therefore it is a perfectly fit subject*[1] of logical predication."

Mill says (*Logic*, ii. 325, 9th ed.), "If the analysis of qualities in the earlier part of this work be correct, names of qualities and names of substances stand for the very same sets of facts or phenomena; *whiteness and a white thing* are

---

[1] The italics are mine.

only different phrases, *required by convenience*[1] for speaking of the same external fact under different relations. Not such, however, was the notion which this verbal distinction suggested of old, either to the vulgar or to the scientific. Whiteness was an entity inhering or sticking in the white substance; and so of all other qualities. So far was this carried that even concrete general terms were supposed to be, not names of indefinite numbers of individual substances, but names of a peculiar kind of entities termed Universal Substances. Because we can think and speak of man in general, that is, of all persons in so far as possessing the common attributes of the species, without fastening our thoughts permanently on some one individual person; therefore man in general was supposed to be, not an aggregate of individual persons, but an abstract or universal man, distinct from these."

It would, I think, be convenient to extend the sense of Determination so that the determination of any name may include the attribute of being called by that name. This is certainly a part, and not an implicit part, of the attribution.

By *Import* I intend *the Denomination together with the Attribution* of a name or term, *i.e.* the complete scope of the term in its quantitive and qualitive aspects. To take examples:—Denomination of (1) *Man* is the more or less permanent existence of all individuals of the human race (Socrates, Plato, Aristotle, Shakespeare, and so on). (The whole of the *characteristics* of *Man* is included in the *attribution* of the word. Existence and Character (Quantitiveness and Qualitiveness) are, of course, inseparably bound up together, though we may think and speak of them separately. The *existence* of each thing is unique, but this uniqueness of existence can only be made clear by its unique *attribution*—and the existence and the attribution involve each other.) Denomination of (2) *Triangularity* is the mere existence of the attribute named wherever it occurs.

Determination of (1) is the attributes of animality and rationality, and (in accordance with the view suggested above)

---

[1] The italics are mine.

it also includes the attribute of being called Man; of (2) is the characteristics of having three angles, and being called Triangularity.

Implication of (1) is that the things to which the name is applied are Subjects of Attributes, have a particular external form, etc.[1] Of (2) that that to which the name is applied is (wherever occurring) an Attribute of Subjects, etc.

The *Import* of (1) is all creatures to which the name applies, considered with reference both to quantitiveness and qualitiveness, they being Subjects of Attributes, having the characteristics of animality and rationality, and being called by the name Man, etc.

Of (2) is the attribute *Triangularity*, as having quantitiveness, *i.e. as occurring* (wherever it does occur) and as having definite qualitiveness (*i.e.* as differentiated *from other Attributes* by having three angles, and by being called Triangularity, and as differentiated *quâ* Attribute of Subjects *from Subjects of Attributes*, etc.).

The Denomination of (1) *All the Greek poets* [are celebrated] means the quantitiveness (*quâ* Subjects) of those things of which *All the Greek poets* is the name—*i.e.* of the individuals Homer, Æschylus, Sophocles, and so on; of (2) *Whiteness* [is the colour of snow, sea-foam, privet-blossom, etc.] is the quantitiveness (*quâ* Attribute—*i.e.* the occurrence in Subjects) of that of which *Whiteness* is the name. (Most Attribute Names do not take a plural, because in them determination is most prominent, and denomination of the singular includes every case of occurrence. The only exception is, groups of Attributes which have such striking similarity that they possess a name in common—*e.g.* colour, virtue.)

---

[1] It would generally be very difficult (not to say impossible) to state at length *the whole* of the implications of any name used with intelligence. It is, I think, to a great extent upon the fulness and vividness with which implications of names are realized in thought, that the force and adequacy of our ideas depend; and the realization of *some* implications is indispensable for understanding. *Such* implications seem to be had in view when it is said that our terms always refer to a certain definite Universe of Discourse. This way of meeting the case, however, does not appear to me to be satisfactory or useful (cf. *post*, Section on Predication and Existence).

The Determination of (1) is the attributes of belonging to the Greek nation, of producing fine poetical compositions, of being the only Greeks who did so, of being called *All the Greek poets*. Of (2) is the attribute common to and distinctive of snow, sea-foam, privet-blossom, etc., and on account of possessing which they are called white, and the attribute of being called *Whiteness*.

In (1) the Implication is that the things named are Subjects of Attributes, of a particular form, speaking a particular language, etc.

The Implication of (2) is that the thing named is an Attribute of Subjects, etc.

The Import of the above terms is given by combining, in each case, the Denomination and Attribution of the term.

The broadest division of Things that language involves and suggests is into I. Subjects of Attributes; II. Attributes. The names which apply to I. may be called Substantival Names, and those which apply to II. may be called Attribute Names.

In the present connection it may perhaps be allowed to distinguish *Subject of Attributes* and *Attributes* as follows:—

A *Subject* is that of which the differentia is to *have* characteristics and not to *be* a characteristic.

An *Attribute* is that of which the differentia is to *be* a characteristic. That it may also *have* characteristics does not destroy its nature as Attribute, any more than being a father abrogates a man's relation as son to his own father.

If we start with *Things* simply, *every* characterization of any *Thing* will without difficulty be allowed to be effected by the attribution of the terms applied to it. But I see no reason why, if we *start* with *Things that are Subjects* and *Things that are Attributes*, we may not (if it is convenient) reckon that in this case *Attribution* begins with such characterization as sets forth the *distinctive kind* of Attribute, or the *distinctive kind* of Subject. I do not see what objection can be made to this, as far as Attributes are concerned (and no one, as far as I know, objects to it with regard to Subjects), by any one who allows that Attributes have distinctive character, to which corresponds Attribution of names. And if any Attribute can have Attributes ascribed to it (and ordinary language certainly countenances, perhaps even necessitates, such a reference), it must be in virtue of its quantitiveness. Any Attribute capable of further characterization by attribution, must be capable of it in virtue of its as yet to some extent uncharacterized existence or quantitiveness, not in virtue of the characterization by attribution which it has already received.

The characterization of Attributes, as well as of Subjects, is largely effected by names of a third kind, which may be called III. Adjectival Names. In these names the *qualitiveness* of the object named is most prominent and some definite characteristics are determined, as in *white, fragrant, organized, beautiful*. Adjectival Names have several important characteristics. (1) They always refer to some Thing (Subject of Attributes or Attribute) previously named, which they help to characterize, and can occur as P of a Categorical Proposition which has either an Attribute Term or a Substantival Term for S; while an Attribute Term can be predicated only of an Attribute Term, and a Substantival Term only of a Substantival Term. (2) They can occur only as P, never as S, of a Categorical Proposition.[1] (3) Attribution (as already implied) is prominent in them.—It is interesting, with reference to this consideration, to notice that in, *e.g.*, modern English,[2] adjectives do not take the sign of the plural, although the things which they qualify may be many. (4) They are applied *because of* certain characteristics in the things to which they apply.—In (3) Adjectival Names resemble Attribute Names; in (4) they resemble Attribute Names and Common Names (cf. Table III.).

What is primary in a Subject is *that* it is ; what is primary in an Attribute is *what* it is: an Attribute Name always

---

[1] Cf. also German in such propositions as, *e.g.*, *Diese Lieder sind wunderschön, Wir sind's nicht gewohnt.*

[2] Cf. Stock, *Deductive Logic*, § 88.

characterizes the Attribute which it applies to so fully that any affirmative Categorical Proposition having Complete Attribute Terms for both S and P must be a Nominal Proposition. A Subject Name may determine nothing more than that what it applies to is called by that name.

Substantival Names are names in which (in isolation or as Subjects) the *quantitiveness* of what is named is most prominent.[1] Here the determination may include definite characteristics, sufficient to enable us to define and apply the name, as in, *e.g.*, *bird, fairy, accident*. Or we may have some characteristics determined, but not enough to enable us to define or apply the name, as *the eldest son of Charles I*. Or it may only be (i.) determined that the thing called by a name has the attribute of being called by that name; (ii.) implied that the thing has, 1st, what is common to *all* Subjects of Attributes; 2nd, unique individuality; 3rd, an unique name—as in, *e.g.*, *Tom Smith*.

Substantival Names may be divided into (*a*) *Common Names*, *i.e.* names of which the application is restricted by the determination only, as *man, fairy, Ragged Robin*.

(*b*) *Special Names*, *i.e.* names the application of which has some definite degree of further restriction, but is not confined to *only one* object or group, as Predicables, *Admiral of the Fleet, Czar of Russia, Friday, September*. Special Names have always more than the minimum of Determination; and there may be an indefinite number of Fridays, Admirals, etc.; but there can be only one Friday in the week, and fifty-two in a year, and, at any given time, only three Admirals of our Fleet, only one Czar of Russia, and so on.

(*c*) *Unique Names*, *i.e.* names of which the application may be said to be restricted to *one* object or group of objects, as, *the sun, father of D., this boy, Julius Cæsar, Mary, Tom, Quellyn Youde, Vancouver's Island,* 1888 A.D., *the children of King Charles I.*

Unique names may have a maximum of determination, as

---

[1] When a Substantival Name is used as P of a proposition, the qualitiveness of what is named becomes most prominent.

the sun, or a minimum, as *Gordon*. Such names as *Gordon, Tom, Muriel*, of course may be, and are, applied to many individuals, but they may still be called Unique, being given in every case with the intention of distinguishing an unique individual—an object of which (without further knowledge than the name affords) we can only predicate (1) what is common to all Subjects of Attributes, (2) unique individuality, (3) an unique name, (4) what that name is. If a "proper name" conveys more to us than this, it is because either (1) we have special knowledge of the individual named, or (2) because the name has, so far, ceased to be a Proper Name.

I have adopted the above distinctions of names in preference to those ordinarily given in logical handbooks for the following among other reasons. The old distinctions form independent couples (*e.g.* General and Singular, Collective and Distributive, Positive and Negative), and they do not lend themselves to a satisfactory classification. Some of them are of no logical importance, *e.g.* Collective (a name that is not collective may be used collectively), Positive and Negative, Relative and Absolute; and the distinction between Categorematic and Syncategorematic is a distinction purely of words, and not even of names, much less of terms (though Jevons, *Elementary Lessons in Logic*, 7th ed. p. 26, uses it as applying to terms). The distinction between Abstract and Concrete is inconsistently treated by logicians, and is, in my opinion, untenable, since it seems impossible to arrive at any valid justification for the adoption of those particular words in their logical use, or at any satisfactory test by which to determine their application. My reasons for this opinion and some discussion of the subject are given in a short consideration of the terms Abstract and Concrete. On the other hand, the division of names which I have adopted appears to correspond to important distinctions either in the objects named or in the aspect of them with which we are concerned; there are no cross-divisions, and a formally good classification is possible. All of them are, I think, of further consequence when we come to the divisions of Terms and of Categorical Propositions.

16 IMPORT OF PROPOSITIONS.

TABLE I.]

ADJECTIVAL TERMS.

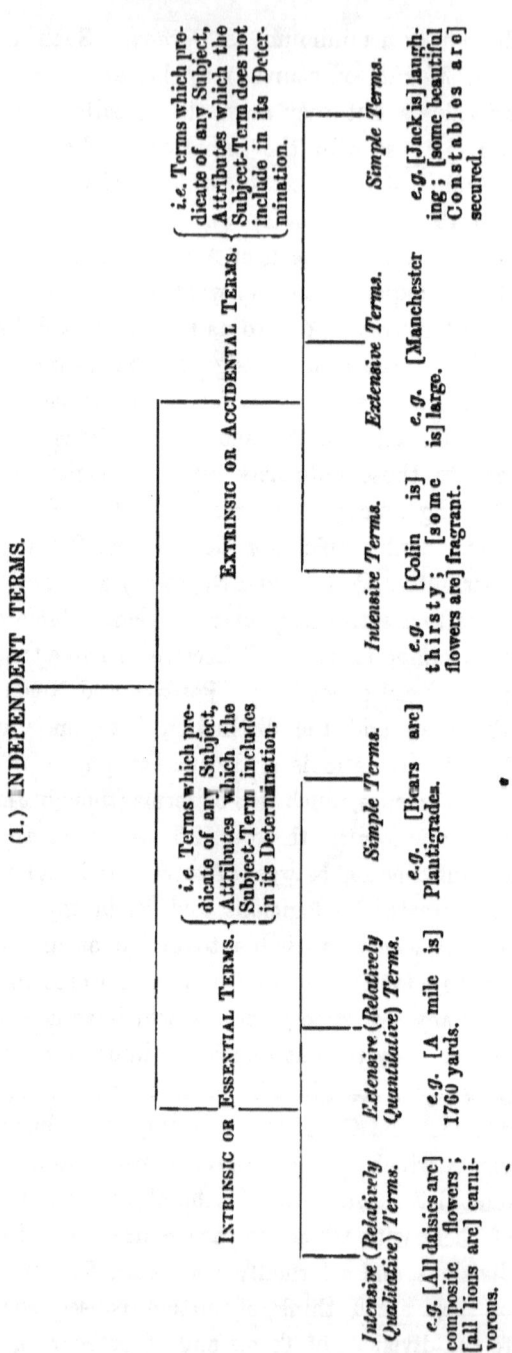

(1.) INDEPENDENT TERMS.

- INTRINSIC OR ESSENTIAL TERMS. { *i.e.* Terms which predicate of any Subject, Attributes which the Subject-Term includes in its Determination.
  - *Intensive (Relatively Qualitative) Terms.*
    e.g. [All daisies are] composite flowers; [all lions are] carnivorous.
  - *Extensive (Relatively Quantitative) Terms.*
    e.g. [A mile is] 1760 yards.
  - *Simple Terms.*
    e.g. [Bears are] Plantigrades.

- EXTRINSIC OR ACCIDENTAL TERMS. { *i.e.* Terms which predicate of any Subject, Attributes which the Subject-Term does not include in its Determination.
  - *Intensive Terms.*
    e.g. [Colin is] thirsty; [some flowers are] fragrant.
  - *Extensive Terms.*
    e.g. [Manchester is] large.
  - *Simple Terms.*
    e.g. [Jack is] laughing; [some beautiful Constables are] secured.

NAMES AND TERMS. 17

TABLE II.] ADJECTIVAL TERMS.

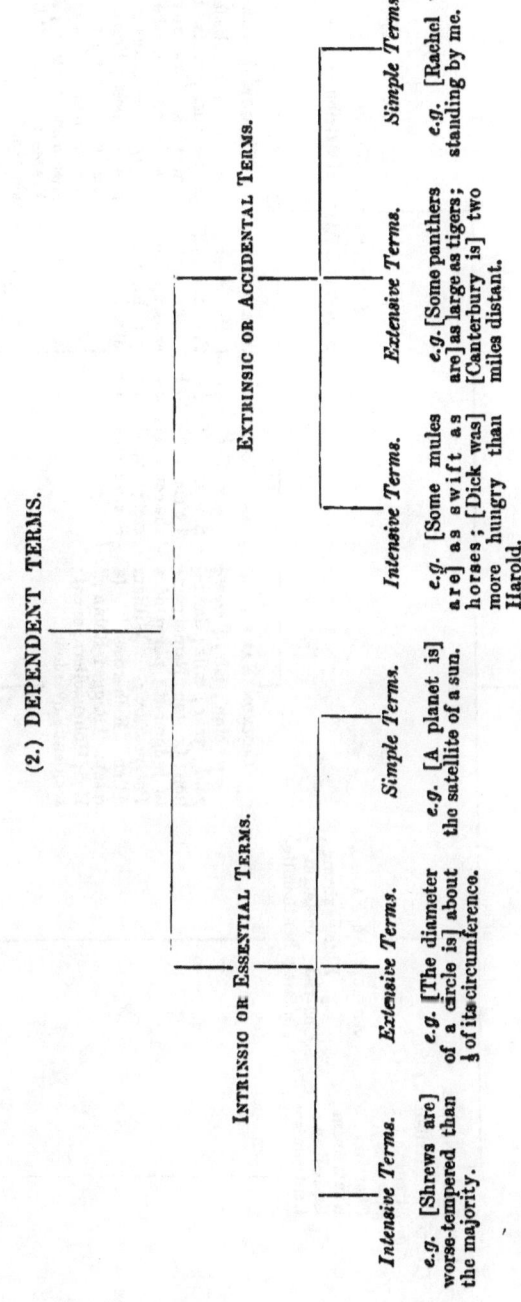

(2.) DEPENDENT TERMS.

- INTRINSIC OR ESSENTIAL TERMS.
  - *Intensive Terms.*
    e.g. [Shrews are] worse-tempered than the majority.
  - *Extensive Terms.*
    e.g. [The diameter of a circle is] about ⅓ of its circumference.
  - *Simple Terms.*
    e.g. [A planet is] the satellite of a sun.

- EXTRINSIC OR ACCIDENTAL TERMS.
  - *Intensive Terms.*
    e.g. [Some mules are] as swift as horses; [Dick was] more hungry than Harold.
  - *Extensive Terms.*
    e.g. [Some panthers are] as large as tigers; [Canterbury is] two miles distant.
  - *Simple Terms.*
    e.g. [Rachel was] standing by me.

B

[TABLE III.] IMPORT OF PROPOSITIONS.

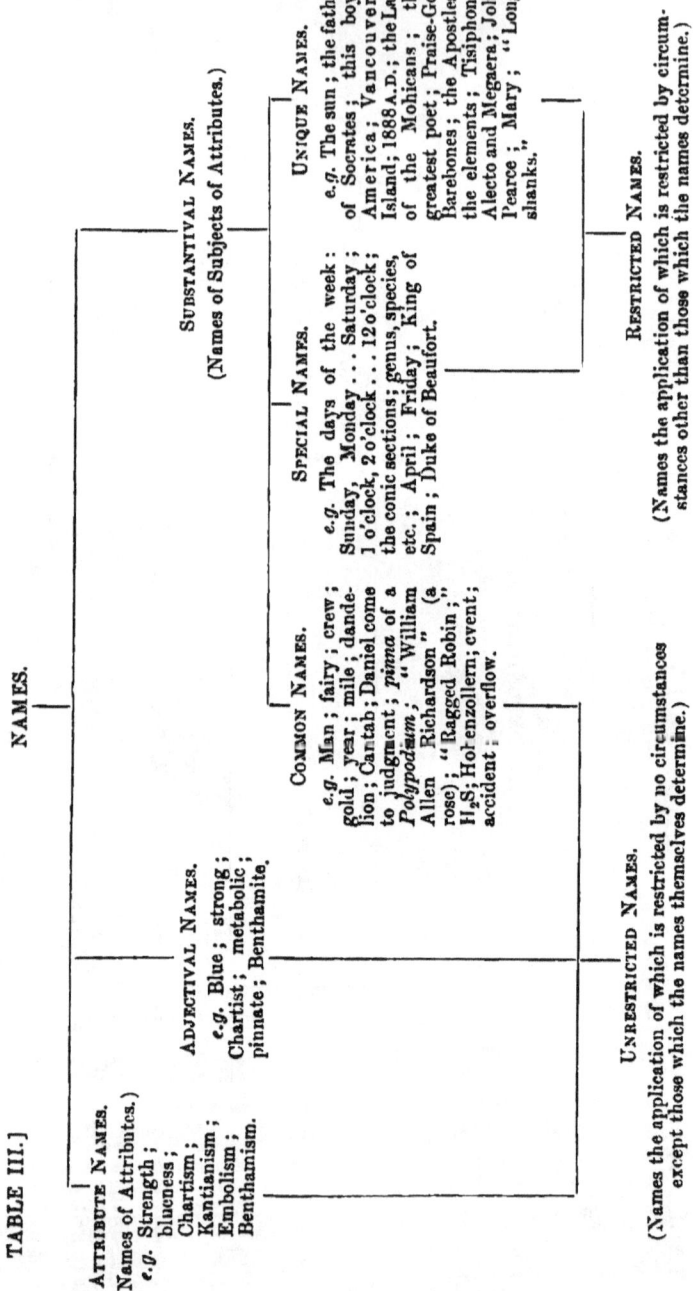

SECTION III.

TERMS.

If we consider Names *quâ* nominal and not *quâ* terminal (cf. Table of Names, p. 18), we shall find some broad distinctions corresponding to differences in the things named, or in the aspect of them which is emphasized—differences which are of importance when we come to the classification of Terms and Propositions. As regards Terms, however, we frequently cannot fully settle their character as Attribute Terms, Substantival Terms, etc., until we have considered what their special force is in the propositions to which they belong. An isolated name can generally be classed on mere inspection as primarily adjectival or substantival, and so on; but the terms of any proposition must be regarded *as parts* of that proposition, and only then, it may be, can they have their character definitely and fully determined—this character, of course, depending on the character of the thing named. For instance, if I am asked to characterize the name *Whiteness*, I have no hesitation in calling it an Attribute Name; but if the word *Whiteness* is given to me as a *Term* or *part of a Term*, and I am required to characterize it, I can only say, Until I know the proposition in which it occurs, I am unable to do so. If, *e.g.*, the proposition is, Whiteness is a colour, then *Whiteness* is an Attribute Term; if the proposition is, This table-cloth is whiteness itself, then I should say that *Whiteness* is part of an Adjectival Term (*whiteness* itself being equivalent to *as white as white can be*); if the proposition is, This whiteness is death-like, I should say that *whiteness* is perhaps part of an Attribute Term, *this whiteness* (*this whiteness* meaning *this pallor of countenance*—for an exactly similar colour on china or on silk, etc., need not be death-like).

It will be found, however, that most of the important distinctions in propositions depend upon differences in their Terms, especially the Subject Terms—*e.g.* any proposition beginning with a class-name qualified by *No* is an Universal Proposition; any proposition beginning with a class-name qualified by *Some* is a particular proposition. I therefore proceed to consider Terms before discussing Propositions.

The accompanying Tables of Terms, pp. 25–34 (containing many important distinctions in addition to those which correspond to the distinctions of names already noticed), exhibit the distinctions of Terms in schemes of Division. The remarks which follow here will be made with reference to these Tables.

The first distinction I have taken is that between what I have called (1) *Uni-terminal* and (2) *Bi-terminal* Terms. (1) Are terms which can only be used as P of Categorical Propositions; (2) are Terms which may be used as either S or P of Categorical Propositions.

All Uni-terminal Terms are *Adjectival*, and the first subdivision here is into what may be called *Vernacular Terms*, *e.g.* red, like X, and *Specific Terms*, *e.g.* lanceolate, pinnate, Chartist, æsthetic, "intense." (These would include what Dr. Venn calls *Special* or *Technical* Terms (*Empirical Logic*, p. 281). He goes so far as to say that it is philosophically more correct to call these terms, not English, but another tongue, *op. cit.* p. 282.) Each of these again may be subdivided into Dependent or Systemic (implying a dependence or relation of objects connected in some system, which may be of any degree of complexity, from the simplicity of a class or of any two related objects to the intricacy of a genealogical tree, or even of the universe itself) and Independent. Any one who has a knowledge of the system referred to by a Systemic or Dependent Term can draw from a proposition containing it a greater variety of inferences than is possible in the case of propositions which contain only Independent Terms (compare, *e.g.*, E is F, and E is equal to F); hence the logical importance of this distinction, and hence also the hopelessness of constructing a "Logic of Relatives." *A fortiori* arguments are simply arguments of which some terms are "dependent." All kinds of Terms are divisible into *Dependent* and *Independent*. *Dependent Adjectivals* are such as like B, before C, equal to D, less pinnatifid than E, out-heroding Herod.

To the division into Uni-terminal and Bi-terminal Terms there corresponds a very important division of Categorical Propositions, namely, that into what I propose to call (1) *Adjectival Propositions* and (2) *Coincidental Propositions*. (1) are Categorical Propositions which have a Uni-terminal Term for P, and can neither be converted nor quantified; (2) are Categorical Propositions which have Bi-terminal Terms for both S and P; most of them can be converted, and those unquantified Coincidentals which have Common Names for Term-names can be both quantified and converted. This distinction will be further considered with reference to Quantification.

The subdivisions of (1) and (2) correspond. It is therefore not necessary to consider them under both heads, and I have accordingly in the Tables of Categorical Propositions (Tables IV.–XVI.) aimed at carrying out the division under one head only, choosing (2) rather than (1) because all (1) are reducible to (2), and it is with (2) that we are concerned in the logical processes of Conversion, Reduction, etc.

The principal division of Bi-terminal Terms is into *Attribute Terms* and *Substantive Terms*. Attribute Terms are further divisible into (1) *Vernacular* and (2) *Specific* Terms; (1) and (2) subdivide into *Complete Terms*—*e.g.* Steadfastness, Stupidity—and *Partial Terms*. The latter may be *Definite* or *Indefinite Singular*—*e.g.* His heroism, Some æstheticism; and *Definite* or *Indefinite Particular*—*e.g.* Their hard-heartedness, Much affection. Particulars are Distributive or Collective. All the above species are *Independent* and *Dependent*.

Under *Substantive Terms* we have the species (1) *Common Terms*, (2) *Special Terms*, (3) *Unique Terms*. *Common Terms* are divisible into *Vernacular* and *Specific Terms*. The *Vernacular Common Terms* of any language include *Universal Terms* corresponding to every Term-name; have determination (can be defined), their determination being a sufficient guide to their application; and are understood by any persons who are said to know the language, without special training or information, whether scientific, artistic, professional, or peculiar to any trade, or section of society, and so on. Vernacular Names form the bulk of any language, and we expect to find them fully enumerated in any good ordinary dictionary. Specific Names (including Technical Names, Slang and Cant words, and so on) also have a maximum of Determination and may be Universal, but to understand them needs some special training or information. We find them partly in special treatises and vocabularies, dictionaries of Slang, of History, of Biography, in local Vocabularies, the Encyclopædia, *Inquire Within*, Hone's *Day Book*, etc.; but they are to a large extent unstatutable language. Of such expressions as *æsthetic*, *Philistine*, *take the bun*, *masher*, *Parnellite*, we should not know where to look for a printed explanation; and such words are specially difficult to translate, while Technical Names are probably the easiest of any. Technical Names supply the material of scientific Nomenclature and Terminology.

The Vernacular words of any language may be recruited from time to time from Specific words, and the departments of the latter, on the other hand, sometimes appropriate Vulgar Terms.

Propositions having Specific Terms may be reduced to propositions having Vernacular Terms, but many of the latter cannot be reduced to the former. It is in this circumstance that I find the justification for introducing this distinction in a *logical* division. It is with reference to Specific Terms that the case for Universes of Discourse seems to me most plausible. It may no doubt conduce to clearness and conciseness that in vocabularies of, *e.g.*, Architectural Terms, Terms of Sport, Slang, and so on, a limitation is expressly introduced once for all (cf., however, *post*, Section on Predication and Existence). But this limitation is itself limited, and the cases in which it applies are generally indicated by a difference of type or some similar device.

Vernacular Terms are divisible into *Partial* and *Total*;

Partial into *Singular* and *Particular*; *Singular* into *Definite* and *Indefinite*; *Definite* and *Indefinite* (and every other penultimate class) into *Independent* and *Dependent*. Particular Terms divide into *Definite* and *Indefinite*, and each of these into *Collective* and *Distributive*. Total Terms (*Universals*) subdivide into *Definite* (*Distributive* and *Collective*) and *Indefinite* (*Distributive*). The Subdivisions of Specific Terms correspond to those of Vernacular Terms. Examples of all these classes, and of those which follow, are given in the Tables of Terms.

By a *Partial Term*, is meant a Term of which the application is not *ex vi termini* the whole sphere of the Term-name; by a *Total Term*, is meant a term of which the application is *ex vi termini* the whole sphere of the Term-name. All *R* includes *every R*, whether we look to determination or application; *some R* may happen to apply to *all the R's*, but cannot have the same determination.

It may be noticed that many technical and other terms which have the form have not the force of Dependent Terms; *e.g.* Fibres of Corti, Basis of Division, Consilience of Inductions, Man-of-war, will of iron.

By Special Terms I mean such terms as *Predicables, Conic Sections, the days of the week*, which resemble Common Terms in that they are fully determinative, and may be used universally—as in, All Conic Sections are curves—and resemble Unique Terms in being members of a limited, and as it were organic system; as in The five Predicables are Genus, Species, Difference, Property, and Accident. Unique Terms are different; for though, *e.g.*, Apostle, Continent are fully determinative, and we can say All Apostles, All continents, we cannot regard *Apostles* and *continents* as being related to *the twelve Apostles, the five continents*, in the same way as all Predicables are related to *the five Predicables*, all Conic Sections to *the four Conic Sections*.

Special Terms are divisible into *Total* and *Partial*; these into *Simple* (similar to Common Terms) and *Synoptical* (regarded as indicating members of limited groups). *Simple*

Totals (Universals) are divided into *Definite (Distributive and Collective)* and *Indefinite (Distributive)*. *Synoptical Totals (Generals)* may be (1) *Summary* or (2) *Enumerative*; (1) subdivides into *Definite (Distributive* and *Collective)* and *Indefinite (Distributive)*; (2) subdivides into *Distributive* and *Collective*. *Partial Simple Terms* are *Singular (Definite* and *Indefinite)* and *Particular (Definite* and *Indefinite, Distributive* and *Collective)*; *Partial Synoptical Terms* are *Unitary (Definite* and *Indefinite)* and *Plurative*; *Plurative* are *Summary (Definite* and *Indefinite, Distributive* and *Collective)* and *Enumerative (Distributive* and *Collective)*. The final division, as before remarked, is into Independent and Dependent in each case.

Unique Terms are subdivided into *Whole* ((*a*) having the application of Term and Term-name the same, or (*b*) no distinction between Term and Term-name) and *Partial*; *Whole* into (*b*) *Individual* and (*a*) *Total*; Individual into *Appellative, Descriptive,* and *Mixed*; *Totals (Generals)* into *Summary* and *Enumerative*; *Total Summary* into *Appellative, Descriptive,* and *Mixed (Definite* and *Indefinite),* and the *Definites* into *Distributives* and *Collectives*; *Total Enumeratives* into *Appellative, Descriptive,* and *Mixed (Distributive* and *Collective)*. *Partial Terms* are divided into *Unitary* and *Plurative*; *Unitary* into *Appellative, Descriptive,* and *Mixed (Definite* and *Indefinite)*; *Plurative* divide into (1) *Summary* and (2) *Enumerative*; (1) into *Appellative, Descriptive,* and *Mixed (Definite* and *Indefinite, Distributive* and *Collective)*; (2) into *Appellative, Descriptive,* and *Mixed (Distributive* and *Collective)*. All *Enumeratives* are, of course, *Definite*.

All Definite Partial Terms have an unique application. Special Terms are (as already indicated) not limited in application to one object or group of objects, or one or some of a particular group, differing in this point from Unique Terms.—By Descriptive Terms, I mean Terms of which the Term-names determine the distinctive characteristics of the objects to which they apply; by Appellative Terms, Terms of which the Term-names are of the nature of (so-called) Proper Names. A Mixed Term is a term which is partly

Descriptive and partly Appellative; as *the Shield of Achilles, George Smith's brother*. Any other (unexplained) names used in this classification are, I hope, self-explanatory. I think that the reason why such names as *Gold, Water, the number 6, the half-sovereign, the word " and," the word " symbol,"* etc., are always or mostly used in the singular number, is because these names apply to things of which the intrinsic quality does not vary from instance to instance. (Compare the corresponding plural use of such names as *peas, beans,* etc.) Attribute Names (cf. *ante*, p. 11) seldom take a plural, but the denomination of Attribute Terms may be limited by the term-indicator—which, however, can never be numerical.

TABLE IV.]

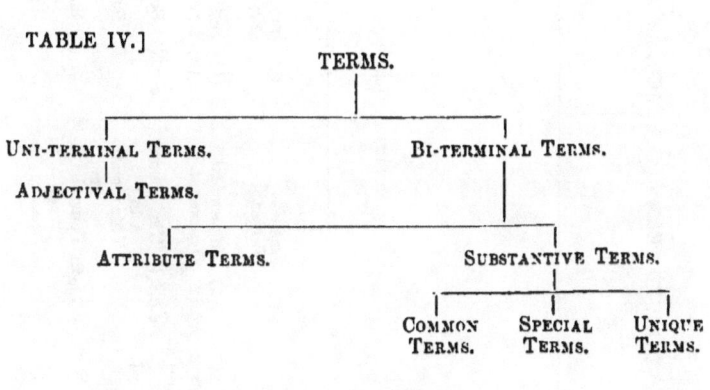

TABLE V.]
ADJECTIVAL TERMS (VERNACULAR AND SPECIFIC).

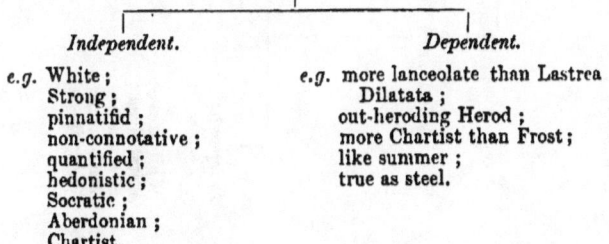

26 IMPORT OF PROPOSITIONS.

[TABLE VI.]

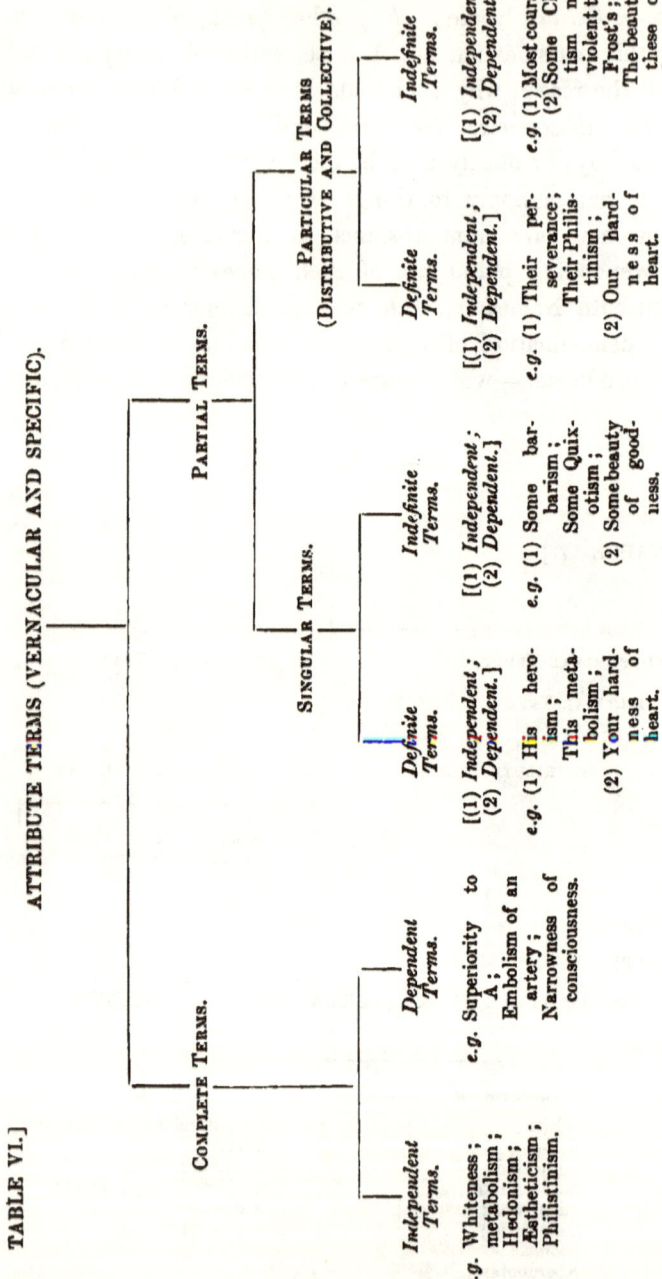

TERMS. 27

TABLE VII.] COMMON TERMS (VERNACULAR AND SPECIFIC).

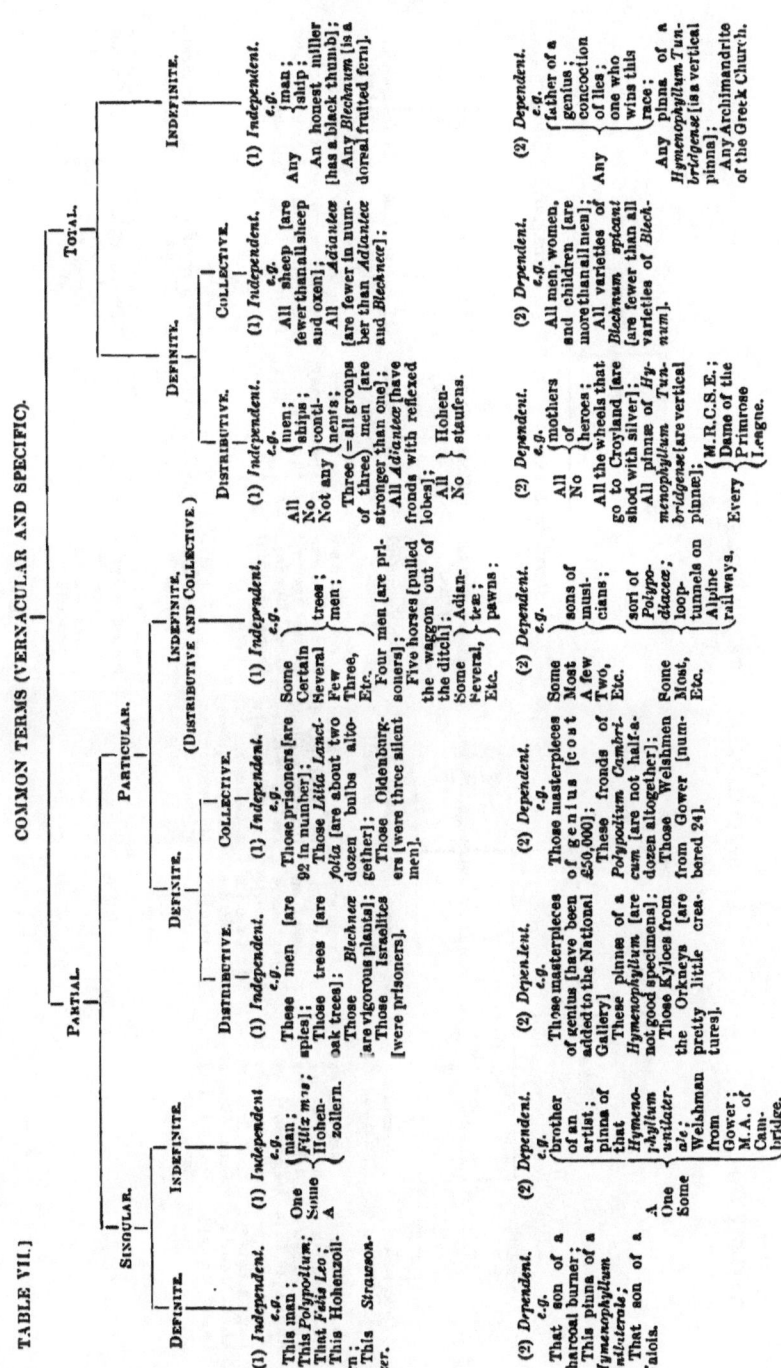

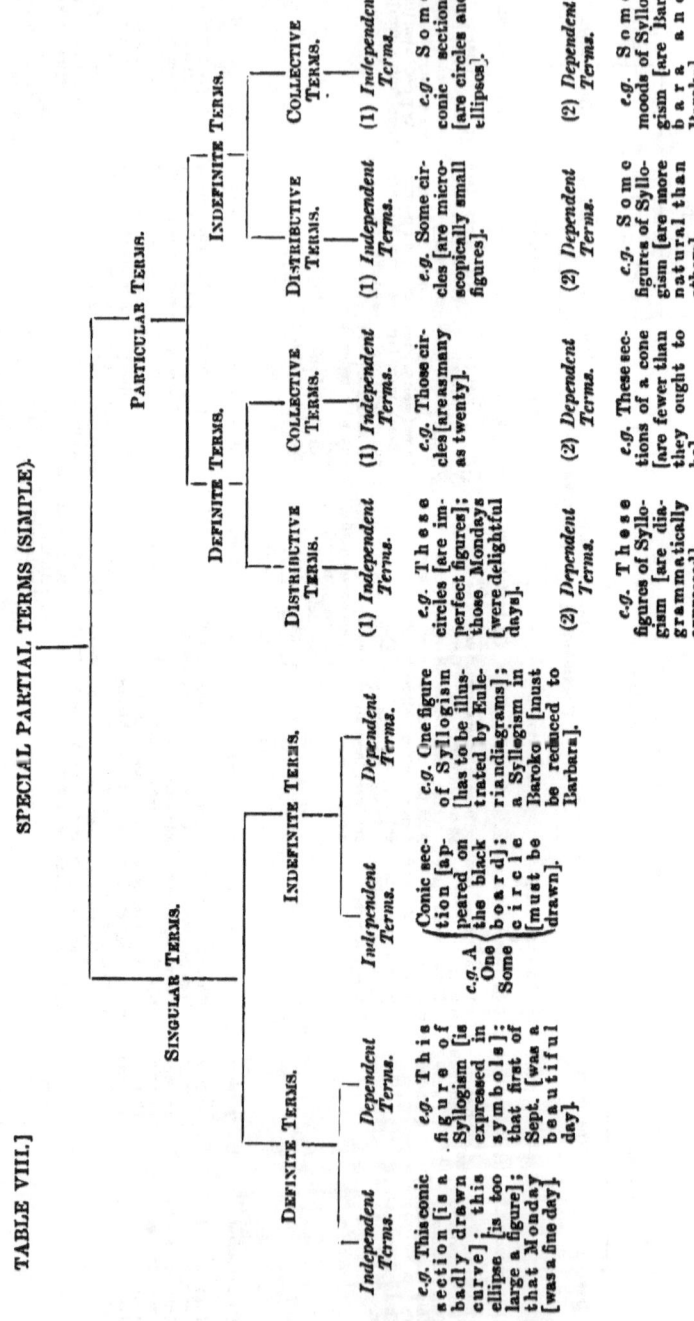

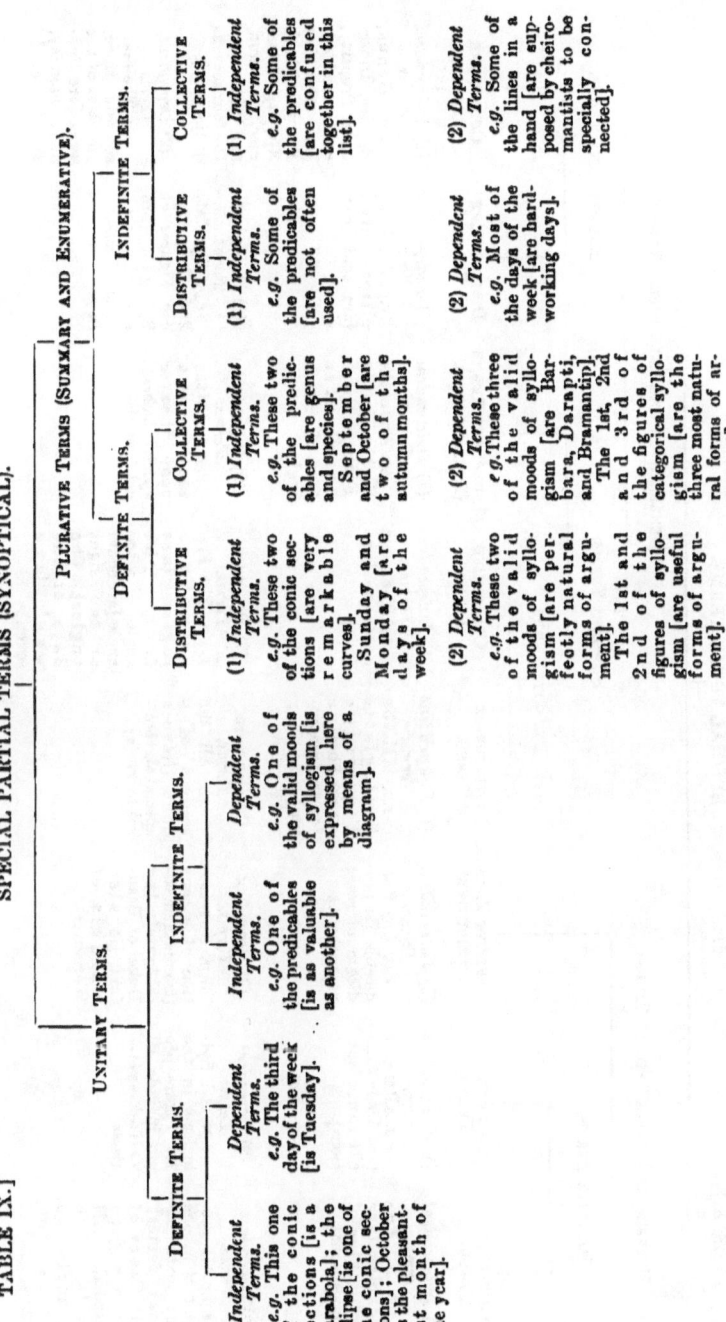

[TABLE X.] 30 IMPORT OF PROPOSITIONS.

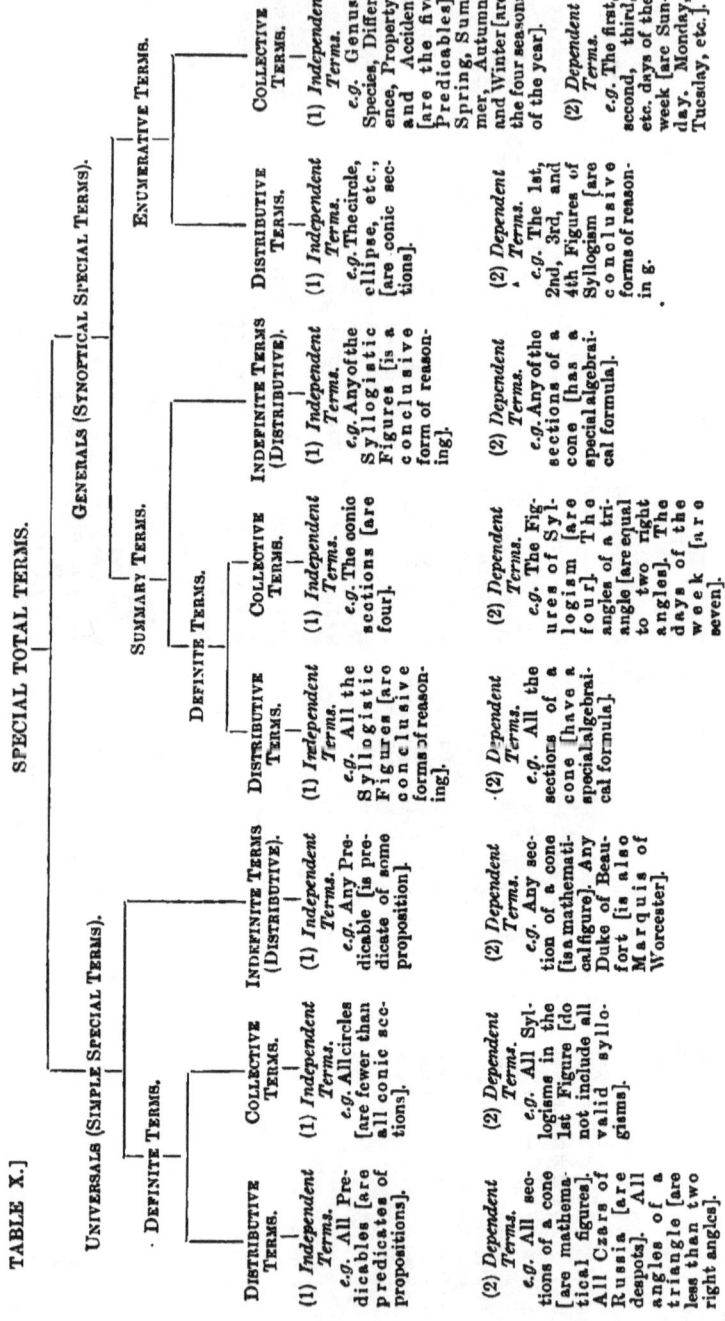

TERMS. 31

TABLE XI.]

INDIVIDUAL TERMS (UNIQUE).

(APPELLATIVE, MIXED, AND DESCRIPTIVE.)

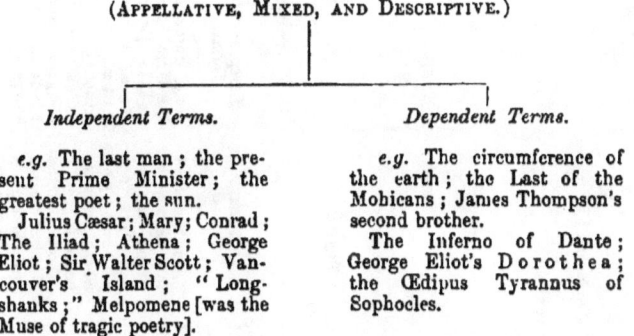

Independent Terms.

e.g. The last man; the present Prime Minister; the greatest poet; the sun.
Julius Cæsar; Mary; Conrad; The Iliad; Athena; George Eliot; Sir Walter Scott; Vancouver's Island; "Longshanks;" Melpomene [was the Muse of tragic poetry].

Dependent Terms.

e.g. The circumference of the earth; the Last of the Mohicans; James Thompson's second brother.
The Inferno of Dante; George Eliot's D o r o t h e a; the Œdipus Tyrannus of Sophocles.

TABLE XII.]

UNIQUE UNITARY TERMS.

(APPELLATIVE, MIXED, AND DESCRIPTIVE.)

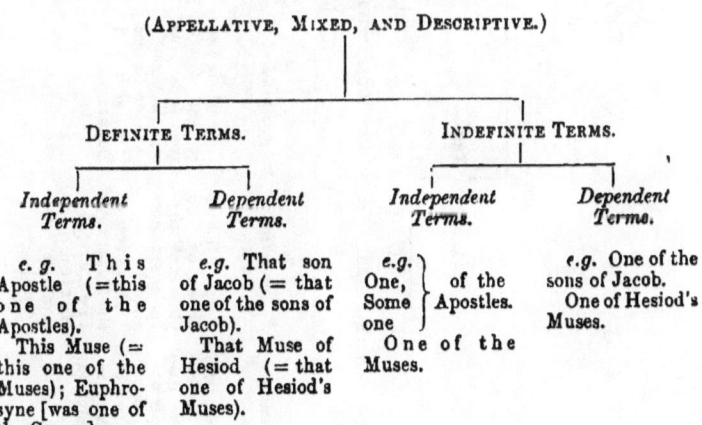

DEFINITE TERMS.

Independent Terms.

e. g. This Apostle (=this one of the Apostles).
This Muse (= this one of the Muses); Euphrosyne [was one of the Graces].

Dependent Terms.

e.g. That son of Jacob (= that one of the sons of Jacob).
That Muse of Hesiod (= that one of Hesiod's Muses).

INDEFINITE TERMS.

Independent Terms.

e.g. One, Some one } of the Apostles.
One of the Muses.

Dependent Terms.

e.g. One of the sons of Jacob.
One of Hesiod's Muses.

TABLE XIII.] UNIQUE PLURATIVE TERMS (SUMMARY).
(APPELLATIVE, MIXED, AND DESCRIPTIVE.)

```
                                    UNIQUE PLURATIVE TERMS
                                    ┌───────────────┴───────────────┐
                            DEFINITE TERMS.                  INDEFINITE TERMS.
                    ┌───────────┴───────────┐            ┌───────────┴───────────┐
            DISTRIBUTIVE TERMS.       COLLECTIVE TERMS.   DISTRIBUTIVE TERMS.   COLLECTIVE TERMS.
            ┌───────┴───────┐         ┌───────┴───────┐   ┌───────┴───────┐     ┌───────┴───────┐
        Independent    Dependent   Independent  Dependent Independent Dependent Independent Dependent
          Terms.         Terms.      Terms.      Terms.    Terms.      Terms.    Terms.      Terms.
```

Independent Terms. — *e.g.* These two of the Greek gods [were important personages]. Those two of the Graces [are often referred to].

Dependent Terms. — *e.g.* Those three of the plays of Æschylus [are masterpieces]. Those two of the Muses mentioned by Hesiod [are favourite goddesses].

Independent Terms. — *e.g.* Those two of the Greek gods [are Zeus and Poseidon]. Those Graces [are Aglaia and Euphrosyne].

Dependent Terms. — *e.g.* Those three of the plays of Æschylus [form the *Oresteia*]. Those Muses of Hesiod [are Clio and Terpsichore].

Independent Terms. — *e.g.* Some of the Greek gods [were frivolous beings]. Some of the Gorgons [are not often mentioned].

Dependent Terms. — *e.g.* Some of the heroes of Greek mythology [are not personages worth remembering]. Some of the Muses of Hesiod [are favourites of the poets].

Independent Terms. — *e.g.* Some of the Greek goddesses [were Hera, Aphrodite, and Athena]. Some of the Gorgons [were Medusa and Euryale].

Dependent Terms. — *e.g.* Some of the heroes of the Arthurian legends [are Galahad, Launcelot, and Geraint]. Some of the Muses of Hesiod [are Clio and Euterpe].

TABLE XIV.]

UNIQUE PLURATIVE TERMS (ENUMERATIVE).
APPELLATIVE, MIXED, AND DESCRIPTIVE.

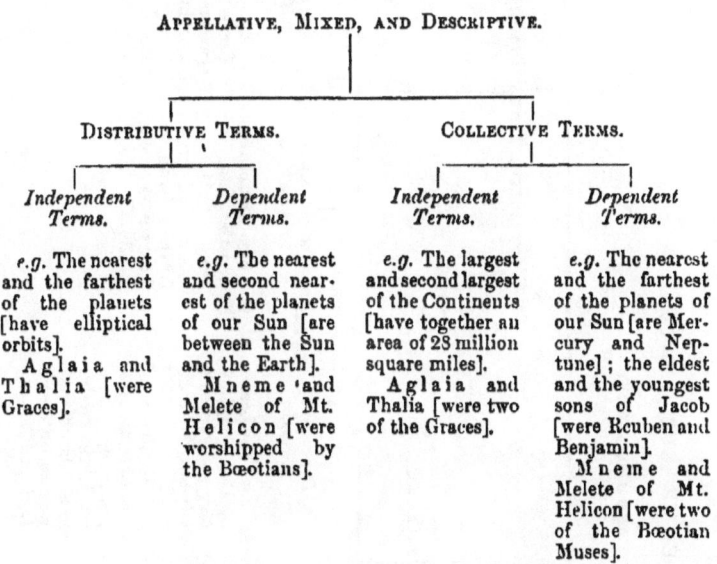

DISTRIBUTIVE TERMS.

Independent Terms.
e.g. The nearest and the farthest of the planets [have elliptical orbits]. Aglaia and Thalia [were Graces].

Dependent Terms.
e.g. The nearest and second nearest of the planets of our Sun [are between the Sun and the Earth]. Mneme and Melete of Mt. Helicon [were worshipped by the Bœotians].

COLLECTIVE TERMS.

Independent Terms.
e.g. The largest and second largest of the Continents [have together an area of 28 million square miles]. Aglaia and Thalia [were two of the Graces].

Dependent Terms.
e.g. The nearest and the farthest of the planets of our Sun [are Mercury and Neptune]; the eldest and the youngest sons of Jacob [were Reuben and Benjamin]. Mneme and Melete of Mt. Helicon [were two of the Bœotian Muses].

TABLE XV.]

UNIQUE TOTAL TERMS (ENUMERATIVE).
APPELLATIVE, MIXED, AND DESCRIPTIVE.

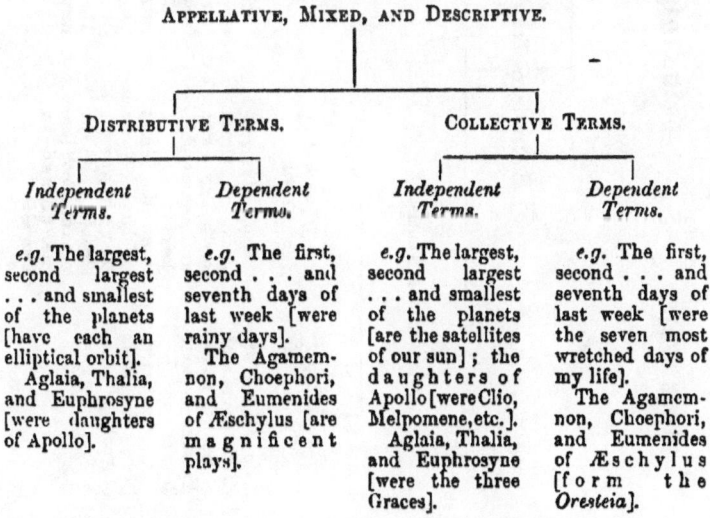

DISTRIBUTIVE TERMS.

Independent Terms.
e.g. The largest, second largest ... and smallest of the planets [have each an elliptical orbit]. Aglaia, Thalia, and Euphrosyne [were daughters of Apollo].

Dependent Terms.
e.g. The first, second ... and seventh days of last week [were rainy days]. The Agamemnon, Choephori, and Eumenides of Æschylus [are magnificent plays].

COLLECTIVE TERMS.

Independent Terms.
e.g. The largest, second largest ... and smallest of the planets [are the satellites of our sun]; the daughters of Apollo [were Clio, Melpomene, etc.]. Aglaia, Thalia, and Euphrosyne [were the three Graces].

Dependent Terms.
e.g. The first, second ... and seventh days of last week [were the seven most wretched days of my life]. The Agamemnon, Choephori, and Eumenides of Æschylus [form the Oresteia].

C

34 IMPORT OF PROPOSITIONS.

TABLE XVI.] UNIQUE TOTAL TERMS (SUMMARY).

(APPELLATIVE, MIXED, AND DESCRIPTIVE.)

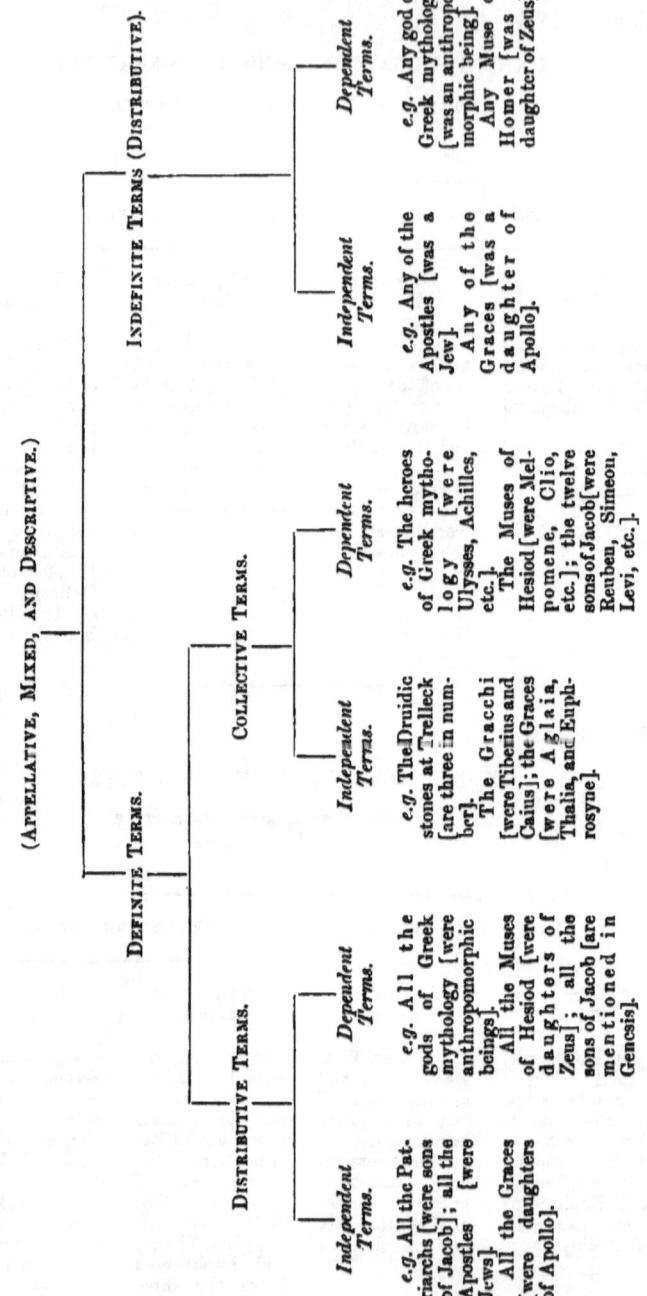

SECTION IV.

NOTE ON DEFINITION AND CONNOTATION.

The Definition of a word, it is said, sets forth its meaning; and the Meaning of a word, as distinguished from its application, is frequently said to be its "connotation."

But what is the connotation of a word or name? According to some, it is the whole of the attributes common to the things called by that name. This is the view of Jevons and some other writers, and, according to Dr. Venn (*Empirical Logic*, p. 183), it is shared by Dr. Bain. Mr. Keynes, however (cf. *Formal Logic*, 2nd ed. p. 26), thinks Dr. Bain's opinion to be that the connotation of a word comprises, not *all* the attributes common to the things to which it applies, but only those which are independent of one another. The difficulty, not to say impossibility, of deciding what qualities (if any) *are* independent, seems to be an insuperable objection to this latter view. The opinion that any name of which we know the application (cf. Jevons, *Elementary Lessons in Logic*, Less. v., etc.) connotes all the "peculiar qualities and circumstances" which we know to belong to the thing named, involves the admission that proper names are among the most connotative of any; and this admission Jevons makes, or rather insists upon. But the proper name of a person *not* known individually, must be allowed, even by Jevons himself, to have only a minimum of connotation, while a class-name applied to any object not known individually may convey a maximum of connotation. Jevons confuses (1) the information conveyed by a name, without any individual knowledge concerning the very thing or things named, and (2) the information gained by individual knowledge of the very thing or things indicated by a name, and consequently associated with and suggested by the name. The view that (2) is included in connotation involves as a consequence that *the same* name may have different connotations to different people. And there is indeed a further confusion here, besides the one mentioned above—a confusion, namely, between (1) the qualities which a thing is *known* to possess, and (2) the qualities which it actually *does* possess (cf. Keynes, *Formal Logic*, 2nd ed. p. 27, distinction between *intension*, *connotation*, and *comprehension*). Taking connotation to include (2), it is clear that we do not, and cannot, *know* the whole connotation of any name whatever. And it is plainly absurd that the *meaning* of a name should be said to be something which no person has ever understood to be conveyed by it.

In the case of any class-name, if it is said that it connotes all the attributes *known* to be possessed in common by the things to which it is applied, it follows that no universal synthetic propositions are possible; and worse than this, that a multitude of significant names must have such a voluminous meaning, and so many words the same meaning, as would make language hopelessly unmanageable and confused. Since our thought is discursive—must proceed by *successive steps* of intuition—we need corresponding conditions in language; that is, we need limited definitions and clearly marked differences of meaning in different words.

It seems best to say that what a name connotes (what is included in its determination) is, *those attributes on account of which we apply the name, and in the absence of any of which we should not apply it.* (Cf. Mill, *Logic*, Bk. i. ch. ii. § 5, p. 38, 9th ed., and Bk. i. ch. viii. § 3, p. 156; also Keynes, *Formal Logic*, 2nd ed. p. 25.) It may happen, and generally does happen, that the attributes connoted by a name are in our experience inseparably connected with *other* attributes which it does not connote; but it is not on account of these latter that we apply the name in question. I believe, indeed, that it is probable that every attribute is one of an unique set, all of which are inseparably connected (cf. Section on *Ground of Induction*), and that the more our knowledge grows, the fuller and surer will be the *suggestions* which, from association, each name carries with it. But this increase of knowledge concerning the things indicated by any name is quite different from increase of the connotation of the name itself; and increase of the former kind takes place to a far greater extent than of the latter kind; though, no doubt, there can hardly be change of connotation except as the result of an increase of knowledge.

SECTION V.

THE MEANING OF *ABSTRACT AND CONCRETE*, AND OF *CONCEPT*.

Reference to the various definitions of Abstract and Concrete Terms given in logical handbooks is sufficient to show that the distinction is one involving some difficulty. In *The Oxford Elements of Logic* (1816) adjectives only—*e.g.* white, round, long—are recognised as Concrete Terms (cf. p. 16); such names as man, house, fairy, are not classed under the head either of Abstract or Concrete. Dr. Abbott in his *Elements of Logic* (1883, cf. pp. 4, 5, 83, 84, etc.) seems undecided how to class adjectives; Jevons, in *Studies in Deductive Logic* (2nd ed. p. 4), omits them altogether; but in his *Elementary Lessons in Logic* (p. 21, 7th ed.) he says that we must "carefully observe that adjectives are concrete, not abstract." Again, while in *Studies in Deductive Logic* (p. 1) he allows only names that can stand as the Subject of a proposition to be Categorematic, thus by implication excluding adjectives from the category of terms altogether, in the *Elementary Lessons* (p. 18) he admits adjectives among the words "which stand, or appear to stand, alone as complete terms." He explicitly says (*Elementary Lessons in Logic*, p. 21; *Studies in Deductive Logic*, ch. i. § 2, pp. 1, 2) that he was conscious of a difficulty, and the presence of this to his mind is clearly betrayed by these inconsistent and confused statements. Jevons' conclusion seems to be that abstractness must be considered "a question of degree" (cf. *Studies*, p. 2). No doubt it is a question of degree if by an *abstract term* is meant a term, the application of which presupposes a process of abstraction—every adjective, every common term, every term applying to an attribute, is applied as a result of abstraction; even a "proper name" is in this sense abstract, for, though not applicable to more than one individual in the same sense, it is applicable to that one at different times and under different circumstances, and in using it as a permanent appellation, abstraction is made from these times and circumstances. This is not, of course, the sense in which Abstract is understood when used in antithesis to Concrete. According to Mill (*Logic*, i. 29, 9th ed.), "A concrete name is a name which stands for a thing ... as John, the sea, this table ... white." "An abstract name is a name which stands for an attribute of a thing," *e.g.* whiteness. Here the distinction seems to depend on discriminating between a Subject of Attributes and Attributes of a Subject. It seems clear that by *thing* as used here, Mill means just a *subject of attributes*. But what reason is there for calling a term which applies to *attributes* Abstract, while a term which applies to a *subject* is called Concrete? *Attribute* implies *subject* as much as *subject* implies *attributes*—as much as parent implies child, or half implies whole. As Mill himself says (*op. cit.* i. 53), "the condition of belonging to a substance" (subject) is "precisely what constitutes an attribute." In what respect is the term *redness*, which applies to an attribute *of red things*, more abstract than the term *red thing*, which applies to a thing which has the attribute? A further difficulty on Mill's view would arise with reference to the predicates of such propositions as, *e.g., Perseverance is admirable*. If adjectives are concrete, we have here a "concrete" Predicate asserted of an "abstract" Subject. Mr. Stock, *Deductive Logic* (1888, pp. 28, 29), says, "Whether *an attributive is abstract or concrete* depends on the nature of the subject of which it is asserted or denied. When we say, 'This man is noble,' the term 'noble' is concrete as being the name of a substance; but when we say, 'This act is noble,' the term 'noble' is abstract, as being the name of an attribute." "Those terms only are called abstract *which cannot be applied to substances at all.*" (*Op. cit.* p. 27. The italics are mine.) Compare also what is said on pp. 24, 25.

If we fall back upon Whately (*Logic*, 9th ed. p. 81), we find that he describes Abstract Term as a term which is applied to a "notion derived from the view taken of any object" when not considered "with a reference to, or as in conjunction with, the object that furnished the notion." As a term applying to an attribute is, *ex vi termini*, considered with such "reference" and "conjunction," we seem driven to the conclusion that what Whately *ought* to mean, and what *must* be meant by Abstract Term as distinguished from Concrete, if there is a consistent meaning in the distinction, is that an Abstract Term is the name of a logical "Concept"—something complete in itself and isolated from all else—*totus teres atque rotundus*, involving no reference to attributes, as a term applying to a subject does, and no reference to a subject, as a term applying to an attribute does. Here there is indeed a very marked distinction between the objects indicated by Abstract Terms and by other terms. But it remains to ask whether it is possible that Terms—that is, the Subjects and Predicates of propositions—can indicate such logical Concepts.

The meaning here assigned to Concept is substantially that recognised by Mansel, who, in common with some other logicians, holds that Logic is concerned with Concepts, and Concepts only. Locke's "Abstract Idea" seems to correspond to Mansel's "Concept," and he says that the "names of abstract ideas" are "abstract words" (Essay, Bk. iii. ch. 8, § 1). But, according to Locke, "all our affirmations . . . are only in concrete" (*loc. cit.*). With this view I agree, only going so far beyond it as to hold that not only our affirmations, but also our negations, are "only in concrete." For of such a "concept" nothing but itself could be asserted, and nothing could be denied but the negative of itself; if isolated and independent, it could have no relations whatever to things in space and time. It would be like one of Leibnitz's Monads, having "no windows" by which anything could get into or out of it; a closed, solitary, impregnable whole, incapable of diminution, increase, or division, or alteration of any kind.

It seems indisputable that a "concept" as thus defined (cf. Mansel, etc.) must be quite incapable of alteration. *Alteration* of any "concept" ABC would mean that some other "concept"—*e.g.* AB, or ABCD—is substituted for it. If not isolated and independent, it would, of course, be related to all other things, like any ordinary idea. Again, if a "concept" were something complete, the name applying to it and determining its character would have to indicate relations to everything in the world, for such relations are among the attributes of every constituent of the universe. Indeed, one such name would describe the universe and all things in it, and there need be only one name at all, and no propositions. But, without pushing the thing to such an extreme, it must be allowed that if all terms applied to independent or complete concepts, all propositions would be reduced to the *A is A* type; any illustration, any bringing into connection, any movement of thought at all would be impossible. Indeed, assertion itself would be impossible; for *A is A*, taken strictly, has absolutely no predicative force, and merely attempts to assert a necessary presupposition of all significant assertion (cf. *post*, p. 52), and even, I think, of thought itself.

I think that not only must it be impossible for names applying to monadic concepts to be the terms of propositions, but also that such concepts could not be objects of thought at all. This seems to follow directly from the acceptance (1) of the Law of Relativity (*Semper idem sentire et non sentire ad idem recidunt*), and (2) of that definition of concept according to which it is *totus* and *teres*—something complete in itself and wholly unrelated. Nothing is an object of knowledge unless it is an identity in diversity, a permanent amid change, and unless it is like some things and unlike other things. Whatever is comparable with other things must be connected with them in some system, *e.g.* in space; but members of a system are doubly related, namely, both to one another and to the unity of which they are members, hence the members of a system can never consist of such essentially isolated entities as concepts.

But the name Concept may be differently defined, *e.g.* as the "mental equivalent of a general name." Of the existence of such mental objects there can be no doubt. But I should demur to this definition, because I should maintain that it draws an arbitrary distinction between the mental equivalent of Common Names and that of other names, *e.g.* Proper Names. Have I not an idea as truly general, corresponding to, *e.g.*, *Alfred Tennyson*, as to *snow* or *horse*? My idea of him must be one that applies throughout all variety of time, place, and circumstance, just as my idea of snow or horse applies under a variety of individual manifestations. And there seem many reasons in support of the view that Common (and Proper) names are not the names of concepts (in the sense of *mental equivalents*). For if they are—(1) we are left without any term for the object from seeing (or in some way knowing) which we have got the idea. (2) When a familiar object, *e.g.* a bird, is seen, some such mental equivalent must accompany the sight of it as accompanies the hearing of the word, otherwise it could not be recognised. (3) In the case of a word having two distinct applications— *e.g.* box, page—we determine which of the applications we are to take by reference, not to a *concept*, but to *a thing of which we may have a concept;* because what any concept is must be determined by what the *thing* is of which it is the concept. (4) The idea called up in the mind by a Common or other name, is an idea which differs widely in different minds, and in the same mind under different circumstances (as of context, interest, etc.). Thus the same name would have an indefinite multitude of different meanings. If we say that in every unit of all this multitude there is some element of similarity, and that it is this which is meant by *mental equivalent*, that a concept is a kind of mental type, *e.g.* a kind of Bird-in-itself, I would ask, Can it be recognised as a *type* unless considered in conjunction with its ectypes, the copies in which it is exemplified? I should say that the person whose mental equivalent of a name (common or other) is most perfect and adequate, is the person in whose mind that name calls up the greatest fulness of well-ordered particulars, so connected and arranged as to give most prominence to what is most important; so presented, in fact, as to exhibit clearly the law or type common to all; here the element or elements of similarity are exhibited in the greatest fulness of relationship. It would be generally allowed, I think, that an expert in any subject is likely to have more perfect mental equivalents of the names special to that subject than those who are comparatively unacquainted with it; or that any one has a better mental equivalent of the name of a person whom he knows well than he has of those with whom his acquaintance is but slight. It seems to me that, for instance, I myself have beyond comparison a clearer, more satisfactory, and, I suppose, truer idea called up by names of things or persons that I am well acquainted with, than by those of things or persons that I do not know, or know but slightly, or am only learning to know. And the superiority seems to consist in the greater fulness and completeness of the corresponding ideas in the first case. Things with which one is familiar become clearer and more real in proportion as one knows more about them—the unity of a system becomes more striking in proportion as one realizes more fully the inter-relations of the plurality which it embraces. This is quite compatible with the fact that an influx of fresh information, especially in an unfamiliar region, may sometimes involve one in great confusion.

As to the mental equivalents which actually occur to people's minds in using names, experiment seems to show that these differ exceedingly in different cases. Such a word as animal, for instance, will call up to one person's mind the name simply printed, or written in a particular handwriting, or printed on the outside of a particular book; or it may call up the image of a "picture alphabet" with illustrations of animals, or some story of animal intelligence, or a pet animal, or the first animal one cared for, or the cat of the house, or an idea of the movements made in speaking the word, or some striking delineation of an animal seen in a magic-lantern exhibition or a picture gallery, or Noah's ark, or a mere shapeless moving mass. If one dwells upon the word, an immense succession of ideas may occur to one; in rapid reading or speaking, probably only one or two. What seems very often to happen in the latter case is, that one just thinks very transiently of the word itself, with a satisfactory, though evanescent, consciousness of understanding its meaning and application. If in reading or listening one meets a word of which one does not know the meaning, one is instantly arrested by a feeling of dissatisfaction, due to the recognition of a hindrance to comprehension. As an illustration of what I mean, I may refer to what happens when, in looking rapidly through a passage in some tolerably familiar language with a view to translating it, one comes here and there upon words of which one does not know the meaning. The translator, the moment he sees the other words, and without any pause to realize their full import, is aware that he knows their signification; and he is aware, just as instantaneously, that he does *not* know the meaning of the strange words. What perhaps often happens to some people, in connection with Common and Proper names, is that these call up in the mind a kind of "generic image." *E.g.* the word *horse* may suggest a sort of vague image, like a horse seen at a little distance in a fog, which is definite enough not to be mistaken for any other creature, but not definite enough to be identified as of this or that breed, colour, size, etc., much less as a definite individual: *quadruped* may suggest merely four vague elementary legs, supporting an elementary body, like a child's drawing—and so on. Our image of many acquaintances, and even friends, may be very vague, just definite enough to enable us to know them when we see them, but by no means definite enough to enable us to accurately draw or describe them, or perhaps even to say by what sign or signs we recognise them.

Butler (Sermon I. note 2) puts the case of a man whom he supposes to " go through some laborious work, upon promise of a great reward, without any distinct knowledge what the reward would be." The state of this man's mind with reference to the reward must, I imagine, correspond in essentials with the state of mind of a person dwelling on a Common Name withdrawn from context; but, of course, names ordinarily occur to us with a context which helps to determine their mental equivalent.

(II.)—*OF PROPOSITIONS AS WHOLES.*

(*A.*)—CATEGORICAL PROPOSITIONS.

SECTION VI.

IMPORT AND CLASSIFICATION OF CATEGORICAL PROPOSITIONS.

Formal (most General) Import of Categoricals.

It seems convenient to discuss Propositions in immediate connection with Terms, the constituents of all Propositions. *Proposition* may perhaps be defined quite generally as a sentence or significant combination of words affirming or altogether denying unity (in difference).

Each of the principal forms of Proposition has, of course, its own special definition. Propositions may be divided into (1) Categorical, (2) Inferential, and (3) Alternative; (2) may be subdivided[1] into Hypothetical, *e.g.* If D is E, D (or F) is G; and Conditional, *e.g.* If any D is E, that D is F. The division is exhibited in tabular form, thus:—

PROPOSITIONS.

Categorical Propositions. Inferential Propositions. Alternative Propositions.

Hypothetical Propositions. Conditional Propositions.

[1] Cf. Keynes, *Formal Logic*, 2nd edition, pp. 64, 65; also *post*, Section on Inferential Propositions.

I assume that any proposition would be admitted to be the expression of a judgment, and capable of being defined as such. This mode of definition is, however, subject to two inconveniences; for, in the first place, until a definition of judgment has been given, we have defined *ignotum per ignotum;* and, in the second place, it tends to a confusion of standpoints if, after having treated Terms, the elements of Propositions, as applying to *Things*, we define Proposition as the mere expression of a psychological process. Unless we apprehended things we could, of course, have neither ideas of them nor names of them; unless we judged we could neither think Propositions nor express them; and it is true that Logic is concerned with "what we ought to think." But Apprehension and Judgment, considered as mental processes, are the concern of Psychology, and Logic is concerned with what we ought to think only because we ought to think of things as they are. There is no more reason for defining Proposition by reference to Judgment, than for defining Term by reference to Apprehension. If Terms are concerned with things, Propositions are concerned with the same things. Our things may, of course, be thoughts, or thoughts of thoughts, and so on, to any degree of "Re-representation," but at any point in the regress what our terms apply to is surely the objects thought about, and not the apprehension of those objects; what our Propositions import is surely something about those things other than the fact (however indisputable) that we frame a judgment concerning them. However re-representative the objects to which our terms apply, our thought of the thing named would be impossible without our having an idea which is something other than the thing intended to be indicated by the name. The presence of such an idea is as inevitable as the nervous change which is supposed to accompany all change of consciousness. For instance, let my term be *King's College Chapel, Cambridge.* Here the object named is a construction of stone and mortar distant, perhaps, more than a hundred miles from my present position in space. But without an idea present to my mind and other than the object named, I could not hear or use the term with intelligence. And if my term is, *the thought which I had two minutes ago of King's College Chapel*, the object named, and the accompanying idea, though not so diverse as in the previous case, are equally distinct.

A Categorical Proposition might be defined as, A Proposition which affirms (or negates) Identity of Denomination in Diversity of Attribution, and is of the form

S copula P.[1]

But this definition would admit Propositions of the form

A is A,

because the second A differs from the first A in implication, since it is *predicated*, while the first A is *predicated of*. *A is A*, however, is a locution which has only the *form* and not the *force* of a Proposition. A *significant* Categorical Proposition, a Proposition in which the Predicate adds something to the Subject, may be defined as, A Proposition which affirms (or negates) Identity of Denomination in Diversity of Determination. (Or if we consider directly the *Things* which are named by our terms rather than the terms themselves, we may define as follows: A Categorical Proposition is a Proposition which affirms (or negates) quantitive Identity in qualitive Diversity.)

Thus a Categorical Proposition asserts complete coincidence or absolute non-coincidence of S and P.

It will perhaps not be superfluous to illustrate the application of my definition by a few simple examples. In *All birds are animals*—a proposition which (understood with an implication of the knowledge which we possess concerning the

---

[1] In a class there is also one-in-many or many-in-one, namely, a qualitive one in a quantitive many, or similarity of character in a plurality of things. There is a third kind of one-in-many, where we have a system of Subjects of Attributes related to each other and to a common whole (a quantitive many in a quantitive one). Mill (*Logic*, ii. 395) considers the importance of the distinction upon which my definition turns—the distinction, namely, between a thing being *identical* (*numero tantum*), and things being *similar* (*specie tantum*). The same distinction is discussed by Dr. James Ward (*Encycl. Brit.* 9th ed., part 77, p. 81a, art. "Psychology"), who uses the terms *individual identity* and *indistinguishable resemblance*.

relation between the classes *Birds* and *Animals*) might be represented as in the first diagram—what is asserted is that the denomination of *All birds* is the very same as the denomination of *animals*. But not of *all* animals, but only of those animals included by circle B—that is, *some animals*. The denomination of *All birds* is found to coincide with, to be in short, the denomination of the *some animals* of the proposition under consideration. This coincidence of denomination of S and P might be represented thus:

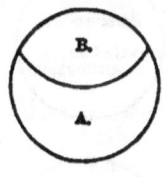

That the determination of *All birds* is different from that of [*some*] *animals* is obvious.

Take again, Some vertebrates are quadrupeds (understood, as the previous example, in its full material signification).

The continued identical existence of the things indicated by *Some vertebrates* is just the same as that of the things indicated by [*some*] *quadrupeds*—that is, the denomination of S and P is identical. The determination of *Some vertebrates* is, of course, different from that of [*some*] *quadrupeds*. In the proposition, Those men are my three brothers, the S denominates the quantitiveness—the continued identical existence—of certain individuals, say, AB, CD, and XY; and the P denominates the very same quantitiveness, the same continued existence under whatever change of attributes—*i.e.* the quantitiveness of the identical persons, AB, CD, and XY. Hence, wherever two terms have identical denomination, their *application* is the same; what the one term is the name of, the other term is the name of. The determination of *Those men* differs, of course, from the determination of *My three brothers*. Again in, This musician is a painter, the

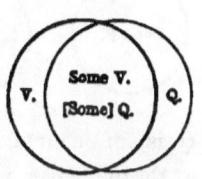

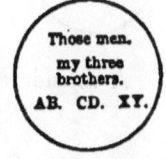

denomination of S is the denomination of P; hence S and P apply to one and the same person. The determination is again different. In Perseverance is admirable, Courage is valour, there is the same identity of denomination and diversity of determination as in the previous examples. The last example differs from the others in this, that (if not interpreted as a definition) the determination of S differs from that of P in *name* only. In *S is not P*, what is denominated by S is declared to be *not* what is denominated by P, the determination of S differs *ex vi termini* from the determination of P.

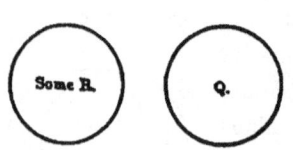

In Some R is not Q, what is asserted is, that the denomination of *Some R* is wholly uncoincident with the denomination of Q. The *determination* of *Some R* and of Q is, of course, different. In, There is no rose without a thorn, what is asserted is that the denomination of *all roses* is wholly unidentical with the denomination of *without a thorn*. And the determination of *all roses* is different from that of *without a thorn*.

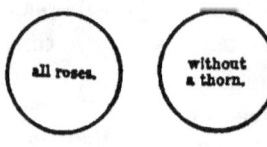

A consideration of the extreme case

A is A (A is-not not-A)

confirms this analysis. For though *A is A* conveys absolutely nothing more than mere *A* does (and this appears to me to be nothing at all, for a mere isolated name is a complete nonentity), the exigencies of assertion introduce difference of position in space or order in time between the Subject A and the Predicate A, in addition to the implication that the SA is *what is predicated of*, while the PA is *what is predicated*. Unless we could speak or write A twice over we could not assert A to be A. Thus in *A is A* there is a formal though valueless diversity of attribution, and this valuelessness becomes if possible more obvious when we use significant terms. And that both A's have an identical denomination (and thus both apply to an identical thing) seems so evident as to be incapable of proof.

If the denomination of SA were different from the denomination of PA, this would have to be expressed by saying that

(S)A is-*not* (P)A.

The *proposition*, *A is not-A*, is comparable to the *terms Aa* (*a* = *not-A*), *Round-Square*, or any other complex of contradictions.

And while in *A is A* the diversity of attribution had shrunk to such a degree as to be purely a matter of form, and incapable of imparting any value to the predication, in *A is not-A* the diversity has become so extreme as to destroy the identity implied by the affirmative copula. In *A is-not A*, though there is a formal diversity of attribution between S and P, the determination is precisely similar, and hence the denomination is identical. The proposition is therefore self-contradictory, the identity involved by the *terms* being negatived by the *copula*.

Unless we admit an indefinite variety of different copulas, I do not see that any insuperable objection can be brought against the above account of Categorical Propositions. This account, involving as it does the view that all terms have both denomination and determination, seems to me of fundamental importance. I have tried to give some further justification of it, both in later passages of this Section and also in the Section on Quantification and Conversion.[1]

[1] I should like to refer here to some passages of De Morgan, Dr. Venn, Mr. Bradley, and Mr. Bosanquet, which seem to me confirmatory or elucidatory of the view of the Import of Categorical Propositions which I advocate. De Morgan says (*Formal Logic*, pp. 49, 50), "Speak of names and say 'man *is* animal;' the *is* is here an *is* of applicability; to whatsoever (idea, object, etc.)

Propositions of the form:

There is X, There are Y's,

are reducible to either—

(1) X is in that place;
Y's are in that place—

For instance, if X = Newton's statue, then There is X = Newton's statue is there (= in some indicated place); if Y's = blackberries, then There are Y's = Blackberries are there (= in some indicated place)—

or (2) X is existent;
Y's are existent.

For instance, if Y's = Green roses, then *There are Y's* may mean, Green roses are existent.[1] Such propositions as,

It is raining, It is cold,

are already in the form *S is P*—*it* apparently being meant to

man is a name to be applied, to that same (idea, object, etc.) animal is a name to be applied. . . . As to absolute external objects, the *is* is an *is* of identity, the most common and positive use of the word. Every man *is* one of the animals; touch him, you touch an animal; destroy him, you destroy an animal."

Dr. Venn (*Empirical Logic*, p. 212) says, "What the statement [Plovers are Lapwings, Clematis Vitalba is Traveller's Joy] really means is that *a certain object* has two different names belonging to it." (The italics are mine.)

The next quotation is from Mr. Bradley (*Principles of Logic*, p. 28): "The doctrine of equation, or identity of the terms, has itself grasped a truth, a truth turned upside down and not brought to the light, but for all that a deep fundamental principle."

"Turned upside down and made false it runs thus: the object of judgment is, despite their difference in meaning, to assert the identity of subject and predicate [when taken in extension]." This "upside down" doctrine—if for *despite* we read *through*—is exactly what seems to me to be the true account of the import of Categorical Propositions (explaining *identity* to mean *tantum numero*). Mr. Bradley's condemnation of this interpretation seems to me to depend on a confusion between identity and similarity, for he goes on to say (p. 29), "In 'S = P' we do *not* mean to say that S and P are identical [= ?]. We mean to say that they are *different*, that the diverse attributes S and P are united in one subject." If in *S is P* the attributions of S and P are diverse, but are "united in one subject," this is exactly what I mean by S and P being identical (where S and P are Substantive Terms).

Mr. Bosanquet says (*Logic*, i. 96), "The content of a judgment is always . . . a recognised identity in differences."

[1] Is the *there* in this case a corruption of *they?* If the original form was, e.g. Green roses, they are = Green roses exist, or are to be found (cf. an old

indicate something vaguely conceived as a causal agent to which P is attributed as effect, or, more vaguely still, a subject to which P is assigned as attribute.

According to the above definition of significant Categoricals (as has been already repeated and illustrated to perhaps a tedious degree), the S and P of an affirmative proposition have always the same denomination and different determinations. If it is allowed that the S and P in any Categorical have denomination, it seems clear that in affirmative propositions they must both have *the same* (= identical) denomination and in negative propositions *different* (= non-identical) denominations. If my S is the name of something having its own quantitiveness, the P which I assert that S is must certainly have the same quantitiveness, and therefore be the same *thing* (subject or attribute, as the case may be) as S, and have the same denomination as S. Of negative propositions the converse holds. The assertion that the S and P of the Categorical must have different determinations is perhaps more likely to be disputed than the assertion that they must, if affirmative, have the same denomination, and if negative a different denomination. (Terms having the same determination must have also the same denomination, therefore the above assertion concerning different determinations holds with reference to negative as well as to affirmative propositions.) In trying, just above, to apply my definition to "Propositions" of the form *A is A, A is-not not-A*, I came to the conclusion that this form of words can have no predicative force. I wish to set forth a little further the reasons for this conclusion, and will therefore ask, What can *A is A, A is-not not-A*, stand for? What thought, what truth, or what assertion is it that can correspond to, or be expressed by, these forms of speech?

There seems to be *prima facie* a case for special examination of these (which have been called Identical) "Propositions"

---

form of inscription in books, *e.g. Stephen Thorp, his book*), it may have passed to They are, (*i.e.*) green roses (are); and then, perhaps for euphony's sake and with some oblivion of the primary meaning and a vague reference to *there* in sense (2), There are green roses. *There* seems sometimes to be pleonastic, as in There is frost to-night, There is nothing to be seen from my window.

—for *A is A*, and *A is-not not-A* differ in the following respects from ordinary propositions of the *S is P, S is-not P* type—(1) they can have no intelligible contradictory; (2) they cannot be divided into Adjectival and Coincidental Propositions; (3) *any* word or combination of words or symbols may stand for S, and for P; (4) S and P in *A is A* must be *precisely* similar; in *A is-not not-A*, S and P differ in being the precise negatives of each other.

Let us take a sentence of the form *A is A*, in which A is significant—and since *A is-not not-A* is reducible to the affirmative form, it need hardly be examined here separately. Let the sentence be, *e.g.*, Whiteness is whiteness, or This tree is this tree. In using these forms of words how do I go beyond what is involved in the mere enunciation of the words *whiteness, this tree?* That *whiteness* and *this tree* should BE *whiteness* and *this tree* respectively seems not a significant assertion, but a presupposition of all significant assertion— as *extension* is a presupposition of *colour*, or *ears* of *sound*. And if, in perceiving *whiteness* or thinking of *this tree*, I ever *need* to assert that *whiteness is whiteness*, or that *this tree is this tree*, do I not just as much need to assert the same sentence separately for both S and P in each case? And at what point is the process to stop? And if identity needs to be asserted for the *terms*, does it not equally need to be asserted for the *copula?* If we need to declare that *whiteness* is *whiteness*, etc., do we not also need to declare that *Is* is *Is?* Unless we can start by accepting terms and copula as having simply and certainly a constant signification, I do not see how we are ever to start at all.

The analysis involved in my definition of Categorical Propositions I believe to be both ultimate and absolutely general, and also to contain the maximum that can be asserted with absolute generality. When the Proposition is analysed into (1) Subject and (2) Predication, there are always two elements distinguishable in (2); namely, (*a*) a constant element (the copula) significant of identity or non-identity, (*b*) a changing element (the predicate). *E.g.* in (*a*) He sleeps, (*β*) He will sleep, (a) = He (is) sleeping in present time, (β) = He (is) to sleep in future time. Hence the analysis into Subject and Predication fails of being ultimate. Hobbes' account of Categorical Proposition—that the Predicate is a name of the same thing of which the Subject is a name—furnishes an absolutely general but a deficient and superficial definition (cf. Mill, *Logic*, i. 99). The Class Inclusion and Exclusion view is neither ultimate nor formal (strictly general). If we say that

>R is Q (1),
>R is not Q (2),

may mean respectively

>R is included in Q (3),
>R is excluded from Q (4),

we give an account which needs explanation even more than that which it professes to explain. For the relation between R and *included in Q, excluded from Q*, in (3) and (4), is precisely the same as that between R and Q (1), *not-Q* (2); and the justification for adding *included in* to the copula in (1) is not clear. Again, this explanation is not properly formal; for there are a multitude of propositions to which it cannot be made to apply at all, *e.g.* Tully is Cicero, Courage is Valour, The word *quadruped* is a word that means *having four legs*. And in the cases where it does apply, it refers to a relation *not* between the Terms, but between the Term-names, for the "relation" indicated by the copula between the *Terms* (Subject and Predicate) of a Categorical Proposition is that of Identity or Non-Identity. And *R is included in Q* is not even *compatible with*

>R is Q,

for what *R is Q* means is, that R and Q are coincident or identical.

As regards Mathematical Equations, they also may be analyzed into

>S copula P (cf. Section X.).

The interpretation which makes

$$(\text{All S is P}) = (Sp = 0)$$

and Mill's view of the Import of Propositions will be discussed in Sections XI. and VIII.

That view of the Import of a Categorical Proposition, according to which it asserts a connection between two *ideas* (which is one of the views discussed and rejected by Mill, *Logic*, Bk. i. ch. v.), results from a particular theory of the import of Terms.

Classification of Categorical Propositions.

In the Tables of Categorical Propositions (pp. 62–76), the first distinction taken is that between (1) *Adjectival Propositions* and (2) *Coincidental Propositions*. As before remarked (p. 21), (1) are Propositions which have a Uni-terminal Term for P, and they cannot, *as Adjectival Propositions*, be converted; but *Adjectival* Propositions can always be replaced by Coincidental Propositions, which *are* susceptible of conversion. And as all the subdivisions of Adjectivals and Coincidentals correspond, I have in the Tables of Categorical Propositions confined myself to Coincidentals. These are propositions which have Bi-terminal Terms for S and P, and they are susceptible of conversion. I have adopted the name *Coincidental* because it seemed a convenient word, and is, besides, suggestive of the identity of denomination which holds between the S and P of all affirmative Categorical Propositions, and is perhaps specially obvious in those in which both terms are bi-terminal.

Coincidental Propositions may be either (1) *Attribute Propositions, i.e.* propositions which have an Attribute Term for S; or (2) *Substantive Propositions, i.e.* propositions which have a Substantive Term for S.

Attribute Propositions subdivide into *Complete* and *Partial Propositions*, and Partial into *Singular* (*Definite and Indefinite*). *Particulars* are *Distributive* or *Collective*. Each of the above, again, may be *Vernacular* or *Specific*; and each of all these subdivisions (in common with every penultimate division in the classification) subdivides into *Independent* and *Dependent*. A Dependent Proposition is a Proposition which has at least one Dependent Term.

The majority of the subdivisions of Attribute Terms seem, however, to be most appropriately, and perhaps even most usually, expressed as *Complete Propositions* (*i.e.* Propositions which predicate concerning the Attribute in its completeness), the modification on which a distinction depends appearing as part of the content of the Predicate. *E.g.* instead of saying, Some perseverance is mischievous, it might (and perhaps most frequently would) be said, Perseverance is sometimes mischievous, or, Perseverance is mischievous in some cases. The corresponding Common Proposition here would be, Some cases (or instances) of perseverance are mischievous. We can say, That courage was remarkable, Some kindness is cruel; but, That instance of courage was remarkable, Kindness is sometimes cruel, are perhaps preferable. Attribute Names have properly no plural, and Particular Definites frequently cannot be expressed as (Particular) Attribute Propositions. *E.g.* Those instances of laziness are nothing out of the common.

In Coincidental Propositions which have Attribute Terms for S and for P, conversion takes place without any modification of the terms; *e.g.* Courage is valour, Generosity is not justice, convert quite simply to Valour is courage, Justice is not generosity. In such propositions as Courage is Valour, the terms have not only the same denomination but also a determination similar in every point except in this, that the object is called by different names in S and P (unless we regard the proposition as making an assertion about the *word* which is the Subject).

In my Table of Categorical Propositions (Table XVII.) the first division is into *Whole* and *Partial*. Whole Propositions include *Complete Propositions* (cf. above), *Individual Propositions*, and *Total Propositions*.

Individual Propositions are divided into *Descriptive*, *Appellative*, and *Mixed* (partly Descriptive and partly Appellative). Total Propositions may be *Universal* (or *Unlimited*) and *General* (or *Limited*). Universals are *Common* and *Special*, and the Common are Vernacular and Specific. Each of these classes of Universals may be Definite (Collective and Distributive) or Indefinite (Distributive).

(All equations of the kind commonly called Mathematical or Quantitative propositions are Dependent.)

The Generals are (1) *Special*, (2) *Unique*. (1) Subdivide into *Summary* (Definite and Indefinite) and *Enumerative* (which here and elsewhere are all Definite). The Definites may be Distributive or Collective; the Indefinite Generals are (here and elsewhere, like the Indefinite Universals) all Distributive. (2) Unique Generals may be Summary or Enumerative, and these again may be Descriptive, Appellative, or Mixed. Those which are Summary further subdivide into Definite and Indefinite, Distributive and Collective; the Enumeratives may be Distributive or Collective.

Partial Propositions (*i.e.* Propositions of which the S has a Term-indicator which is not Universal nor General) are divided into *Single* (referring to one individual, species, or specimen of a class or quantity) and *Multiple* (referring to more than one such individual, species, or specimen). Single Propositions subdivide into *Singular* (Attribute, Common, and Special) and *Unitary* (Special and Unique). Common Singulars may be Vernacular or Specific, and each of these and Special Singulars subdivide into Definite and Indefinite. Unique Unitaries may be Descriptive, Appellative, or Mixed, and each of these, and Special Unitary Propositions, may be Definite or Indefinite. Multiple Propositions are *Particular* (Attribute, Common, and Special) and *Plurative* (Special and Unique). Such propositions as, Some bread is unwholesome, Some air is bracing, Some gas has escaped, should, I think, be classed rather as Multiple than as Single, since where the *Some* is not equivalent to *certain kinds, certain specimens,* or *certain* (somehow indicated) *quantities,* it can always be said that what is referred to is quantity that may be divided without losing its specific character, and that it may therefore be regarded as Multiple rather than Single.

Particular Common Propositions may be either Vernacular or Specific, and each of these is subdivided into Definite and Indefinite, and these into Distributive and Collective. The subdivisions of Particular Special Propositions are the same as those of Vernacular and Specific Particulars.

Plurative Propositions are Special and Unique, and both subdivide into Summary and Enumerative. The Special Summary Pluratives are Definite and Indefinite, Distributive and Collective. The Enumeratives are either Distributive or Collective.

Unique Plurative Propositions are Summary and Enumerative. Each of these may be Descriptive, Appellative, or Mixed.

The different kinds of Summary Propositions subdivide into Definite and Indefinite, Distributive and Collective; the Enumerative Propositions into Distributive and Collective. A Distributive Enumerative Proposition may be looked at as a combination of propositions (cf. Jevons' *Elementary Lessons in Logic*, 7th ed. p. 90—a "compound" sentence, consisting of " co-ordinate propositions ").

Important differences in use, depending on differences of relation to other propositions, are connected with the differences that are apparent on a mere inspection in the propositions of the Tables, pp. 62–76. The following may be noticed here—A Distributive Universal Proposition is the only one from which both Universals and Particulars can be deduced by Immediate Inference (Collective Universals have the form without the force of Universals). It is only Distributive Universals— such as, *All particles of matter attract each other*—and Special Generals—such as, *The three angles of a triangle* (the three angles of any one triangle) *are equal to two right angles* (a proposition which, though Collective in form, has distributive force)—that are capable of expressing a Law,—a Law being a statement of some uniformity of coexistence or succession (depending on coexistence) in things. In expressing Universality these propositions express also Necessity, since the rule which has not at any time or place an exception, states something which cannot anyhow be otherwise—while conversely, *what must be*, is something to which there is nowhere an exception. Every Categorical Syllogism expressing a so-called "Inductive" reasoning—a reasoning in which by help of particular instances we reach and establish a new law—has an Universal proposition for major premiss and conclusion (cf. *post*, Section XVIII. 3rd note, and Table XXXVI.); every Syllogism by which any law is deduced from other laws has Universals or Special Generals for premisses and conclusion. Indefinite Universals (*e.g.* Any R is Q) are not directly subject to the ordinary rules of Immediate Inference and Opposition. *Any R is Q* converts most naturally to Some Q's are R's. There is no negative form specially corresponding to this Indefinite Universal. It is, of course, denied in *Some R is not Q* (contradictorily), and in *No R is Q* (contrarily); but these forms are the recognised correspondents of *All R is Q*, the Definite Affirmative Universal. In General, as in Universal Propositions the S-term applies to all the objects to which the S-name applies; but in Generals the sphere of the S-name is restricted. As regards the Term-names of the Unique Terms, their application is fixed and limited once for all, but as regards Special Names, it may increase under certain conditions. For instance, the application of *Muse* or *picture by Rembrandt* can never be increased, while that of, *e.g.*, *Sunday*, or *April*, or *picture by J. E. Millais*, may. It is only to Definite Distributive Universals and Indefinite Distributive Particulars that the ordinary rules for Conversion, and therefore, of course, for Reduction also, apply; and the forms of Syllogism (Barbara, Celarent, etc.) recognised by the traditional Formal Logic are concerned with these only. To Singular Propositions (though they can be treated in some respects as Definite Universals) the same rules of Conversion and Opposition do not apply; and with regard to propositions of the form *Some Q is R*, understood as

Singular—*e.g.* Some jockey broke his horse's back over the first fence (1), similar remarks may be made. Some (= a, one, a certain) jockey broke, etc., may perhaps be denied by a proposition of this form, Some (= a, one, a certain) jockey did not break, etc. (2), but this could not be said of, *e.g.*,

> Some jockeys are rascals,

which no one could hold to be incompatible with

> Some jockeys are not rascals.

I admit that (1) would be most ordinarily and naturally negatived by

> No jockey broke, etc. (3),

but (1) might be incompatible, I think, with (2); the reason for denying (1) by (3) rather than by (2) appears to be that while (1) is the most indefinite form of affirmation concerning an individual that can be used, implying that he is merely pointed out as just one of a class, (3) is the most indefinite possible form of negation concerning an individual—in it the denial is made of him simply as a member of the class—whereas (2) rather implies reference to an individual indicated more specially than as a mere member of his class.

When General (Definite) and Plurative Propositions are converted, the Predicate Terms of the new propositions got by this conversion must have indicators which are the same as, or equivalent to, those which they had as Subject-Terms of the old (converted) propositions; *e.g.*,

All of my pupils have passed, converts to *Some who have passed are all my pupils; The planets are bodies having an elliptical orbit,* converts to *Some bodies having an elliptical orbit are the planets; Some of Rembrandt's pictures are masterpieces,* converts to *Some masterpieces are some of Rembrandt's pictures.* The converses of General and Plurative propositions differ from Particular Propositions in this, that if in any converse of the former the Term-Indicator of the new predicate is omitted, the force of the proposition is quite altered.

In the common examples of what is called Inductive

Syllogism,[1] or Perfect Induction, the Minor Premiss is a Collective Enumerative Proposition, and the Major Premiss a Distributive Enumerative Proposition; the conclusion being Summary and Distributive; *e.g.*,

Sunday, Monday, . . . and Saturday are all (*omnes*) twenty-four hours in length;

Sunday, Monday, . . . and Saturday are all (*cuncti*) the days of the week;

∴ All (*omnes*) the days of the week are twenty-four hours in length.

It may be remarked that this Syllogism is incorrect in form, the Minor Term being taken collectively in its premiss, distributively in the conclusion. I do not remember to have seen this inaccuracy noticed. Mansel (Mansel's *Aldrich*, 4th ed. p. 221), Whately (*Logic*, 9th ed. p. 152), and Jevons (*Elementary Lessons*, 7th ed. pp. 214, 215), among others, offer as instances of Perfect or Aristotelian Induction, arguments exactly corresponding in form to the one I have given, without any remark on their formal incorrectness.

To reach by Inference (Mediate or Immediate) an Universal Proposition, we must always start from an Universal; and to reach a General we must always start from a General. Particulars are immediately deducible from Universals and Particulars, and Pluratives from Generals and Pluratives; Singulars from Universals or Particulars or Singulars; Unitary Propositions from General or Plurative or Unitary propositions. From Individual or Singular Propositions only Individuals and Singulars, and from Particular Propositions only Particulars and Singulars can be obtained. Complete Propositions can be got only from Complete Propositions or their converses; and these, and Singular and Individual Propositions, convert quite simply, and admit of only one mode of negation. In Traduction as described and illustrated by Jevons (cf. *Elementary Lessons in Logic*, 7th ed. pp. 211,

---

[1] I should propose to call this (in an amended form) a Limited Deductive (Categorical) Syllogism.

222), both of the premisses and the conclusion are Singular or Individual Propositions. I should like to extend the application of the term so as to include Syllogisms of which either (*a*) all the terms are Singular or Individual, or (*b*) the Subjects of both premisses are Definite Partial Terms.

Although in Universal and General Propositions the distributive *all* may have the same force as *any* in the majority of propositions, yet there are certain differences—for *any* may occur as Subject-indicator in a proposition in which, by determination of S or P, the application of the Subject is restricted to *one* individual. *E.g.* Any one who wins this race will have a silver cup, Any person whom the Committee choose will be appointed Secretary, Any one may have my ticket (we could not here replace *any* by *all*). *Any* is equivalent to the *a* or *an* in many proverbial sayings—*e.g.* A woman's mind and winter's wind change oft, An honest miller has a golden thumb, An ill plea should be well pleaded. The force of *any X* seems to be this:—A thing, and the only condition of acceptance is Xness. Hence it follows that *any* is equivalent to all, wherever more than one is in question. From the statement that *any X is Y* it follows that *all X's are Y* (if there be more than one X), *because* Xness is connected with Yness. And, conversely, from *all X's are Y* it follows that *any X is Y*, *because* from every X being Y there may be inferred a connection between Xness and Yness.

[TABLES.

IMPORT OF PROPOSITIONS.

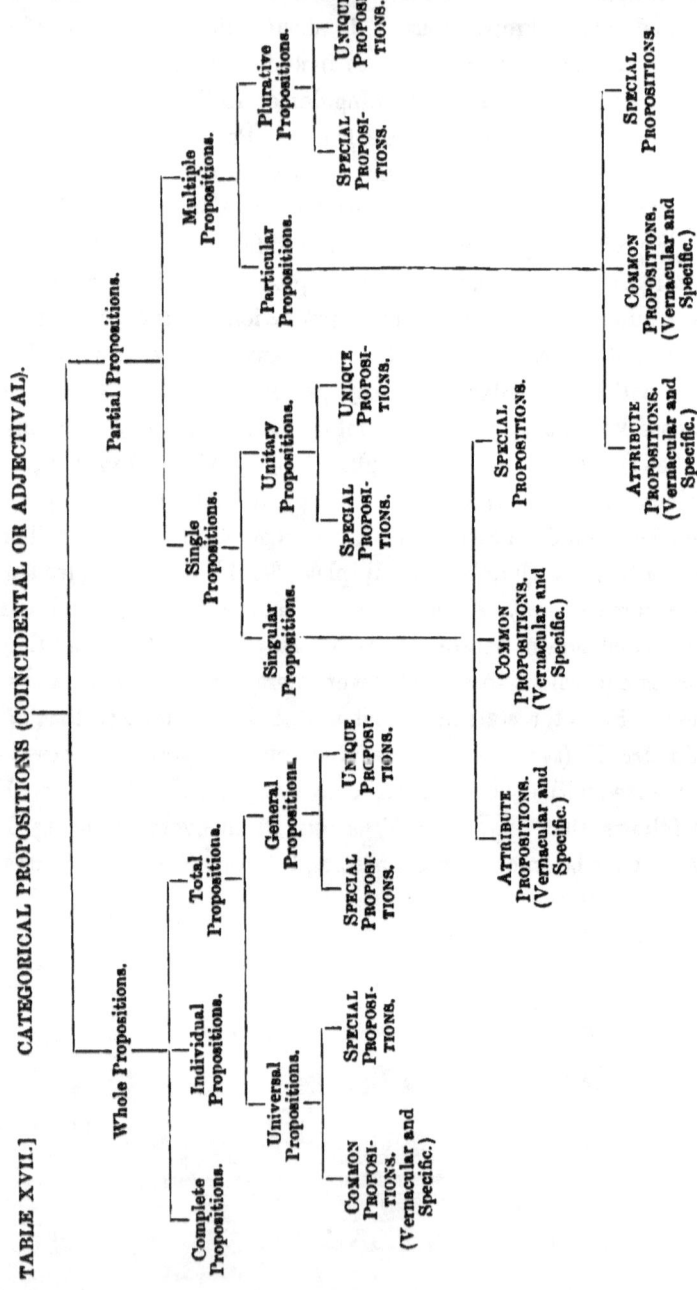

TABLE XVII.] CATEGORICAL PROPOSITIONS (COINCIDENTAL OR ADJECTIVAL).

IMPORT AND CLASSIFICATION OF CATEGORICAL PROPOSITIONS. 63

TABLE XVIII.]   ATTRIBUTE PROPOSITIONS.
(VERNACULAR AND SPECIFIC.)

```
                                    ATTRIBUTE PROPOSITIONS
                                              |
                    ┌─────────────────────────┴─────────────────────────┐
              COMPLETE                                              PARTIAL
            PROPOSITIONS.                                        PROPOSITIONS.
                                                                      |
                                                    ┌─────────────────┴─────────────────┐
                                               SINGULAR                             PARTICULAR
                                             PROPOSITIONS.                        PROPOSITIONS.
                                                                           (DISTRIBUTIVE AND COLLECTIVE.)
                                          ┌───────┴────────┐                ┌───────┴────────┐
                                     DEFINITE         INDEFINITE       DEFINITE         INDEFINITE
                                   PROPOSITIONS.     PROPOSITIONS.   PROPOSITIONS.     PROPOSITIONS.
```

(1) *Independent*; (2) *Dependent.*

e.g. (1) Gentleness is a virtue; generosity is not justice; pity is sometimes injurious; Benthamism is not gaining ground; Philistinism is difficult to define.

(2) Likeness of tastes is a bond of friendship; superiority to A is more than B can claim; colour-blindness is a frequent phenomenon; note-deafness is occasionally met with; the narrowness of consciousness accounts for many psychological facts.

(1) *Independent*; (2) *Dependent.*

e.g. (1) His courage was a splendid example.
(2) Such beauty of character is a great power.

(1) *Independent*; (2) *Dependent.*

e.g. (1) A great kindness has been received.
(2) Some bitterness of feeling has been caused.

(1) *Independent*; (2) *Dependent.*

e.g. (1) Their perseverance is a reproach to me.
(2) Our narrowness of view imposes an arbitrary limit.

(1) *Independent*; (2) *Dependent.*

e.g. (1) Some Æstheticism is a nuisance.
(2) Much rudeness of manner proceeds from shyness; the liberality of these three brothers has had a great effect.

TABLE XIX.]

INDIVIDUAL PROPOSITIONS (APPELLATIVE, DESCRIPTIVE, AND MIXED)

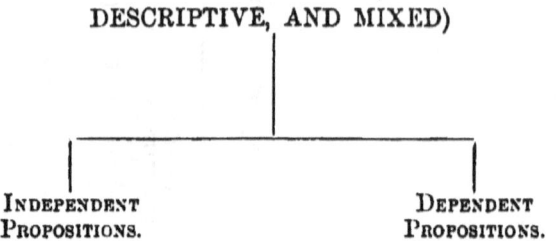

INDEPENDENT PROPOSITIONS.	DEPENDENT PROPOSITIONS.
e.g. The sun is not a planet; the present Czar is a tyrant; Praise-God Barebones is one of Sir Walter Scott's characters; Monmouthshire is not a Welsh county; Aglaia was a Greek goddess; Jack is a fidgety child; Tom Smith, the boy I speak of, has a ferret.	*e.g.* The *Œdipus Tyrannus* of Sophocles is an unsurpassed tragedy; the *Inferno* of Dante has not been satisfactorily translated into English; the year 1888 A.D. was a year remarkable for its bad weather; the youngest child of that poor woman has just died of whooping-cough; Jane Smith's eldest boy has scarlet fever; the *P.S.* to your letter yesterday was not of much consequence; the circumference of the earth is about 24,000 miles; *Bacon of Verulam* seems to be the denomination by which Francis Bacon is commonly known to Germans; the greatest poet of the Elizabethan age was Shakspeare.

IMPORT AND CLASSIFICATION OF CATEGORICAL PROPOSITIONS. 65

TABLE XX.]

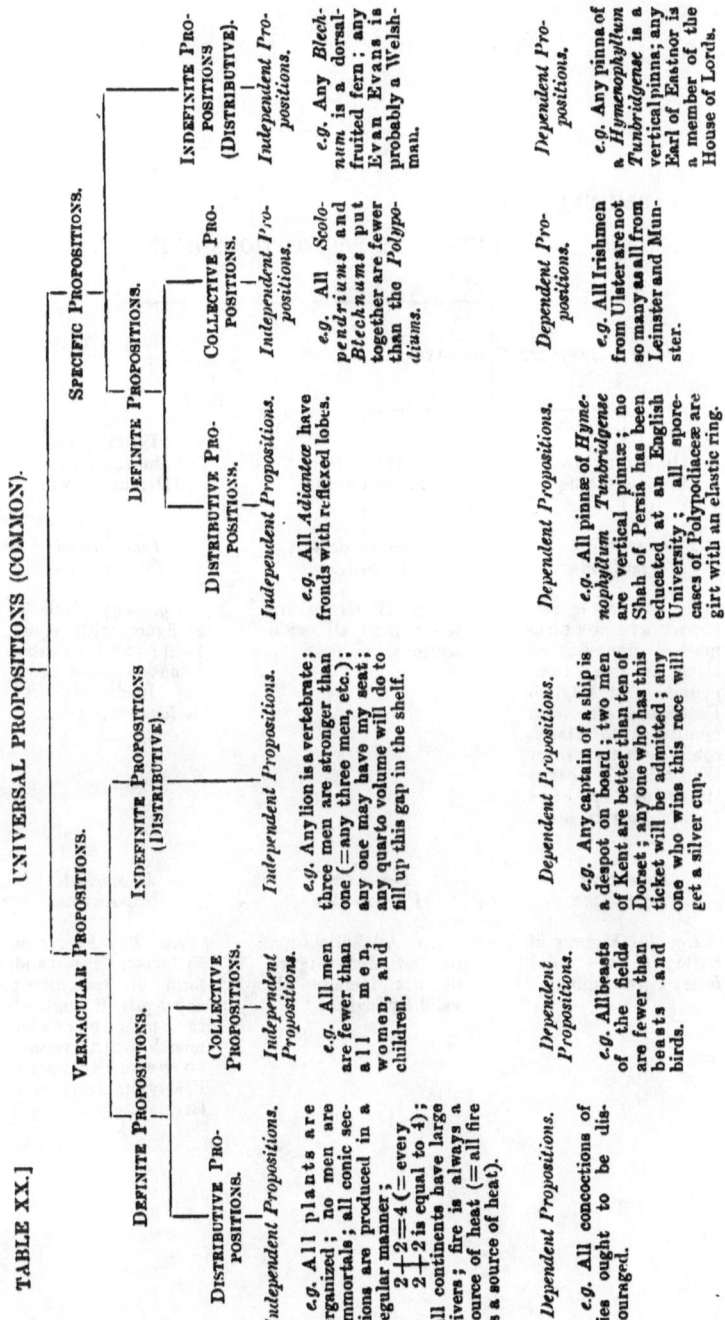

[TABLE XXI.]

UNIVERSAL PROPOSITIONS (SPECIAL).

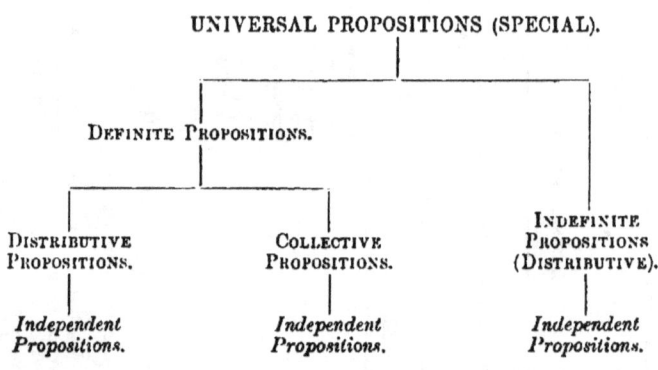

DEFINITE PROPOSITIONS.

DISTRIBUTIVE PROPOSITIONS.	COLLECTIVE PROPOSITIONS.	INDEFINITE PROPOSITIONS (DISTRIBUTIVE).
Independent Propositions.	*Independent Propositions.*	*Independent Propositions.*
e.g. All conic sections are mathematical figures ; no elements are compounds; no English Decembers are warm months ; no March could be more wintry than this July ; *genus* includes *species* (= every genus, etc.).	*e.g.* All circles are fewer than all conic sections.	*e.g.* Any circle is a figure with equal radii ; any Predicable is out of place here ; any Predicable will do for illustration.
Dependent Propositions.	*Dependent Propositions.*	*Dependent Propositions.*
e.g. All Figures of Syllogism are valid forms of reasoning.	*e.g.* All Syllogisms in the first Figure do not include all valid Syllogisms.	*e.g.* Any Figure of Syllogism is a valid form of reasoning ; any April in England is an uncertain month with regard to weather; any Friday in Lent is a fast day.

IMPORT AND CLASSIFICATION OF CATEGORICAL PROPOSITIONS. 67

[TABLE XXII.]

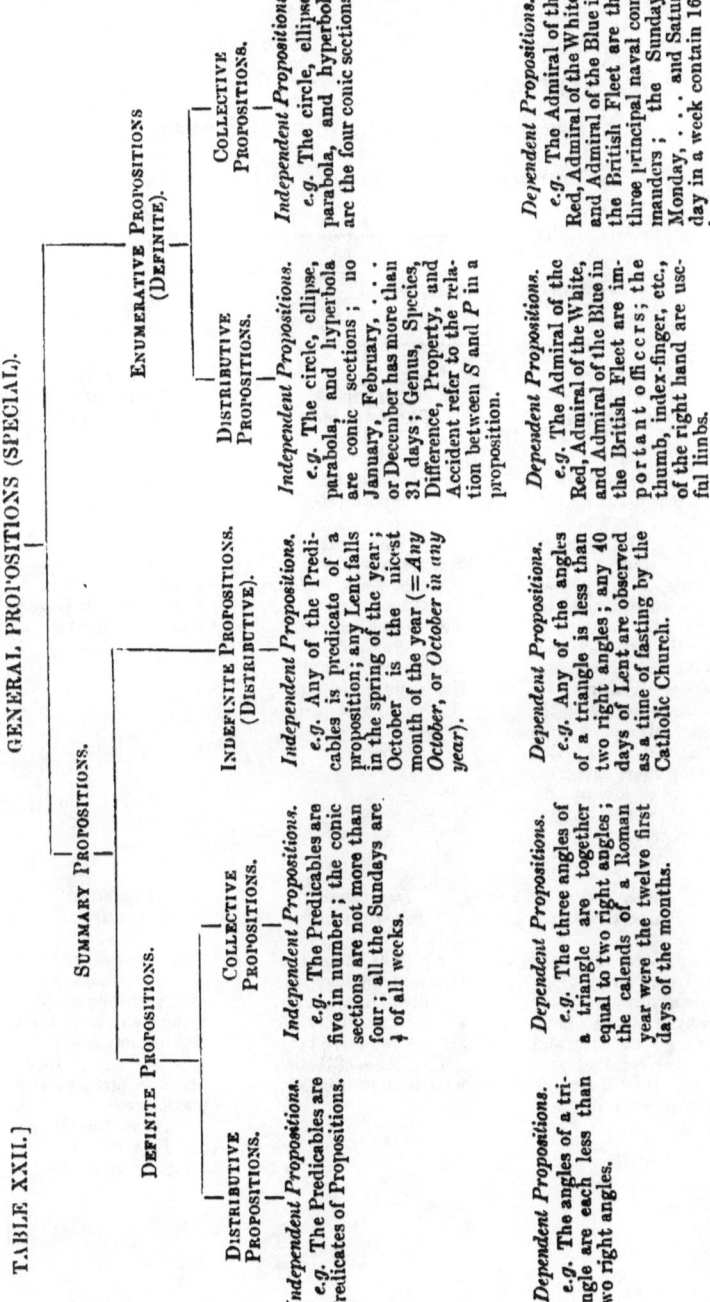

GENERAL PROPOSITIONS (SPECIAL).

- SUMMARY PROPOSITIONS.
  - DEFINITE PROPOSITIONS.
    - DISTRIBUTIVE PROPOSITIONS.
      - *Independent Propositions.*
        e.g. The Predicables are Predicates of Propositions.
      - *Dependent Propositions.*
        e.g. The angles of a triangle are each less than two right angles.
    - COLLECTIVE PROPOSITIONS.
      - *Independent Propositions.*
        e.g. The Predicables are five in number; the conic sections are not more than four; all the Sundays are ¼ of all weeks.
      - *Dependent Propositions.*
        e.g. The three angles of a triangle are together equal to two right angles; the calends of a Roman year were the twelve first days of the months.
  - INDEFINITE PROPOSITIONS. (DISTRIBUTIVE).
    - *Independent Propositions.*
      e.g. Any of the Predicables is predicate of a proposition; any Lent falls in the spring of the year; October is the nicest month of the year (= *Any October, or October in any year*).
    - *Dependent Propositions.*
      e.g. Any of the angles of a triangle is less than two right angles; any 40 days of Lent are observed as a time of fasting by the Catholic Church.
- ENUMERATIVE PROPOSITIONS (DEFINITE).
  - DISTRIBUTIVE PROPOSITIONS.
    - *Independent Propositions.*
      e.g. The circle, ellipse, parabola, and hyperbola are conic sections; no January, February, ... or December has more than 31 days; Genus, Species, Difference, Property, and Accident refer to the relation between *S* and *P* in a proposition.
    - *Dependent Propositions.*
      e.g. The Admiral of the Red, Admiral of the White, and Admiral of the Blue in the British Fleet are important officers; the thumb, index-finger, etc., of the right hand are useful limbs.
  - COLLECTIVE PROPOSITIONS.
    - *Independent Propositions.*
      e.g. The circle, ellipse, parabola, and hyperbola are the four conic sections.
    - *Dependent Propositions.*
      e.g. The Admiral of the Red, Admiral of the White, and Admiral of the Blue in the British Fleet are the three principal naval commanders; the Sunday, Monday, ... and Saturday in a week contain 168 hours.

TABLE XXIII.]

GENERAL PROPOSITIONS (UNIQUE SUMMARY).

(DESCRIPTIVE, MIXED, AND APPELLATIVE.)

DEFINITE PROPOSITIONS.

DISTRIBUTIVE PROPOSITIONS.	COLLECTIVE PROPOSITIONS.	INDEFINITE (DISTRIBUTIVE) PROPOSITIONS.
Independent Propositions.	*Independent Propositions.*	*Independent Propositions.*
e.g. All the patriarchs were sons of Jacob; all the planets have an elliptical orbit; all the days of my life are [few and] evil; all the Greek heroes were men of courage; each of the nine Muses was a daughter of Apollo; all of those cattle are Kyloes; all of the birds in that aviary are parrots.	e.g. The twelve patriarchs were Reuben, Simeon, Levi, Judah, Issachar, Zebulon, Joseph, Benjamin, Dan, Naphtali, Gad, and Asher. The three Furies were Tisiphone, Alecto, and Megæra.	e.g. Any of the patriarchs was a son of Jacob. Any of the Graces was a daughter of Apollo.
Dependent Propositions.	*Dependent Propositions.*	*Dependent Propositions.*
e.g. All the gods of Greek mythology were anthropomorphic beings; all the wheels that go to Croyland are shod with silver. All the Muses of Homer were dwellers in Olympus.	e.g. The heroes of Greek mythology were Achilles, Ulysses, etc.; all the days of my life are few [and evil]. The Muses of Hesiod were nine in number.	e.g. Any god of Greek mythology was an anthropomorphic being; any of $B's$ set is a person not to be trusted; any of Rembrandt's pictures is a masterpiece. Any of the Muses of Hesiod was a daughter of Zeus.

TABLE XXIV.]

GENERAL PROPOSITIONS (UNIQUE ENUMERATIVE).

(DESCRIPTIVE, MIXED, AND APPELLATIVE.)

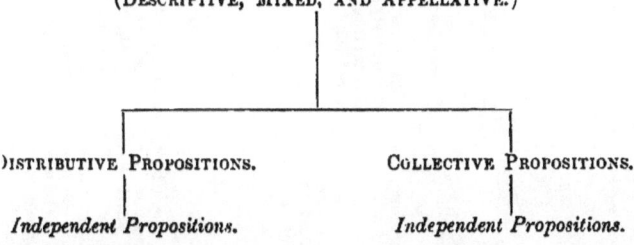

DISTRIBUTIVE PROPOSITIONS.

Independent Propositions.

e.g. The largest, second largest . . . and smallest of the planets have each an elliptical orbit.
Aglaia, Thalia, and Euphrosyne were daughters of Apollo.

COLLECTIVE PROPOSITIONS.

Independent Propositions.

e.g. The largest, second largest . . . and smallest of the planets are the satellites of our sun; the first, second, third, and fourth of the Cardinal Virtues were Wisdom, Courage, Justice, and Temperance.
Aglaia, Thalia, and Euphrosyne were the three Graces.

Dependent Propositions.

e.g. The first, second . . . and seventh days of last week were rainy days.
The Agamemnon, Choëphoræ, and Eumenides of Æschylus are splendid plays.

Dependent Propositions.

e.g. The first, second . . . and seventh days of last week were the seven most wretched days of my life; the daughters of Henry VIII. were Mary and Elizabeth.
The Agamemnon, Choëphoræ, and Eumenides of Æschylus form the Oresteia.

TABLE XXV.] SINGULAR PROPOSITIONS.

COMMON PROPOSITIONS (VERNACULAR AND SPECIFIC).

DEFINITE PROPOSITIONS.

Independent Propositions.

e.g. This man is a spy; this finger has been scratched by the cat; this horse is not an Arabian.
This Conservative Home Ruler made a tedious speech; that *Lilium Lancifolium Album* is a most beautiful flower; this *Ophioglossum* is a vigorous plant.

Dependent Propositions.

e.g. That receiver of stolen goods has been sent to prison.
This frond of *Polypodium Cambricum* is a good specimen; that son of a Valois is not a credit to his name.

INDEFINITE PROPOSITIONS.

Independent Propositions.

e.g. One prisoner has escaped; one patient has recovered; a } spy has been taken prisoner; one } militia-man is not to be found; a gold medal as big as a crown piece is the prize.
A Master in Lunacy was summoned before the Court; an *Asplenium lanceolatum* was killed by the frost; one *Cystopteris* is a sickly plant; a Hohenzollern was then on the throne of Germany; a *General Jacqueminot* is not mentioned.

Dependent Propositions.

e.g. One warder of a prison is missing; one officer of an artillery regiment is a prisoner; one of my friends is not a ratepayer; a spire of a church has been struck by lightning.
A guardian of the poor ought to be a discriminating person; a frond of *Allosorus Crispus* is the best preserved specimen in my collection; a Welshman from Gower sang at the Eisteddfod; a syllogism in Baroko must be reduced; a colonel of engineers is a prisoner; one reduction from the 4th Figure to the 1st has not been attempted.

SPECIAL PROPOSITIONS (SIMPLE).

DEFINITE PROPOSITIONS.

Independent Propositions.

e.g. This hyperbola is a very queerly drawn figure; that conic section is drawn in red ink.

Dependent Propositions.

e.g. That Monday in August was a terrible day; that syllogism in the 4th figure sounds very far-fetched; this Simple Converse of an *A* proposition is a mistake.

INDEFINITE PROPOSITIONS.

Independent Propositions.

e.g. A circle has been described about the given centre; a conic section occupied the blackboard.

Dependent Propositions.

e.g. One section of a cone must be drawn and defined.

IMPORT AND CLASSIFICATION OF CATEGORICAL PROPOSITIONS. 71

TABLE XXVI.]

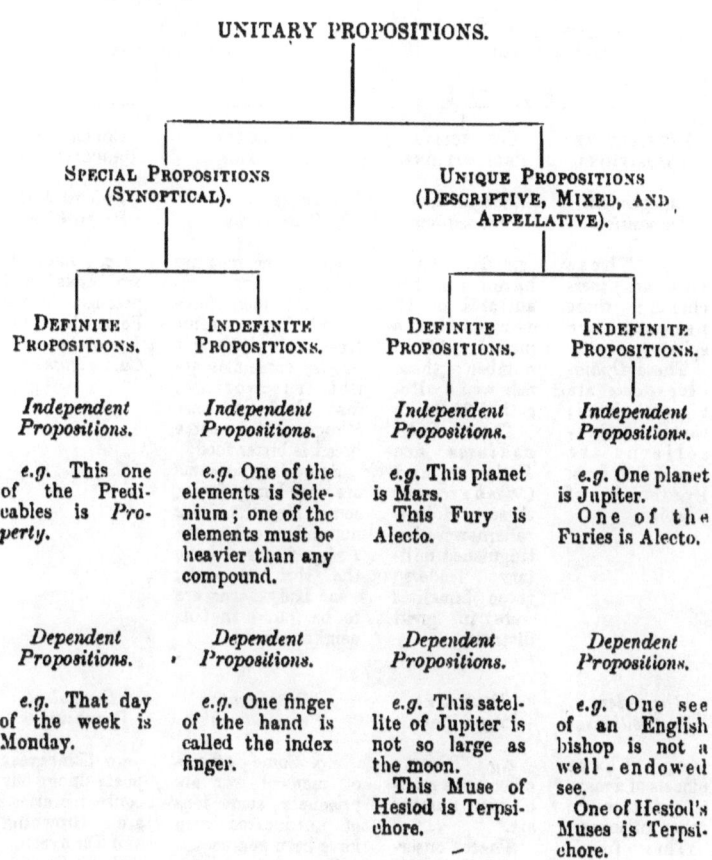

[TABLE XXVII.]

PARTICULAR PROPOSITIONS (COMMON).

(VERNACULAR AND SPECIFIC.)

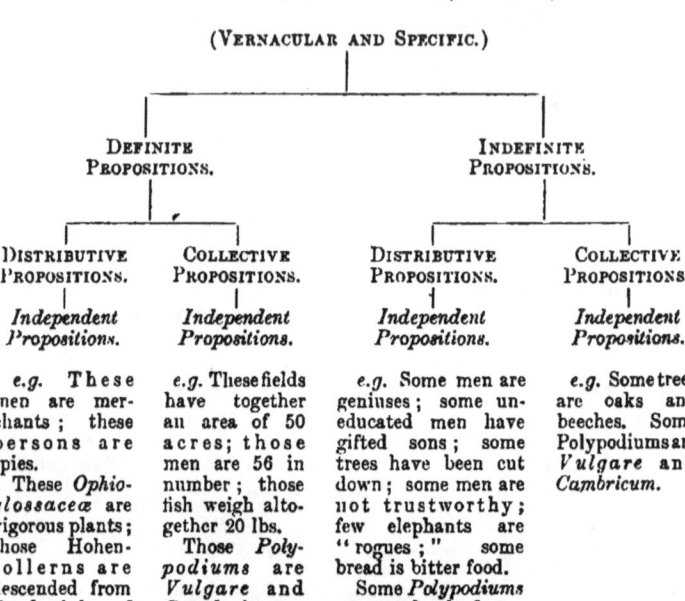

	DEFINITE PROPOSITIONS.		INDEFINITE PROPOSITIONS.	
	DISTRIBUTIVE PROPOSITIONS.	COLLECTIVE PROPOSITIONS.	DISTRIBUTIVE PROPOSITIONS.	COLLECTIVE PROPOSITIONS.
Independent Propositions.	e.g. These men are merchants; these persons are spies. These *Ophioglossaceæ* are vigorous plants; those Hohenzollerns are descended from Frederick of Suabia.	e.g. These fields have together an area of 50 acres; those men are 56 in number; those fish weigh altogether 20 lbs. Those *Polypodiums* are *Vulgare* and *Cambricum*; these Hohenzollerns were distinguished military leaders; those Israelites were in great distress.	e.g. Some men are geniuses; some uneducated men have gifted sons; some trees have been cut down; some men are not trustworthy; few elephants are "rogues;" some bread is bitter food. Some *Polypodiums* are very hardy ferns; some Hegelians are not understood; some *Polypodiums* have the sori exposed; some Lady Ferns are to be found in this neighbourhood.	e.g. Some trees are oaks and beeches. Some Polypodiums are *Vulgare* and *Cambricum*.
Dependent Propositions.	e.g. Those officers of a man-of-war were taken prisoners. These fronds of *Polypodium Cambricum* are good specimens; those Liberal Unionists of Glamorganshire have not done much.	e.g. Those officers of a man-of-war number six. These Conservative Unionists of Monmouthshire are John Allen Rolls and George Griffin Griffin; these pinnæ of *Hymenophyllum* are deflexed.	e.g. Some officers of men-of-war are prisoners; some sons of uneducated men have been geniuses. Some *prime donne* at the London Opera Houses make good incomes; some sulphites of soda are not poisons; some sori of *Polypodiaceæ* are without indusia; few nervous systems of vertebrates are so complex as that of the elephant.	e.g. Some great poets among our contemporaries are Browning and Tennyson. Some Conservative Unionists of Monmouthshire are A. B. and C. D.

IMPORT AND CLASSIFICATION OF CATEGORICAL PROPOSITIONS.

TABLE XXVIII.]

PARTICULAR PROPOSITIONS (SPECIAL).

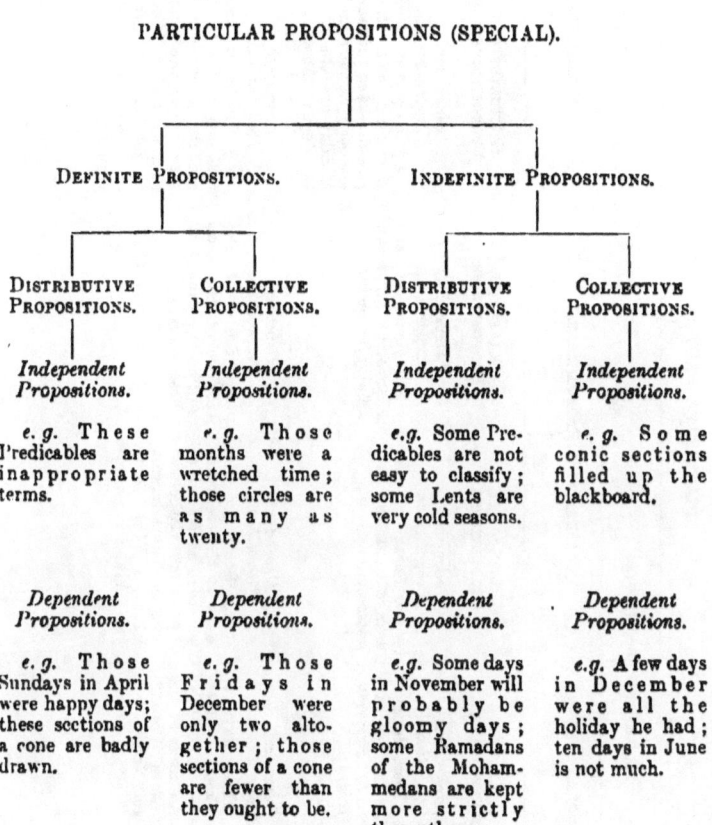

- **DEFINITE PROPOSITIONS.**
  - **DISTRIBUTIVE PROPOSITIONS.**
    - *Independent Propositions.*
      e.g. These Predicables are inappropriate terms.
    - *Dependent Propositions.*
      e.g. Those Sundays in April were happy days; these sections of a cone are badly drawn.
  - **COLLECTIVE PROPOSITIONS.**
    - *Independent Propositions.*
      e.g. Those months were a wretched time; those circles are as many as twenty.
    - *Dependent Propositions.*
      e.g. Those Fridays in December were only two altogether; those sections of a cone are fewer than they ought to be.
- **INDEFINITE PROPOSITIONS.**
  - **DISTRIBUTIVE PROPOSITIONS.**
    - *Independent Propositions.*
      e.g. Some Predicables are not easy to classify; some Lents are very cold seasons.
    - *Dependent Propositions.*
      e.g. Some days in November will probably be gloomy days; some Ramadans of the Mohammedans are kept more strictly than others.
  - **COLLECTIVE PROPOSITIONS.**
    - *Independent Propositions.*
      e.g. Some conic sections filled up the blackboard.
    - *Dependent Propositions.*
      e.g. A few days in December were all the holiday he had; ten days in June is not much.

74 IMPORT OF PROPOSITIONS.

TABLE XXIX.]

PLURATIVE PROPOSITIONS (SPECIAL).

SUMMARY PROPOSITIONS.

DEFINITE PROPOSITIONS.

DISTRIBUTIVE PROPOSITIONS.

Independent Propositions.
e.g. These two of the conic sections are most important curves.

Dependent Propositions.
e.g. These six of the days of the week are working days.

COLLECTIVE PROPOSITIONS.

Independent Propositions.
e.g. These three of the Predicables are *Difference, Property,* and *Accident.*

Dependent Propositions.
e.g. Those days of the week are Wednesday and Saturday; those Admirals of the Fleet were Collingwood and Nelson.

INDEFINITE PROPOSITIONS.

DISTRIBUTIVE PROPOSITIONS.

Independent Propositions.
e.g. Some of the conic sections are closed curves.

Dependent Propositions.
e.g. Some of the days of the week are observed as fast days by strict Catholics; two of the Admirals of the Fleet distinguished themselves.

COLLECTIVE PROPOSITIONS.

Independent Propositions.
e.g. Some of the elements have an affinity for each other.

Dependent Propositions.
e.g. Some of the sections of the cone will be the subject of these lectures.

ENUMERATIVE PROPOSITIONS (ALL DEFINITE).

DISTRIBUTIVE PROPOSITIONS.

Independent Propositions.
e.g. Summer and Autumn are the pleasantest of the four seasons; Sunday and Monday are the first two days of the week.

Dependent Propositions.
e.g. The thumb and first finger of a hand are its most useful members; the first and second of the figures of syllogism are useful forms of argument.

COLLECTIVE PROPOSITIONS.

Independent Propositions.
e.g. The circle and ellipse are two of the four conic sections; September and October are two of the autumn months.

Dependent Propositions.
e.g. The first and second of the days of the week are Sunday and Monday; the first, second, and third of the figures of categorical syllogism are the three most natural forms of argument; Sunday and Monday in any week contain 48 hours between them.

IMPORT AND CLASSIFICATION OF CATEGORICAL PROPOSITIONS. 75

TABLE XXX.]

PLURATIVE PROPOSITIONS (UNIQUE SUMMARY).

(DESCRIPTIVE, MIXED, AND APPELLATIVE.)

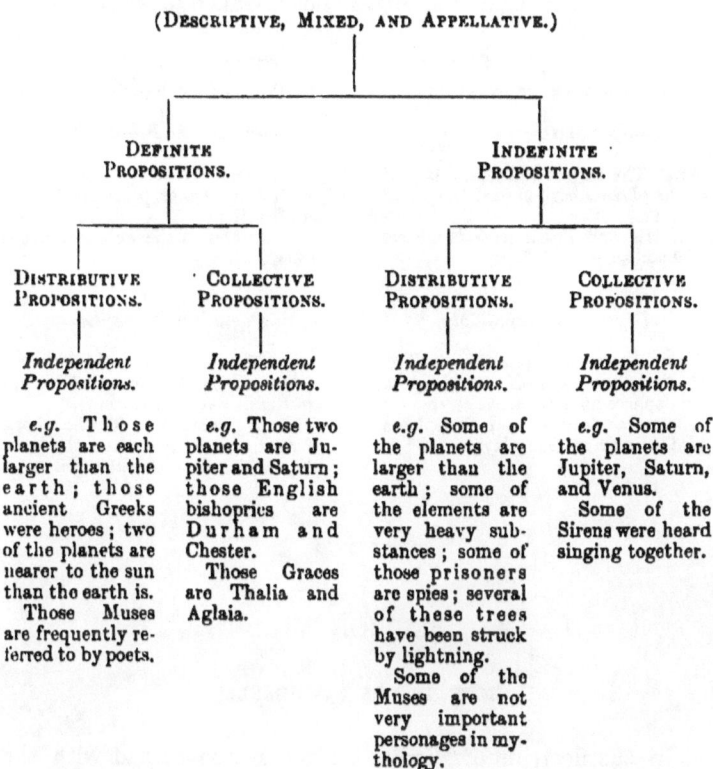

Definite Propositions.		Indefinite Propositions.	
Distributive Propositions.	Collective Propositions.	Distributive Propositions.	Collective Propositions.
Independent Propositions.	*Independent Propositions.*	*Independent Propositions.*	*Independent Propositions.*
e.g. Those planets are each larger than the earth; those ancient Greeks were heroes; two of the planets are nearer to the sun than the earth is. Those Muses are frequently referred to by poets.	*e.g.* Those two planets are Jupiter and Saturn; those English bishoprics are Durham and Chester. Those Graces are Thalia and Aglaia.	*e.g.* Some of the planets are larger than the earth; some of the elements are very heavy substances; some of those prisoners are spies; several of these trees have been struck by lightning. Some of the Muses are not very important personages in mythology.	*e.g.* Some of the planets are Jupiter, Saturn, and Venus. Some of the Sirens were heard singing together.
Dependent Propositions.	*Dependent Propositions.*	*Dependent Propositions.*	*Dependent Propositions.*
e.g. Those two of the continents of the Eastern hemisphere are immensely larger than Australia; three members of the present Cabinet are D.C.L.'s; these plays of Euripides are masterpieces. Those Muses of Hesiod are favourite deities of the poets.	*e.g.* Those continents of the Western hemisphere are North and South America; those grandsons of Queen Victoria are soldiers and sailors. Those Muses of Hesiod are Clio and Euterpe.	*e.g.* Some of the great rivers of America are larger than any in Europe; some of his pupils are not geniuses. Some of the Muses of Hesiod are better known than the others.	*e.g.* Some of the great rivers of Europe are the Volga, the Danube, the Rhine, and the Loire. Some of the Muses of Hesiod were Clio, Melpomene and Terpsichore.

TABLE XXXI.]

PLURATIVE PROPOSITIONS (UNIQUE ENUMERATIVE).

(Descriptive, Mixed, and Appellative.)

DISTRIBUTIVE PROPOSITIONS.

Independent Propositions.

e.g. The largest and second largest of the planets both exceed the earth in bulk.
Aglaia and Thalia were daughters of Apollo.

Dependent Propositions.

e.g. The largest and the smallest of the continents of the Eastern Hemisphere have immense rivers.
The Agamemnon and Choëphoræ of Æschylus are fine plays.

COLLECTIVE PROPOSITIONS.

Independent Propositions.

e.g. The greatest and second greatest of German poets are Goethe and Schiller.
Aglaia and Thalia were two of the Graces.

Dependent Propositions.

e.g. The largest and the smallest of the independent States of Europe are Russia and San Marino.
The Agamemnon and Choëphoræ of Æschylus are two out of the three plays which form the Oresteia.

SECTION VII.

NOTE ON THE PREDICABLES.

In the doctrine of Predicables we are concerned with the *matter* of propositions, since it is impossible to say of propositions expressed in symbols, under which Predicable-head the Predicates come. This subject of Predicables is full of confusion, and emphatically illustrates Carlyle's saying that "mixing things up is the great bad."

It does not seem to me possible to reduce the accounts of Predicables to a form that would have practical or theoretical value; but it may clear up the subject a little to indicate the different elements and points of view which, without clearly discriminating one from another, they seem to include. We may distinguish (1) a division of Predicates regarded from a particular point of view—*i.e.* in relation to their Subjects—or, more accurately, a division of Predicate-names regarded in relation to their Subject-names. (2) A scheme of division, and subdivision by dichotomy ("the matchless beauty of the Ramean tree"), from which a series of definitions "per genus et differentiam" and the relations of the positive members in a hierarchical classification are deducible. (3) A view of the relations between classes of natural objects and between individuals and their classes, resulting from and only compatible with a peculiar doctrine of the constitution of nature. (4) The relation between what the Subject-name applies to and what the Predicate-name applies to. (Cf. Genus and Species, which refer to relations between classes: cf. also Aristotle's division into Predicates which are (*a*) convertible (Definition and Property), (*b*) not-convertible (Genus and Accident) with the Subject; in (*a*) there is identity, in (*b*) there is not identity of denomination of S-name and P-name.) (5) The relation between what the Subject-name denominates and what the Predicate-name determines (cf. Difference, Property, Accident, which refer to relations of Subjects and their Attributes—cf. Mill (*Logic*, i. p. 134, 9th ed.), confusion between class-relations and relation of Subject and Attribute); (6) A division of General Names corresponding to differences of classes (cf. Mill, *Logic*, Bk. i. ch. viii. § 2—I. 134, 9th ed.).

If we take the Tree of Porphyry, and make a table of Predicates according to the suggestion which it affords, we get an intelligible division of Predicates into

(*a*) Genus (wider containing class).

(*b*) Species (narrower contained class).

(*c*) Difference (mark by which Species is distinguished from Genus).

But except on the Realist view, or where the Difference is unique, Genus is not distinguishable, in predication, from Difference (as in, *e.g.*,

All men are rational,
All men are animals);

unless we say that Genus is understood to refer to denomination and Species to determination. Genus + Difference, when predicated of Species, give the Definition—*e.g.* Man is a rational animal—here there is *identity* of the classes referred to. The omission of this head of Predicables seems a defect in the Scholastic account of Predicables.

If I say, *Cæsar* is a man, I predicate Species—Species prædicabilis. But if I say, *This animal* is a man, what is it that I predicate (on any view of the Predicables)? I do not see under which head of Predicables this Predicate is to be brought. If I say, All negroes are men, I predicate Species too, on the Realist (or on Mill's) view. But if we are to take this view, nothing but exhaustive knowledge can enable us to know in any case under which Predicable-head our Predicate comes. If I say, All men are animals, I predicate Genus, and *All men* is a Species subjicibilis. In, *These animals* are rational animals, I do not know what Predicable I predicate. And if I say, All rational animals are men, what is my Predicate? Not Genus (that would be *animals*). Not Species, for that would be *rational animals*, Species it is said consisting of Genus and Difference. Not Difference, because *rational* would be the Difference. Not Definition, because here the Definition of the *Predicate* is given by the *Subject*. Not Property (for Property *flows from* essence, and *men* contains the whole of the essence). Not Accident (because *men* is essential).

Coincidence of two classes in extension (of two class-*names* in application) can hardly be called a *relation* of classes (*i.e.* a relation of the extension of classes or application of class-names) at all (cf. *post*, p. 80, note 1).

Difference, Property, and Accident either do not express class-relations (which are relations of extension), or they are resolvable into Genus or Species. Genus and Species are properly understood in denomination (quantitively); but Difference, Property, and Accident are properly taken (if they are distinctive at all) in determination (qualitively). (Cf. Jevons, *Principles of Science*, p. 699, 9th ed. "Difference, it is evident, can be interpreted in intension only.")

SECTION VIII.

MILL'S VIEW OF THE IMPORT OF PROPOSITIONS.

Any further general differences in (unquantified) Categorical Propositions, beyond those already noticed, depend, I think, wholly upon determination, upon—

1. Relations of determination between S-name and P-name—here we get the distinctions between Analytic and Synthetic, Real and Verbal. Mill says that Verbal Propositions only inform us as to the meaning of names; and I should like to take him as nearly as possible at his word, and restrict the term "verbal" to Definitions and Propositions asserting Synonymity of names. Such a Proposition as *Courage is Valour* (1) may mean (*a*) The *word* Courage is a *word* having the same application as the *word* Valour (in which case it is verbal), or (*b*) The *thing named by the word* Courage is *the same as the thing named by the word* Valour. I should propose to group together (*a*) and (*b*) with Definitions, as Nominal Propositions, thus :—

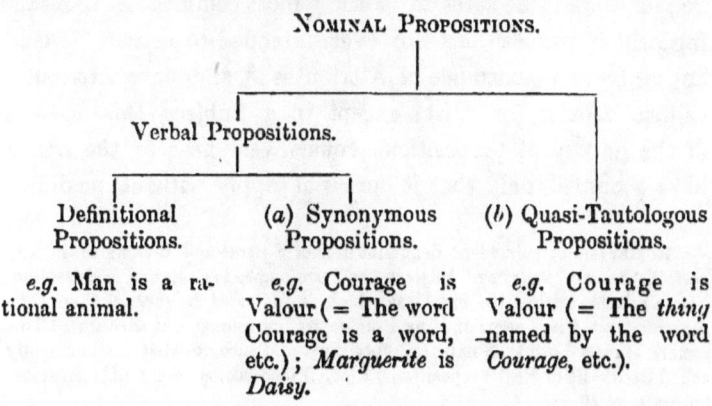

Understood as (*a*), (1) is plainly a question of names; understood as (*b*), not only is the denomination of S and P the same, but also *no* difference can be pointed out in the determination of S and P respectively, *except* that the object named is referred to by one name in S and by a different name in P.[1]

2. Determination of S-name or P-name, or both. Under this head must certainly be reckoned Mill's division of propositions into Propositions of

>Existence.
>Coexistence.
>Sequence.
>Causation.
>Resemblance.

(Cf. Mill, *Logic*, i. 116, 9th ed.) With reference to this list, Prof. Bain says that Mill "enumerates five ultimate *predicates, or classes of predications*" (Bain, *Logic*, i. 106, 2nd ed.); but though it seems to me to be true that Coexistence, etc., and such Existence as *can* be expressed, are most commonly expressed in the *Predicate* of a proposition, Mill's account of the heads of *Coexistence* and *Succession* is by no means in accordance with this view. He analyses, as an example apparently of both Coexistence and Sequence, the proposition, "A generous person is worthy of honour" (cf. *Logic*, i. 110–112). What he here means by Coexistence (? and Sequence), and declares to be the "most common . . . meaning which propositions are ever intended to convey," would appear to be Coexistence of Attributes;[2] and since Attributes cannot coexist (or exist) except in a Subject, this account of the import of propositions comes very near to the one I have proposed, only that it does not apply without modifica-

---

[1] In all cases of coincident denomination of S-name and P-name in a Categorical, the only "relation" between the Term-names is a relation of *determination*, a relation within the *one* class which is indicated by *each* of them. In *denomination*, the S-name and the P-name are not *related*, but *identical*. This remark applies both to Nominal Propositions and also to what are commonly called Synthetic or Real Propositions, *e.g.* All food-cookers are risible creatures (cf. *ante*, p. 79).

[2] This, which may be accepted as Mill's view of the Formal Import of Propositions (in as far as it is to be gathered from the *Logic*), appears to be connected with his view of Logic generally, as concerned pre-eminently with Induction, with passing to *new* truths, for it is only by fresh enlightenment as to the *connections* of attributes that an increase of knowledge respecting classes of objects can be gained.

tion to what I have called Quasi-Tautologous Propositions,[1] and that Mill (though somewhat doubtfully) interprets partly in Sequence as well as in Coexistence (cf. *op. cit.* i. pp. 113, 114, § 6). Again, according to Mill (*op. cit.* i. p. 116), this proposition, "The sensation I feel is one of tightness," is among the propositions which assert *Resemblance*. But this proposition does not seem to have any distinctive characteristic justifying that title. The Category of Causation he reduces to Sequence. As one example of a proposition asserting "a sequence accompanied with causation," Mill gives "Prudence is a virtue" (pp. 119, 120). Here we may perhaps say, that if *this* proposition asserts "a sequence accompanied with causation," then of any proposition with Common or Attribute Terms we may give the same account.

Mill's application of his Categories to the Import of Propositions seems to me extremely strained, and the mixture here of Formal and Material (non-formal) points of view very confusing. Categorical Propositions which in any ordinary sense would be said to assert Coexistence, Sequence, Causation or Resemblance, assert it in virtue of the *content* of the terms (generally of the Predicate); and thus understood, there are other Categories which might make good their claim to be added to Mill's list; *e.g.* the Categories of Inclusion, Exclusion, Intersection, Coincidence, etc. Then there are the Categories of Identity (and Non-identity) and Diversity, which apply directly to all Categorical Propositions without exception; the Categories of Inherence and Subsistence, which apply to all Adjectival propositions, such as, *e.g.*, *Trees are green;* the Category of Inference, which applies to all Hypothetical and Conditional Propositions; the Categories of Relations of Magnitude, Part and Whole, and so on.

[1] According to Mill himself, its application would be very much more restricted.

SECTION IX.

SYSTEMIC OR DEPENDENT PROPOSITIONS.

I mentioned above (cf. *ante*, p. 20) the connection between what are called *à fortiori* arguments and Dependent or Systemic Terms. A proposition which has one such term for S or P or both, besides the ordinary purely formal Immediate Inferences which can be drawn from it in just the same way as from Independent Propositions, furnishes other Immediate Inferences to any one *acquainted with the system to which it refers*. These inferences are not purely formal, inasmuch as they cannot be drawn except by a person knowing the "system;" on the other hand, they are not material in the ordinary sense, since no knowledge is needed of the objects referred to, except a knowledge of their place in the system, and this knowledge is in many cases almost coextensive with intelligence itself; consider, *e.g.*, the relations of magnitude of objects in space, of the successive parts of time, of family connections, of number. From such a proposition as

The son of C is the father of D,

in addition to the purely formal inferences which may be drawn (*the father of D is the son of C*, etc.), it is possible for any one having the most elementary knowledge of family relationship to infer further that

C is the grandfather of D,
C is the father of D's father,
D is the son of C's son,
D is the grandson of C, etc.

From

C is equal to D (besides *Something equal to D is C*, etc.) it can be inferred that

D is equal to C,
C is not less than D,

SYSTEMIC OR DEPENDENT PROPOSITIONS.

D is not greater than C,
C is not greater than D,
Whatever is greater than C is greater than D,

and so on. (Cf. also, *C is an inference from D*, etc.)

In each of the above examples we are not dealing solely with one object or group in the same way as in Independent Propositions, *e.g.*—

All men are mortal,
Tully is Cicero,
The sky is blue—

we are considering, besides the identity of denomination of S and P, two objects quantitively distinct, namely C and D. The S and P of each proposition have, of course, as just remarked, the same denomination, but an inspection of the Terms (where they are understood) enables us to know that in each case we are concerned with two things (two Subjects or two Attributes) related in a certain way, while of the examples last given this cannot be said. In each of the Dependent Propositions given, what is predicated of S is its relation to another object, and we are able to take that other object and predicate of it its relation to the first object. And where we have two Dependent Propositions as premisses, we are concerned with *three* distinct objects, and the relations between them; and the point of union may be in one of the objects, to which both of the others are related. These considerations seem to me to account for the reputed anomalous character of *à fortiori*, etc., arguments. Every such argument can, I think, be expressed (at greater or less length) by help of Immediate Inference or by rigid Syllogism, or by a combination of both, propositions being used that state explicitly principles or laws of the systems referred to, which, in the ordinary conveniently abbreviated form, are only implied. *E.g.* in

A is greater than B,
B is greater than C,
―――――――――――――
A is greater than C

(where we have four term-names), the reasoning may be expressed by a Conditional Syllogism, thus :—

If any thing (A) is greater than a second thing (B), which (B) is greater than a third thing (C); that thing (A) is greater than (C) :

A thing (A) is greater than a second thing (B), which (B) is greater than a third thing (C) :
_____
That thing (A) is greater than (C).

This Conditional may, of course, but with increase of awkwardness, be reduced to Categorical form.

When Mansel says that *à fortiori*, etc., arguments as they stand are material, *i.e.* are arguments in which the conclusion follows from the premisses solely by the force of the terms (Mansel's *Aldrich*, pp. 198, 199), but that they are reducible to strict syllogistic form, he appears to me to be right.

Among the most important of Dependent Propositions are Mathematical or Quantitative Propositions.

SECTION X.

NOTE ON MATHEMATICAL PROPOSITIONS.

My question here is, What is the quantity of the terms, and what the force of the copula, in Mathematical Propositions?

Take, *e.g.*,

(*a*) $\{2 + 3 = 6 - 1\}$, and let $2 + 3$ and $6 - 1$ mean, $2 + 3$ and $6 - 1$ of *an assigned unit*.

Taking = as signifying *is equal to*, and $2 + 3$, etc., as signifying 2 *units together with* 3 *units*, etc., may we read (*a*), with the subject taken distributively, as

$$\text{any } (2 + 3) = \text{some } (6 - 1)$$

(i.e. any *2 + 3* is *equal to some 6 − 1*, of the assigned unit)?

NOTE ON MATHEMATICAL PROPOSITIONS.

We cannot have
$$\text{any } (2+3) = \text{any } (6-1),$$
because the objects denoted by the Predicate in that case might be the *very same objects* denoted by the Subject, in which case the copula $=$ would be inappropriate, since a thing cannot be said to be *equal to itself*.

And if, taking S and P collectively, we interpret (*a*) to mean
$$\text{all } (2+3) = \text{all } (6-1),$$
on this view we might have
$$1 = (1 + 2 + 3 + \text{etc.})$$
$$(1+1) = 1 \text{ (cf. Boole), and so on;}$$
for *all 1's* taken collectively embraces *all units*, however grouped.

But this would not be admissible in Mathematics, and the appropriate copula here (cf. the Multiplication Table) would be *is*, not $=$. (But cf. Monck, *Introduction to Logic*, p. 19.)

If, however, we say (cf. *ante*, p. 84) that (*a*) means
$$\text{any } (2+3) = \text{some } (6-1),$$
there arises the difficulty that Simple Conversion (as commonly applied with the copula $=$) would give us a proposition of this form,
$$\text{some } (6-1) = \text{any } (2+3),$$
which would not be valid, for the reason which prevented our accepting
$$\text{any } (2+3) = \text{any } (6-1).$$

We might have
$$\text{some } (2+3) = \text{some } (6-1),$$
or
$$\text{these } (2+3) = (\text{those } 6-1), \text{ etc.}$$

But here the universality which we attribute to Mathematical propositions is wanting.

If we interpret $=$ as meaning *is-equal-to-or-identical-with*, then we can say

$$\text{any } (2+3) = \text{any } (6-1),$$

and our proposition is true, universal, and convertible.

It may be remarked that the copula

is-equal-to-or-identical-with

has the same force as

is-or-is-equal-to.

If, on the other hand, we hold the figures in question to have the most general or abstract application possible, and take

$$2+3 = 6-1$$

to mean

The numbers $2+3=$ the numbers $6-1$;

the difficulties above referred to do not arise. Thus understood, $2+3=6-1$ is equivalent to

any $(2+3)$ *is equal to* any $(6-1)$.

I take *equal* to mean *exactly similar quantitatively*, and *identical* to mean *the very same quantitively* (*numero tantum*). Thus a thing would be *equal* to some *other* thing, *identical* with *itself*. (Cf. *post*, Section XXVII.)

SECTION XI.

PREDICATION AND EXISTENCE.

The point discussed under this heading is indicated by Dr. Venn (*Symbolic Logic*, p. 128) as the question whether a "logician who utters a proposition of the form 'All X is Y' can reasonably refuse to say *Yes* or *No* to the question, Do you thereby imply that there is any X and Y?" (cf. below, "assert or imply").[1]

---

[1] The subject here considered is treated of by the following writers (among others):—Jevons, *Deductive Logic*, pp. 141, 142; Dr. Venn, *Symbolic Logic*,

I wish to inquire, first, what can this question mean, and what answer can be given to it, as long as we do not mean by "existence" merely *membership of the Universe of Discourse?* (cf. Keynes, *Formal Logic*, 2nd ed. pp. 137, 138).

If we say that *every* term is the name of *something*, or if we say with Mill (*Logic*, Bk. i. chs. ii., iii.), that whatever can have a name given to it is a *Thing*, and that all names are names of *Things*, then we must either answer *Yes* to Dr. Venn's question, or we must say that there may be *Things* nameable and named which are absolutely non-existent. That this latter answer should be given is perhaps suggested in the question, "Whether when we utter the proposition 'All X is Y' we either assert or imply that there are such things as X or Y, that is, that such things exist *in some sense or other?*"[1] (*Symbolic Logic*, p. 126). It is, at any rate, Dr. Venn's view (cf. *Symbolic Logic*, ch. vi. *e.g.* pp. 130, 131, 136, 137) that Universal Categorical Propositions *do not* (while Particulars *do*) imply the "existence" of what is referred to by S and P. (The view that the meaning of "All X is Y" is expressed by Xy=0—adopting Jevons' notation—refers the *non*-existence which is here predicated not to X or to Y, but to Xy.)

I should maintain that the Things spoken of *must exist in some sense or other*, and that those who assert the contrary may reasonably be called upon to produce and justify a definition of Thing which *excludes existence in every sense whatever*. Indeed Dr. Venn himself in his most recent work[2] seems to allow this, for he says (*Empirical Logic*, p. 232) that "mere logical existence cannot be intelligibly predicated, inasmuch as it is presupposed necessary by the use of the term." Mere logical existence means, I suppose, merely such existence as is involved in a thing's being thought about and

---

ch. vi., and *Empirical Logic*, chs. ix., x. ; Mr. Keynes, *Formal Logic*, Part ii. ch. viii. ; Mr. Bradley, *Principles of Logic*, note at end of ch. v. of Bk. i.

[1] The italics are mine.

[2] In which, however, he by implication confirms the account of Predication and Existence given in the *Symbolic Logic* (cf. *Empirical Logic*, pp. 230, 257).

named, which seems to necessitate some reference beyond the momentary thought of the thinker.[1] Dr. Venn also says (*Empirical Logic*, p. 141), "I incline therefore to say decisively with Mill that the reference of names is to be carried beyond the notion or concept to the objects or things from which the notions are derived or should be derived." And again, p. 158, "Each separate word, whatever the sense through which it is conveyed, is to be taken as an indivisible whole, and referred directly to the corresponding idea, or rather . . . to the phenomenon itself." Again, "People do not speak with an intention to mislead, nor do ordinary adults talk habitually of nonentities" (p. 275). It is but the barest minimum of "existence" of any kind whatever— mere That-ness—that I contend for (no other more determinate existence *could* be involved in the use of *all* terms), and "logical existence" must certainly involve this minimum.[2] Whoever affirms that any term can be *devoid of denomination* (and hence have no application, not be *the name of* anything), would allow, I suppose, that such a term must have *determination* (meaning); but I am quite unable to see how a term can have determination and not denomination—that is to say, that it can signify *character*—a combination of attributes—but not "existence;" this seems like saying that it can signify some *kind of existence* but not *existence itself*. I can only conceive of the world as consisting of Subjects (more or less permanent) and Attributes (more or less transient), each having at least a minimum of "existence"—by which I understand a capacity of affecting or being affected: such a capacity belongs to even the most fleeting idea of the feeblest mind. No term, it appears to me, can be the name of any-

---

[1] Cf. Bosanquet, *Logic*, i. 18, 19: "A name always refers to something." "That which is named is recognised as having a significance beyond the infinitesimal moment of the present and beyond the knowledge of the individual . . . It is, in short, characterized as an object of knowledge."

[2] The "existence" that I mean is, I think, what is meant by Professor William James when he says, "In the strict and ultimate sense of the word existence, everything which can be thought of at all exists as *some* sort of object, whether mythical object, individual thinker's object, or object in outer space and for intelligence at large" (*Mind*, lv. 331).

thing other than some of these Subjects or Attributes, and to some of these Subjects or Attributes any term must apply. It might be said, I suppose, that when I mentally construct the plan of a building, a picture, a story, I am merely putting together "combinations of attributes" which have no "existence;" I should say, however, that so far from having no existence, these objects of thought may have an extremely potent and influential existence, for they may be the archetypes and part-causes of constructions having a *visible* and *tangible* existence. It appears to me that they may have more energy of existence, and therefore more reality, than visible and tangible objects which *once had* physical existence, but which, in the form in which they are thought about, have altogether ceased to be, except in thought. And indeed the same may be said of objects of thought which are not archetypal of any constructions in the material world. The existence of anything, and the thought of that existence, are of course two distinct things, and also existence in one case may differ in *character* from existence in another case; but these admissions are not inconsistent with the view that all thought is of something to which *some* existence is ascribed, and which actually *has* some existence—though it may very well be that the existence *ascribed to it* may be a different *kind* of existence from that which it has.

If by terms having *determination and not denomination* is meant terms which apply to *concepts*—logical (or monadological) concepts, that are complete in themselves and altogether isolated—it appears to me that even supposing such concepts to exist as ideas, and to have names by which they are called, these names could never be the terms of propositions. (Cf. *ante*, Section V.)

If it is admitted that all terms are names of something, but maintained that the *Things* which are named may be "non-existent," the answer to Dr. Venn's question with which we started may, of course, be in the negative. But (besides the difficulty as to the meaning of *Thing*, and besides the difficulty there seems in affirming or denying anything of what has absolutely *no existence whatever*, or in making one affirmation or denial in preference to another) how, on this view, are we ever to posit *existence pure and simple* at all? Unless an implication of existence is contained in the mere enunciation of the S and P of a proposition, I do not see how it *can* be "implied or asserted." It is not existence pure and simple which is ever asserted in the P of any proposition,[1] but only some *mode* of existence, that is, some characteristic; the bare "existence" of which, of course, depends upon the "existence" of that of which it is the characteristic. *E.g.* if I say—

Fairies are non-existent,

the existence that I deny is not existence of *every kind*, since fairies have a certain kind of existence in fairy tales and in imagination. This *existence in imagination* is, of course, distinct from the so-called *mental image* which accompanies not only our comprehension of the terms of propositions which we understand, but also our apprehension of objects which we recognise. What is denied to them in the above proposition is (perhaps) "ordinary phenomenal existence and at the time present."

If I say—

Ideals of conduct exist,

the existence that I affirm is not *bare existence*, nor, *e.g.*, the kind of existence just denied to fairies, but existence *in men's thoughts*. Unless it is admitted that mere existence is intended to be implied in the very enunciation of the terms of a proposition, the interpretation of our proposition

---

[1] Cf. Bain, *Logic*, i. 59, 107, 2nd ed.: "There is nothing correlative to the supposed Universe, existence, the absolute; nothing affirmed when the supposed entity is denied." "With regard to the predicate *Existence* occurring in certain propositions, we may remark that no science, or department of logical method, springs out of it. Indeed all such propositions are more or less abbreviated or elliptical."

Cf. also Venn, *Empirical Logic*, p. 198: "Existence, in every case where it need be taken into account, can be regarded as being *of the nature of an attribute*." A "special kind of existence" is not "implied by the use of the term; is not conveyed by the ordinary copula; it is a real restriction . . . and therefore it is a perfectly fit subject of logical predication" (*op. cit.* p. 232).

is liable to involve us in an infinite regress; we have no ποῦ στῶ.¹

Take a proposition of the form—

All R is Q

interpreted on the view that Predication (at any rate in the case of an Universal proposition) is *not* intended to involve existence.

All R is Q (1),

it is said, is equivalent to

$$Rq = 0 \ (2)^2$$
$$= \text{There is no } Rq \ (3).$$

If we remove the ambiguity of *is*, (3) appears to be equivalent to

No Rq is existent (4),
(4) = All Rq is non-existent (5),

and (5), interpreted in the same way as (1), is equivalent to

No Rq-existent is existent (6),

and this process may be carried on indefinitely (compare the result of interpreting *S is P* to mean *S is P is true*). Besides which, (6) is a contradiction in terms.

It is said that in reducing *All R is Q* to $Rq = 0$, Subject and Predicate are taken strictly in extension ("denotation"). But since *All R is (some) Q* is pronounced to be equivalent to (not

All-R-not-(some)-Q = 0

but)

$$Rq = 0,$$

---

[1] It seems to me that in just that "existence" of the things named by a term which is "presupposed necessary by the use of the term," the "reference to reality" is involved, of which Mr. Bosanquet speaks (*Logic*, Bk. i. ch. i. § 2) as essential in judgment. And then every *proposition* by its very nature and constitution lays claim to be true—it cannot help itself—and it can only be called in question or contradicted by *another* proposition also claiming to be true. But unless the terms of propositions are the names of something having *some kind of existence* or *other*, one does not understand how this inevitable claim of propositions can have even so much significance as to be capable of being rejected.

[2] Cf. Venn, *Symbolic Logic*, pp. 25, 144, etc.

it is clear (1) that it is R and Q, and not *All* R, (*some*) Q, that have been dealt with; (2) that R and Q have been taken in determination.[1]

A further point is, that unless the very positing of a term signifies the *existence* of something *named by the term*, we could never say, *S is P*, since the mere symbol S is certainly not the symbol P. And when our terms are synonyms, or our proposition declares a definition, as in, *e.g.*,

> Courage is valour,
> The word *man* is a word meaning *rational animal*,

the analysis into Sp = O seems peculiarly inappropriate.

I think that some of the difficulty of this subject arises from the circumstance that there is often confusion between the following two questions:—(1) Does a term necessarily imply *some* "existence" of *something* to which it refers? (2) Do people when they use terms *mean to imply* that those terms apply to things having the characteristics *usually attributed* to the things named by the terms (or their constituents)? In particular, it seems that a confusion about *time* is often involved; for instance, when it is said that any assertion, All R is Q, leaves (or is meant to leave) the existence of R doubtful, it is not always clear whether the doubt refers to all (any) time, or some particular time. If the doubt does refer to *all time*, we are simply taken back to the question about bare existence, and can only ask, If it is doubtful whether there is, or ever was or will be, any R, what is the meaning of talking about R at all, and what can we be entitled to affirm or deny of R? (And unless the S and P are symbols of something other than themselves, we could not even *say*, All R *is* Q.) If the doubt refers to some particular time, then it refers not to mere existence, but to a certain determination of existence. If this is expressed, it will occur as part of the attribution of S or P. If not so occurring, it can only be supposed to refer to the present moment, since the copula certainly contains no reference to

[1] Cf. *post*, Section on Quantification and Conversion.

past or future time. On this view, if we take, *e.g.*, the proposition—

All Albinos have pink eyes,

our assertion must contain—(*a*) A declaration of an universal connection (namely that between being an Albino and having pink eyes). (*b*) A doubt whether there are any Albinos living at the present moment. It seems to me not only that any one making the assertion would not be naturally conscious of (*b*), but also that the presence of (*b*) to the mind is not even apparent on reflection—that, in fact, it is quite irrelevant.

Or take—

All cases of shooting through the heart are cases of death.

Or—

If a man is shot through the heart he dies immediately.

Is there any implication of doubt about the existence of present cases of shooting through the heart?

As regards the general question, Do people when they use terms *mean to imply* that those terms apply to things having all the determination usually signified by the terms or term-constituents?, I should be inclined to say in answer to it that any proposition detached from context and tone of assertion must inevitably be understood to have such an implication. (Context or tone may, of course, so affect a proposition as to make us aware in any particular case that *S is P* is meant to convey *S is-not P*.[1]) A remark of Mr. Bosanquet's (*Logic*, i. p. 78), though directed to another point, seems confirmatory of this view. He says, "In every judgment, as Mill incisively contends, *we profess*[2] to speak about the real world and real things." That we *do* always so speak, cannot, of course, be maintained. But I think that we do so in more cases than are at first apparent. For instance, we

---

[1] *E.g.* if one says to a very unpunctual person, "*You* are always in time."
[2] The italics are mine.

not uncommonly assert a proposition from knowledge (real or supposed) of the relation of the *negatives* of the terms which we use—as is no doubt the case in such sayings as, An honest miller has a black thumb—inferred from, and meant to express, the supposed truth that All white-thumbed millers are not-honest. All the wheels that go to Croyland are wheels shod with silver, is another instance of the sort.

It is possible (though not common except when we are using symbols) to combine a plurality of Subjects to form a fresh Subject, and a plurality of Predicates to form a fresh Predicate, or, in other modes, to construct complex Subjects and Predicates. We may, of course, in this way construct terms which determine attributes that never have been, and never will be, and even never *can* be, conjoined in a single Subject—*e.g.* we may combine

$$A \text{ is } b$$

and

$$B \text{ is } a$$

and get the proposition

$$Aa \text{ is } Bb$$

or

$$AB \text{ is } ab.$$

Here not only denomination, but also determination, proposition, and term would vanish altogether if we could refer the contradictory determinations to one and the same Subject.

But if the determinations remain as separate as the term-constituents which express them, denomination lasts as much as determination; but it is a mere collocation of denominations (as well as of determinations) in the case of each "term."

A further objection to the view under discussion is that it does not afford an *ultimate* analysis. For let it be admitted that

$$\text{All R is Q}$$

means

$$Rq = 0,$$

then what does Rq = O mean? It must be read off as either—

(1) R-not-Q (is) nought (=*Something* is *nothing*),

or—

(2) R-not-Q (is-equal-to) nought.

But (1) is in the form *S is P*, and (2) is reducible to that form, unless we hold the complexity introduced into the copula to be a step in analysis. So we seem brought back to the point from which we started.

Nor does the above interpretation of Categorical Propositions furnish a *general* analysis; for, giving a widely different interpretation of Universals and Particulars (according to which Particulars involve "existence" while Universals do not), it does not and cannot say what *S is P* means where S and P may stand for *any* term (*e.g.* Some R, All R, this R, one R, etc.). If the copula is unvarying, must not the connection between S and P in *all* propositions be the same? And how could we *interpret*

All R is Q   (1)

into

Rq = O   (2)

unless we had first understood (1) in its ordinarily accepted (or some other) affirmative sense? We have in (2) two elements—the Predicate and a constituent of the Subject—which do not appear at all in (1). Whence do we obtain (R)q and O? and what are our data for the assertion of (2) unless we have first understood (1) to assert concerning *All R* that it is *Q*? If a distinction is to be drawn between propositions which do, and those which do not, make explicit reference to the actual existence, definitely determined in time, of what is indicated by S and P, I think the line should be between those having Proper Names and Singular and Particular Definites—*e.g.* This R, Those R's, etc.—for S, on the one hand, and all other propositions on the other.

Again, treating our propositions as Coincidentals (which

for symbolic purposes, and indeed wherever we use uninterpreted symbols, we are bound to do), if (1)

All R is Q

is expansible to

All R is some Q ;

if (2) what affirmative Categoricals express is identity of denomination of S and P (in diversity of determination); and if (3) *some* implies "existence;" must not the "existence" of *All R* be implied in

All R is Q ?

If not, *some* as qualifying the Predicate-name differs in the most extreme way from *some* as qualifying the Subject-name. And I do not know on what grounds such a divergence of meaning can be justified.

Some exponents of the view which I am disputing, however, hold a different form of the doctrine. They hold that the "existence" here in question is not *bare* or *mere* existence, but a *particular kind* of existence—existence in (= membership of) some region to which we are referring, and which is our *Universe of Discourse.* We must, it is said, know in all cases what our *Universe of Discourse* is. But *how* are we to know this in dealing with uninterpreted symbols—*e.g.* R's and Q's ? In such cases we must (1) define our Universe by reference to our terms, or (2) take the Universe as all-embracing. Or (3) we must admit that we do not know how to describe or indicate our Universe. If it is asked why we do not admit a fourth alternative, and call our Universe, *e.g.* X, or Y, or Z, without defining X, Y, or Z by reference to R or Q, I reply that since our symbols are uninterpreted, we are not justified in referring R and Q to any one such Universe symbolically indicated rather than to any other, if X, Y, Z have any distinctive force at all. And if it is said that they have not, and that taking, *e.g.*, X, as our Universe-term in reference to All R is Q, simply changes All R is Q (1) into All RX is QX (2), then on the proposed interpretation of (1) (since $X=1$ and $O=x$), we get

$$(RXq = O) = (RXq = x)$$

which is a contradiction in terms. (And must not RX and QX have a Universe Y, and so on?)

On supposition (3) we must be unable to say whether anything belongs, or does not belong, to the Universe of Discourse, and in this case the Universe cannot affect our assertions in any way.

On supposition (1) our Universe is a region containing (*a*) R, r, Q, q, or (*b*) some selection from these. If (*b*), we are forced to transcend the Universe (cf. *post*); and case (*a*) resolves itself into (2) where the Universe is all-embracing. Here, too, we are involved in difficulties. For let the Universe-Term (indicating the region which includes R, r, Q, q) be X; then we can say,

Everything is an X.

But this is no more than to say,

Nothing is x;

and here we have transcended our Universe, and need some term which will include X and x. In *mentioning* our Universe we always make it possible to transcend it. And when we *do* transcend it, is it any longer our Universe *of Discourse?* What is it that entitles X rather than x to that appellation? I do not see how, here, the so-called Universe-Term differs from a mere Class-Term.

And in working with limited and indicated Universes, we encounter similar difficulties. If we take any limited Universe X, calling any member of it an X, we are immediately liable to transcend X, and in the interpretation of

All R is Q,

(referred to the Universe X) as

$$(Rq = O) = (Rq = x)$$

we *must* transcend it. Here X seems obviously nothing more

than a Class-term. I do not see that in affirming or denying it one does anything more than affirm or deny membership of a *class;* or that when one has affirmed x, one is any longer entitled to speak of X as one's Universe of Discourse.[1]

Again, let us take as our Universe the region of Animal life, and referring to this, say, *e.g.*—

All lions are tawny (1).

According to the interpretation I have been disputing

$$(1) = (Lt = 0) \ (2)$$
$$= (Lt = a) \ (3).$$

But we were supposed to be referring to the region of A, and the *Lions* spoken of were A (stone lions, marble lions, etc. need not be tawny),

$$\therefore (3) = (Lt \ A \quad a) \ (4).$$

But this is a contradiction in terms, not to mention that again the Universe A is transcended.

If we adopt (2) as the interpretation of (1), and refer Lt to the region A, our "Universe," I do not see how we can avoid arriving at (4); for, unless we interpret O as meaning unqualifiedly "nothing" or "non-existent," we must interpret it as meaning "not occurring in the region A;" but "not occurring in A" means "occurring outside A," and therefore being a (unless (1) A is all-embracing,—which by supposition it is not,—and (2) "not occurring in A" indicates what is absolutely non-existent; and I have, I think, given sufficient reason for refusing to admit this interpretation). The fact seems to me to be that in

$$Lt = 0$$

both our terms refer to the region *a*, not to the region *A*. If we say that we *start* with the Universe A in

All lions are tawny,

---

[1] The objections to the expression Rq = O as an interpretation of All R is Q, are not altered if we explain Rq = O to mean, not Rq = x, but Rq = some x.

we have certainly in
$$Lt = 0$$
transferred ourselves to the region a, and here, as long as we equate to O we remain. But O only has meaning with reference to A, therefore we have to take both A and a into our Universe, and it is not merely reference to the class A, but reference *to that class and to its contradictory* that enables us to interpret

All lions are tawny

into
$$Lt = 0.$$

Thus reference to the Class A as Universe of Discourse seems necessarily to allow both inclusion in that class and exclusion from it, involving free use of the terms A and a, and free movement in the regions indicated by those terms. But I have never understood logicians who advocate the use of Universes of Discourse to mean that the Universe A includes also a; and, moreover, A and a embrace *the whole* Universe taken in the widest sense.

Thus, as it appears to me, the attempt to use restricted Universes breaks down.

Even supposing that we *could* use them, I do not think it would be convenient in ordinary life and thought. I think that in any ordinary conversation, or book, or newspaper, what happens is that we constantly refer in the same paragraph, if not in the same sentence, to more than one restricted "Universe." If I say, "I had a strange dream last night; it reminded me of a scene in *Romola*," I refer to the Universes of spiritual and material fact, of illusion and fiction. If I read, "In the beginning God created the heavens and the earth . . . and the Spirit of God moved upon the face of the waters," I again find many Universes (in the narrow sense) referred to. And it is the same everywhere; no one keeps, or feels any need of keeping, consistently to one Universe. But notwithstanding this, we do not generally fear, nor perhaps risk, confusion. What saves us from this (in as far as we are saved) is not, I think, the apparatus of Universes which seems awkward and inadequate, but that presupposition of thought which the so-called Law of Identity is sometimes interpreted to mean.[1] This is perfectly simple, and fully adequate to the purpose. There is no fear of confusion or mistake in the use of terms as long as we give always *the same value* to our terms; though what our terms *are* can generally only be settled by some reference to context. No doubt we often use *implicitly* qualifications of terms which are indispensable to understanding, and in this danger may lurk. But the risk must be run; and these implicit qualifications must always be capable of being made explicit on demand. It seems to have been with a view to such implicit qualifications that the idea of Universes of Discourse has been introduced. The case for Universes seems most plausible when we are concerned with Technical, etc., Terms. We do, of course, have dictionaries of Technical Terms, and treatises bristling with Technical Terms, and something is gained by the information given us to start with, that we are going to be specially concerned with a particular class of objects. But in no such case are we really confined to the limited region indicated; multitudes of Common Terms must be used, explanations must refer to a variety of outside objects, illustrations may be taken (without formal notice) from almost any region.

The interpretation of

(a) All R is Q,
(b) No R is Q,

to mean

$$Rq = 0,$$
$$RQ = 0,$$

involves, it is said, the admission that (a) and (b) may both be true together—in the case, that is, where there is no R.[2] But if this is so, then if our Universe is all-embracing, *Everything is r*, which seems inadmissible; and if our Universe is

---

[1] Cf. *ante*, p. 3, and *post*, Section on the Laws of Thought.
[2] Cf. *Symbolic Logic*, p. 145.

restricted, let it be X. Then it is with reference to X that we say that

All R is Q,
No R is Q—

in other words, that

R is Q and q.

But if all X is destitute of R's, if the whole of it is r, what is meant by saying that X is our Universe of Discourse when we assert

All R is Q,
No R is Q

(meaning that there is no R within the region X)? How can we call that our Universe of Discourse which is absolutely destitute of the things to which our terms apply?

Suppose I say—

All green lions are African,
No green lions are African,

and assert that my Universe of Discourse is the Zoological Gardens, and that the meaning of my two propositions is to deny the "existence" of green lions (that is, their presence in the Zoological Gardens). Is there not force in the objection that, since what I am talking of is *not* in the Zoological Gardens, that region is *not* my Universe of Discourse? Must not my Universe of Discourse in this case be some region where there *are* green lions, *i.e.* a region of imagination; and in this region contradictions are excluded as well as in regions of material existence. If I imagine green lions, I cannot imagine them as being both African and not African. Mr. Bradley (*Principles of Logic*, p. 154) objects to allow that A and E may be asserted together, and says that the view that they may be so asserted is due to a confusion between possibility and existence. I should rather say that it is due to a confusion between different kinds of existence (or existence in different regions). In as far as it is not this, but an actual contradiction (or contrariety) within a specified region, it involves a breach of the Law of Contradiction, which (besides being, as it seems to me, a pillar of Logic) is as self-evident as any principle in the world can be, and is accepted because of its self-evidence, because its truth is "clear and distinct." And no proposition whatever can be supported by better evidence than this; hence to question the Law of Contradiction is to question the very foundations of Logic, the very possibility of truth, and to open the door to limitless doubt.

One further point in connection with the subject recurs to me forcibly here. Logicians who hold that since *all* does not imply existence while *some* does, Particulars cannot be deduced from Universals, hold also that *some* does not exclude *all*. The point here is, I suppose, that *some* is taken to apply to matter of finite experience, while the Universal *all* is not. If this is so, how is it possible that *some* could ever be admitted to apply to *all?* It appears to me that the Universal *all* both includes and transcends experience, so that *some* may legitimately be deduced from it, but can never be *intended to have*, though, as a matter of fact, it *may have* the same application. Nor even if *all* means merely a completed quantity or number, can *some* ever be *intended* to be equivalent to it—though it may turn out to have an identical application—as if, having taken apples out of a basket of apples and pears in the dark, I say, "Some apples are decayed," meaning all that I have taken out, and find on further investigation that, as a matter of fact, there are no apples left.

But taking either sense of *all*, and regarding *some* as *possibly* equivalent to it (in application), how can we deny the inferribility of *some* from *all?* The truth seems to be that *some* and *all* have diverse determinations, but may in any given case happen to have an identical application.

SECTION XII.

(B.) INFERENTIAL PROPOSITIONS.

PROPOSITIONS of the form

If E is F, E is H,
If E is F, G is H,
If any E is F, that E is H, etc.,

are commonly called Hypothetical or Conditional (*E is F*, *any E is F*, are Antecedents; *E is H, G is H, that E is H*, are Consequents).

My reason for wishing to adopt the name Inferential is twofold. In the first place, it seems to me that the differentia of such propositions is to be found in a relation between A (Antecedent) and C (Consequent), such that C is inferred from A. In the second place, I accept the differentiation of "Hypothetical" from "Conditional" Propositions (cf. Keynes, *Formal Logic*, pp. 64, 65, 2nd ed.) suggested by Mr. W. E. Johnson and accepted by Mr. Keynes, and it seems desirable to have a generic term for these two species. This distinction itself seems to me of great value, corresponding to a fundamental difference, and allaying, at the same time that it explains, the dispute as to whether Hypotheticals and Conditionals are, or are not, reducible to Categoricals having S and P corresponding to the A and C of the original propositions.

I propose to define as follows:—

An Inferential Proposition is a proposition expressing a relation between Antecedent and Consequent, such that an identity (or identities) *expressed or indicated* by the Consequent is an inference from an identity (or identities) *expressed or indicated* by the Antecedent. (Cf. Keynes, *Formal Logic*, p. 164, 2nd ed.; also *post*, Mixed Inferential Syllogisms, Table XXXVIII.)

As I have mentioned above, I accept the view according

to which the propositions which I wish to call Inferential may be divided into two distinct species, called respectively

    (1) Hypothetical.
    (2) Conditional.

(Cf. Keynes, *Formal Logic*, pp. 64, 65, 67, etc., 2nd ed.)

(1) Differ from (2) in this, that both A and C express or indicate a complete Categorical Proposition, capable of being asserted in isolation (cf. *op. cit.* p. 65), *e.g.*,

    If you are right, he is a good man;
    If E were F, G would be H.

Hence the *A* and *C* of Hypotheticals might be called *absolute assertions;* whilst the *A* and *C* of Conditionals might be distinguished as *relative assertions;* for each refers to the other and is in itself incomplete. Take, *e.g.*,

    If any flower is scarlet, it (= that flower) is scentless.

Any flower is scarlet, the *A* of this Conditional, if asserted in isolation, is equivalent to *all flowers are scarlet;* but this is not the meaning which it has as Antecedent. And *that flower is scentless*—the Consequent—has obvious reference to that which has gone before, and is obviously incomplete in itself.

A Conditional Proposition may be defined as—

> A Proposition which asserts that any object which is indicated by a given class-name and distinguished in some particular way, may be inferred to have also some further distinction. (Cf. *post*, p. 111.)

A Hypothetical Proposition may be defined as—

> A Proposition in which two (expressed or indicated) Categoricals (or combinations of Categoricals) are combined in such a way as to express that one (Consequent) is an inference from the other (Antecedent). Cf. Keynes, *Formal Logic*, p. 164.

It may be observed that this inferential relation can only obtain between propositions that differ from each other, but are not incompatible.

The import of an Inferential may, I think, be nearly expressed in a Dependent (or Systemic) Categorical—*e.g.*,

If E is F, G is H

is expressible as

G is H is an inference from *E is F* (1).

This proposition may be compared to such a proposition as

E is larger than F (2).

In both cases there are two non-identical elements (G is H—E is F, E—F) having a certain relation to each other; and from both certain fresh propositions may be inferred in addition to those inferrible from *all* Categoricals (cf. *ante*, Section IX.).

The following are examples of equivalent Inferentials and Categoricals:—

(1) If you are disappointed, I am sorry.
(2) If all men were perfect, all men would be infallible.
(3) If any bird is a thrush, it is speckled.

(1) = That I am sorry is an inference from your being disappointed.

(2) = That all men are infallible is an inference from all men's being perfect (perfect creatures being infallible).

(3) = That any bird is speckled is an inference from its being a thrush.

(2) May be regarded as enthymematic. (Cf. *post*, pp. 106, 107.)

Hypothetical Propositions may be divided as follows:—

(1) Hypotheticals in which the Consequent is an inference from the Antecedent alone (*e.g.* If all R's are Q's, some R's are Q's)—these I call *Self-contained Hypotheticals*. They are further divided into Independent and Dependent.

(2) Propositions in which C is inferred not from A alone, but from A taken in conjunction with some other unexpressed proposition or propositions. These I call *Referential Propositions*. They may refer to either (*a*) only one unexpressed proposition, as in

If M is P, S is P [∴ S is M];

and these I have called *Enthymematic;* or they may refer (b) to more than one unexpressed proposition, as in

> If that rope did not break, the knot must have come undone.

These I call *Elliptical.* Both (a) and (b) may be Independent or Dependent. This account of Hypothetical Propositions involves the view that the terms contained in any Hypothetical are all to be identified in application, either *directly* as in (1), or *indirectly* as in (2). In the latter case the identification is effected by means of Middle Terms; this indirect identification may perhaps be called Integration.

My use here of the terms *Inferential, Enthymematic,* and *Elliptical* perhaps needs some further justification and explanation. As regards Hypotheticals, I think that Mr. Keynes' definition is in support of the view that these propositions assert a relation between A and C, such that C is inferrible from A. For he explains the import of a Hypothetical proposition to be "that the truth of C follows from that of A"[1] (*Formal Logic*, p. 164, 2nd ed.). That C *follows from* A seems to me equivalent to saying that C *is an inference from* A. And reference to the Hypothetico-Categorical Syllogism affords further confirmation; for, having asserted

> If A, C;

we ask no more than the Categorical assertion of A, in order to go on to the Categorical assertion of C. And in a Conditional of the form

> If *any D* is E, *that D* is F,

what is asserted seems to be, that the presence of E with D is *sufficient ground* for expecting the further presence of F— that is, that wherever we find DE, we may *infer* F. (Cf. Mill's *Axiom of Syllogism.* Whatever has any mark (DE), has that (F) which it (DE) is a mark of.) I admit that frequently in Hypotheticals the A does not *express* the *whole justification* for C which it *implies.* In

> If M is P, S is P,

[1] I have substituted A and C for P and Q.

one unexpressed proposition (namely, S is M) is necessary in order to give the whole ground. (It is because of the exact correspondence between this inference and the Categorical Enthymeme that I have called Hypotheticals of this kind *Enthymematic.*) And in such a Hypothetical as,

If X is Y, S is P,

it is clear that *more than one* Categorical proposition is necessary to *justify* the assertion of S is P *on the strength of* X is Y. And since these other Categoricals are unexpressed, the Hypothetical as a whole is *elliptical.*

If the application of the term *Inferential* to these Hypotheticals is objected to on account of the incomplete expression in A of the ground of C, then on this view we ought, I think, to deny that there is an inference in such assertions as: This is iron, and therefore liable to rust; or, This is a square on that side of a right-angled triangle which subtends the right angle, and therefore it is equal to the squares on the other two sides.

Conditional Propositions may be divided into (1) *Divisional Propositions*, in which it is asserted that if any member of a specified class belongs to a subdivision indicated by the P-name of *A*, it may be inferred to belong to one indicated by the P-name of *C*; *e.g.*,

If any goose is not grey, it is white.

If any peer is not a duke, he must be a marquis, or an earl, or a viscount, or a baron.

If any Briton is not English, Welsh, or Irish, he is Scotch.

These correspond to, and are derivable from, *Divisional Alternatives*—to which also they may be reduced.

(2) *Quasi-Divisional Conditionals.* In these the class indicated by the S-name of the *A* is not (as in Divisionals) exhaustively subdivided by the negative of the P-name (or names) of *A*, and the P-name (or names) of *C*; but the species got by combining the Term-names of the S and P of the *A* is referred to the class indicated by the P of *C*, and the division indicated by the P-name of *A* is coincident with,

or included in (not co-ordinate with), that indicated by the P-name of C.

The following are examples of (2):—

If any violet is white, it is fragrant;
If any fowl is a Spangled Hamburgh, it is Silver or Golden;
If any fowl is a Plymouth Rock or a Spangled Hamburgh, it is a handsome bird.

The distinction between Hypothetical and Conditional Inferentials becomes very marked when a proposition of either kind is taken as major premiss in a syllogism which has a Categorical minor and conclusion.

With a Hypothetical we get—

$$\frac{\text{If } A, C;}{A \text{ (or not } C);}$$
$$C \text{ (or not } A).$$

If, *e.g.*, A = Honesty is not the best policy,
C = Life is not worth having,

our syllogism runs—

If Honesty is not the best policy, life is not worth having;
Honesty is not the best policy (or Life is worth having);
Life is not worth having (or Honesty is the best policy).

But, taking a Conditional Proposition as major premiss, we do not for minor simply affirm the A or deny the C, nor for conclusion simply affirm the C or deny the A. A significant syllogism having a Conditional major and a Categorical minor and conclusion is always reducible (though the reduction may be troublesome) to the form—

If any D is E, that D is F;
XD is E (or XD is not F);
XD is F (or XD is not E).

The S of the A of any Conditional is always indefinite— the S-name of the minor and conclusion generally has either a definite Term-indicator, or is distinguished from the S-name of the A by some distinctive attribute. We *may* have a syllogism of the form—

> If any D is E, that D is F ;
> Some D is E ;
> ---
> Some D is F ;

but it is unusual.

If we allow Inferentials of the form

> If M is F, N is H

to represent both Hypotheticals and Conditionals, then we cannot, if we are absolutely precise, use propositions of this form in Immediate Inference. For the only distinctive Immediate Inference that can be drawn from an Inferential is what is called the Contrapositive (cf. *post*, Section XIX.); and given that

> If M is F, N is H (1)

is a Conditional, and therefore (cf. *post*, p. 111) reducible to the form

> If *any E* is F, *that E* is H (2),

the denial of the C will not give us precisely what is wanted for the A of the Contrapositive, nor will the denial of the A give us precisely what is wanted for the C of the Contrapositive. For the Contrapositive would be

> If *any E* is not H, *that E* is not F.

And, similarly, if it is allowed that

> If A, C (3)

represents indifferently Conditionals and Hypotheticals, then

> If A, C

cannot furnish the precise Contrapositive of the Inferential, any more than an Attributive Categorical symbolized as

> S is P

can directly furnish a Converse.

Also if (1) and (3) may symbolize both Hypotheticals and Conditionals, they cannot be used (without further information) as Major Premiss in Inferentio-Categorical Syllogisms; for in the case in which they stand for Conditionals, the A cannot be simply affirmed nor the C simply denied. This obviously follows from the reciprocal dependence of the A and C in a Conditional proposition.

We can, however, and constantly do, use the above forms as representative of both species of Inferentials; and no doubt we are substantially justified in doing so.

A proposition of the form

If any E is F, that E is H (4)

is unmistakeably Conditional; as unmistakeably Hypothetical is one of the form

If E is F, E is H (5)

(containing, that is, two absolute assertions, having three, and only three, terms between them; cf. Table XXXII. "Referential Hypotheticals").

We might perhaps consider (4) as the best symbolic form for Conditionals, accepting (5) and (1) as representing varieties of Hypotheticals, and (3) as representative of both (5) and (1).

The Categorical, I think, that best expresses a Conditional is of this form—

Any E that is F is H;

which is apparently equivalent to

If any E is F, that E is H.

Mr. Keynes and Mr. W. E. Johnson hold that, while Hypothetical Propositions are not equivalent to Categoricals nor reducible to them, Conditional Propositions *are* both reducible to and precisely equivalent to Categoricals—that the relation between A and C in a Conditional, and the relation between S and P in a Categorical, are exactly similar (cf. Keynes, *Formal Logic*, pp. 162, 163, 2nd ed.). With this I agree to a great extent, but not entirely. I think that Hypotheticals are not reducible to Categoricals in the sense in which Conditionals are;[1] but that Conditionals lose something of their force in reduction to a Categorical of the form, Any DE is F, and that such a Categorical gains some addition of meaning by reduction to a Conditional—that thus Conditionals and such Categoricals are not precisely equivalent, and that certain Categoricals are not reducible to Conditionals at all. On analysis, a Conditional Proposition resolves itself, I think (though not in all cases very readily; cf. cases where we refer directly to events), into the assertion that if anything called by a class-name has a distinctive given attribute, *that* member of the class has, it is to be inferred (and inferred from the combination of the distinctive attribute with the attribute determined by the class-name), also another attribute. In—

> If a child is just recovering from measles, he ought not to be at school,

we have the assertion simply and directly made. In—

> If you pull the trigger of a gun, it will go off,

we may resolve into—

> If a gun has its trigger pulled by you, that gun will go off.

> If he told you anything, it is true,

resolves into—

> If anything was told you by him, that thing is true.

In all these cases the P of C is obviously inferred from the qualification of the S of A by the P of A. And I do not see that this is obvious in a Categorical of the form All (or Any) DE is F. No doubt all Conditionals *can* be reduced to Universal Categoricals of this form; and such Categoricals may, if significant, be reduced with the greatest ease to Conditionals; but if we are given such a Categorical

---

[1] Of course, any statement or statements whatever may be expressed in Categorical form; but the point is that when Conditionals are reduced, the S and P of the resulting Categorical correspond substantially to the A and C of the given Conditional, while this is not the case with Hypotheticals.

expressed in symbols, we cannot be sure of getting a valid result when we reduce it to a Conditional. The order of Constituents in a complex term is indifferent, and it would be quite possible to take the proposition, Any BT is S, to transform it to If any T is B, it is S; and to find on interpretation that our Conditional means—

If any *thrush is a bird*, it is speckled.

If we take *any* Categoricals with a simple S-name, and *any* Particular Categoricals, it will appear that they cannot be expressed as Conditionals. Take, *e.g.*,

(1) All lions are quadrupeds.
(2) Some birds are speckled.

It may be said that

(1) = If any creatures are lions, they are quadrupeds (3).

But turn this into a Categorical again and we get, not (1) but

All creatures that are lions are quadrupeds (4).

And supposing it is said that

(1) = If lions, then quadrupeds (5),

I remark that this reduction is not satisfactory, since (5) is either unmeaning, or elliptical and obscure.

(2) Might perhaps be said to be equivalent to

Sometimes when a thing is a bird, it is speckled.

or,—

Some things that are birds are speckled;

but such propositions seem purely Categorical, incapable of transformation to any Conditional, and compatible with the corresponding O propositions (cf. Some rational animals are engineers, Some rational animals are not engineers).

If, however,

Some R is Q

may be expressed as

XR is Q (*i.e.* All XR is Q),

then particulars need not be differently treated from Universals with complex S-names. But as we cannot get a Conditional out of a Categorical unless it has a complex S-name, nor reduce any but such a Categorical to a Conditional, we must either admit *some* point of difference between Categoricals and Conditionals, or divide Categoricals into two classes, distinguished from each other by certain differences.

What any Conditional Proposition—

If any D is E, that D is F (1)

—seems to me to assert is, that the F-ness of *any* D is an inference from its being an E. Thus any Conditional would be universal and affirmative. I think also that (1) *implies* the existence of some D's that are *not* E.

I may, of course, assert something to be an inference, either in a Hypothetical or a Conditional, when as a matter of fact it is not so; just as in a Categorical I may affirm identity of the objects indicated by S and by P, when such identity does not exist; but what we are interested in, in discussing the formal import of propositions, is *what the proposition asserts*, not what is actually true.

The distinctions between Enthymematic and Elliptical Propositions, and between Divisionals and Quasi-Divisionals, cannot be regarded as properly *formal*.

[TABLES.

114　IMPORT OF PROPOSITIONS.

TABLE XXXII.

HYPOTHETICAL PROPOSITIONS.

SELF-CONTAINED PROPOSITIONS.

Independent Propositions (having no Dependent Term).

e.g. If all R's are Q's, some Q's are R's; if some R's are Q's, one R is a Q; if S is P, P is S; if A is B, and B is not C, A is not C; if M is P, and S is M, S is P.

Dependent Propositions (having at least one Dependent Term).

e.g. If all captains of ships are despots on board, this captain of a ship is a despot on board; if the son of N is the father of L, the father of L is the son of N.

REFERENTIAL PROPOSITIONS.

ENTHYMEMATIC PROPOSITIONS (C inferrible from A together with one other proposition, which, with A, constitutes the premisses of a syllogism of which C is the conclusion).

Independent Propositions.

e.g. If all M's are P's, all S's are P's (∵ all S's are M's); if Homer wrote the *Iliad* he was a genius; if some men are noble, some men are to be reverenced; if all men are fallible, all men should be modest; if XY is a liar, he is not to be trusted.

Dependent Propositions.

e.g. If D is equal to E, D is equal to F (because E is equal to F); if all moments of time are quantities, they are infinitely divisible.

ELLIPTICAL PROPOSITIONS (C inferrible from A together with more than one other Proposition).

Independent Propositions.

e.g. If this statesman is honest, he is deluded; if that parcel is not books, it is papers; if the rope did not break, the knot must have come undone; if Shakespeare is not the greatest poet, Goethe is; if you push me, I shall fall; if *one* person stays at home, that will be sufficient; if *Fritz* is a blunderer, it is not surprising; if *this* man is tolerant, he is heroic; if A is B, and C is D, E is F.

Dependent Propositions.

e.g. If the author of that work is not Bacon, he is Shakespeare; if you lifted that box you must be stronger than *you* look; if Jack's friend is pleased, Jack will be satisfied; if Mary has the key of the door, she will open it for you; if E is equal to F, G is equal to H; if G is equal to H, E is equal to F, and F is equal to G.

ALTERNATIVE PROPOSITIONS.

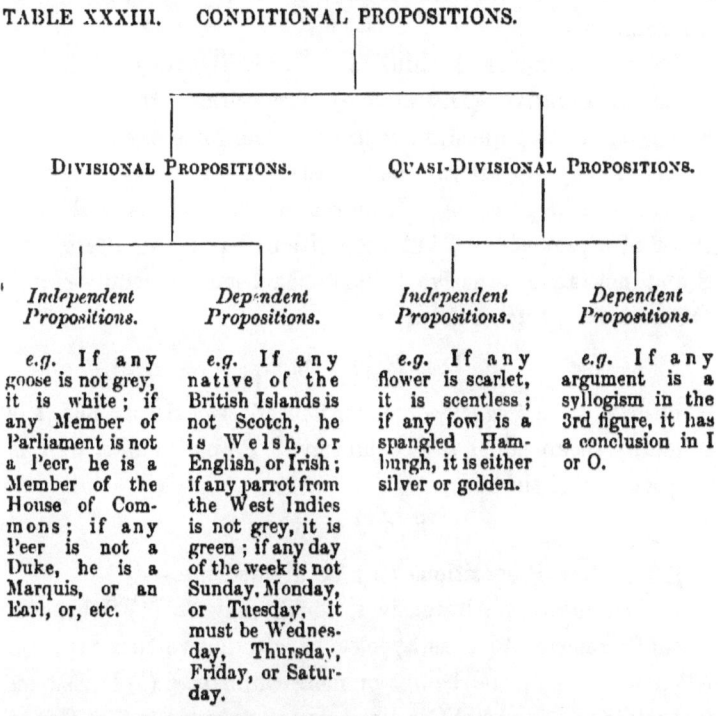

TABLE XXXIII. CONDITIONAL PROPOSITIONS.

SECTION XIII.

(C.) ALTERNATIVE PROPOSITIONS.

I should like to call propositions of the form

$$S \text{ is } Q \text{ or } R$$

Alternative rather than *Disjunctive*, because the *differentia* of these propositions is that they consist of elements connected alternatively, and because the name *disjunctive*, in its untechnical sense, seems as applicable to propositions of the form

$$D \text{ is neither } E \text{ nor } F$$

as to those of the form

$$D \text{ is } E \text{ or } F.$$

The one question which has been considered of importance here is whether the members of an alternation are exclusive or unexclusive.

There has never, I think, been any dispute or difficulty about Alternative (Disjunctive) Propositions that has not arisen out of this question concerning the force of *or*.

There may apparently be alternation—I. between *terms*; II. between *propositions*. I. may occur in the S as well as in the P of a proposition; but propositions having an alternative S and not an alternative P have not been commonly called Disjunctive. Such a form as

D is E, or F is G,

is clearly an *alternative combination of propositions*, but it is generally reckoned as a "Disjunctive" Proposition, as well as propositions of the form

S is Q or R.

Alternative Propositions may be divided into—

I. Classificatory Alternatives, which may be (*a*) Subsumptional (S referred to P as Species to alternative Genera); *e.g.* All men are spiritual beings or mere animals. (*b*) Divisional (reducible to Divisional Conditionals—S referred to P as Genus to alternative (constituent) Species); *e.g.* Any parrot is green or grey. In Divisional and Quasi-Divisional Alternatives, and in them alone, the disjunction is not a disjunction of ignorance or indetermination.

II. What may be called Quasi-Divisional Alternatives (reducible to Quasi-Divisional Conditionals); *e.g.* Any flower is scentless or it is not scarlet.

III. A class which, for want of a better word, I call Contingent Alternatives (corresponding to Elliptical Hypotheticals); *e.g.* The author of those plays is Bacon or Shakespeare, A is B or C is D.

It may be said that what *A or B* means is simply *not* [*a and b*] (using Jevons' notation, according to which $a = \text{not-}A$). But even supposing that we admit this to be true in all cases without exception, it is still possible that it may be as insufficient an account of the meaning of alternation as Hobbes' account of a Categorical Proposition, according to which what the proposition asserts is " [the belief of the speaker] that the predicate is a name of the same thing of which the subject is a name." This is true in all cases without exception, but it is not the *whole* of what is true in each and every case, and it would admit propositions (so called) of the form *A is A*. And so it may be with the above interpretation of A or B. Though *A or B* be granted to mean at least *not (a and b)*, the question may yet remain, Is *or* to be taken exclusively or unexclusively?

Various reasons may be adduced in support of the view that where we have two (or more) Alternatives separated by *or*—*e.g. A or B*—these alternatives ought to be understood as mutually exclusive (as well as together exhaustive).

The view of educated persons as to the usual meaning of *or* ought to be of some weight here. To take first *experts*. There are a large number of distinguished logicians who hold that *or* is exclusive.[1] Kant, Hamilton, Thomson, Boole, Bain, and Fowler take this view (cf. Keynes, *Formal Logic*, 2nd ed. p. 167, note 2). Examples brought forward in support of the unexclusiveness of *or* by other logicians do not seem to afford very powerful confirmation. Take, for instance, Jevons' well-known example (*Pure Logic*, pp. 76, 77), "A peer is either a duke, or a marquis, or an earl, or a viscount, or a baron." This instance, it is said, disproves the exclusiveness of *or*, because a peer may have any combination of the alternative titles. But I think that what the proposition really means is, Any person, in order to be a peer, *must be* a duke or a marquis, etc. A peer may indeed, as a matter of fact, *have* every one of the five titles enumerated; but if he is a peer in virtue of one title, he is not a peer in virtue of any other. One title gives all the privileges of peerage, and all the titles in Burke can do no more. Or take the proposition (which occurs in a "Previous" examination paper), "Every ragged person either is poor or wishes to be thought poor." This seems to me an extremely ingenious

---

[1] The authorities on the other side will be mentioned later.

example, and at first sight very telling on the side of unexclusiveness; but if its full meaning were expressed, would it not run as follows: Every ragged person *is ragged* either *because* he is poor, or *because* he wishes to be thought poor? and in this case the alternation is clearly exclusive.

In legal documents, as I am informed, *or* is understood as exclusive, *e.g.* "A. B. is entitled to a sheep or cow," would be taken to mean that A. B. is entitled to *only* a sheep or *only* a cow. (My authority here is a Chancery lawyer of much learning and experience.)

I have asked a number of persons (not experts) whom I know, whether they think that in using *or* they mean it to be exclusive or unexclusive; and to the best of my remembrance, not one understood it as unexclusive. When I turn to my own experience, it seems to me that this is my own case too, and that when I use *or* I always think of it as having an exclusive force. Where the terms used are not, *in fact*, exclusive, it might perhaps be said that the alternation is elliptical, the current form of speech being an abbreviated one, due to the desire for conciseness, or to the fact that the full expression of the meaning would be intolerably awkward, or to the circumstance that the particular case in question occurs so seldom that the exact expression for it has not got minted, as happens with the adjectival forms of names not often needed except in the substantive form. It might, in fact, be said that in such cases the *alternation* is taken to mean more than it actually expresses, as the form *A is A* does in, *e.g.*, "A man's a man," "Cards are cards" (Sarah Battle); or as Indesignate Propositions do, *e.g.* Birds sing.

But all this, though it has some weight, needs confirmation by the results of reflection. The confirmation which it seems to me to receive from reflection is as follows:—

In as far as the members of any alternation (if *terms*) are taken in determination and are similar in determination, are taken in denomination and are identical in denomination, or (in the case of propositions) have the same signification,

(1.) The formal alternation has no alternative force. It

may be said, in fact, that there *is* no alternation in the matter except an alternation of words or symbols merely. *A or A* has no more title to be called an alternation than *A is A* has to be called a categorical proposition. *A is A* tells us nothing, and *A or A* tells us no more than A. Or—

(2.) The affirmation of one member involves the affirmation of the other, and the denial of one member involves the denial of the other, which is incompatible with interpreting *A or A* to mean *not (a and a)*. Or—

(3.) The denial (or affirmation) of a term or proposition justifies us in proceeding to its affirmation (or denial). This involves a contradiction. Or—

(4.) Neither member of the alternation can be denied (nor affirmed, if affirmation of one member involves the denial of the other). In this case an Alternative proposition cannot be the major premiss of a syllogism having categorical minor and conclusion.

I am bound to admit that an answer to (2) and (3) has been suggested to me by which (4) is obviated, the case in which neither member can be denied being seen to be merely a case of the general rule that *not both* can be denied. But if it is only in virtue of the alternation that we can assert that *not both* can be denied, while at the same time the "alternation" *A or A* is said to be equivalent to *A*—that is, to have no alternative force—we seem to fall upon a fresh difficulty.

The reasoning of (1) remains in force, but it may be said that it does not entitle us to deny that alternatives are unexclusive, for their being unexclusive means no more than this, that we are not in all cases entitled to pass from the affirmation of one alternative to the denial of the other— all that *A or B* means is, that *we cannot deny both A and B*. (And we cannot deny both, *because* the denial of *either* member entitles us to affirm *the other* member.)

This is obvious, and admitted by every one when such a case is proposed, as, Some parishes in the east of London are peopled by paupers or criminals; Fruit is unwholesome unless it is ripe or cooked. No one can say that in these and similar instances it is impossible for the determination of both alternatives to coexist in one individual subject. And that these cases are comparatively infrequent is not to the point. It may, however, be said that even here there is an exclusiveness of determination, though not of denomination. And if we admit alternation in which the members are *wholly* unexclusive, *e.g.*,

$$\text{A is B or A is B (1)},$$

we must, it seems to me, give up the equivalence between Hypotheticals and Disjunctives, for the Hypothetical answering to (1) is—

$$\text{If A is not B, A is B (2)},$$

which is self-contradictory, and has therefore no assertive force; whereas if (1) is equivalent to A is B, and (2) is equivalent to (1), (2) means A is B.

I cannot therefore help concluding that although alternative terms may sometimes be identical in denomination—and it is perhaps in view of such cases that Whately, Mansel, Mill, and Jevons (cf. Keynes, *Formal Logic*, 2nd ed. p. 167, note 2) insist upon the non-exclusiveness of alternation—yet alternatives must always have *some element of exclusiveness*, that otherwise they have no logical value whatever. There is no escaping the admission that in as far as any form of words *has* alternative force, the alternatives are rigidly exclusive; also that *in as far as any* alternation cannot be reduced to a strictly exclusive form, the alternation vanishes—just as in S is P, the proposition would vanish if P turned out to be not S. For the members, in as far as not exclusive, are one —a denial of either involves denial of the other, contrary or contradictory. *E.g.* in

$$\text{All R is Q (1), or this R is Q (2)},$$

contrary denial of (1) involves denial of (2), and denial of (2) involves contradictory denial of (1). Cf. *post.* pp. 151, 152.

So, if by alternatives being unexclusive is meant only that

the affirmation of one member (or members) does not justify the denial of the rest, then alternatives are unexclusive; if by alternatives being unexclusive it is meant that they may be without any element of exclusiveness, then they are *not* unexclusive.

An Alternative Proposition then may, I think, be defined as—

> A proposition in which a plurality of differing elements (connected by *or*, and called the alternatives) are so related that *not all* of them can be denied, because the denial of some justifies the assertion of the rest.

Hence from (1) the denial of some elements we can proceed to (2), the affirmation (categorical or alternative) of the rest—(2) is inferrible from (1). Thus all Alternations are reducible to Inferential Propositions (cf. Keynes, *Formal Logic*, p. 170, 2nd ed.), and, conversely, all Inferential Propositions are reducible to Alternations. Divisional and Quasi-Divisional Alternatives reduce to Divisional and Quasi-Divisional Conditionals, *e.g.* Any goose is grey or white, reduces to, If any goose is not white it is grey. Any flower is scentless or it is not scarlet, reduces to, If any flower is scarlet it is scentless.

Subsumptional and Contingent Alternatives reduce to Hypotheticals, *e.g.* All parts of space are infinitely divisible, or they are not continuous quantity; That bird is a Guillemot or a Razorbill; S is P or P is not S; reduce to, If all parts of space are continuous quantity, they are infinitely divisible; If that bird is not a Razorbill it is a Guillemot; If P is S, S is P.

[TABLE.

122 IMPORT OF PROPOSITIONS.

TABLE XXXIV. ALTERNATIVE PROPOSITIONS.

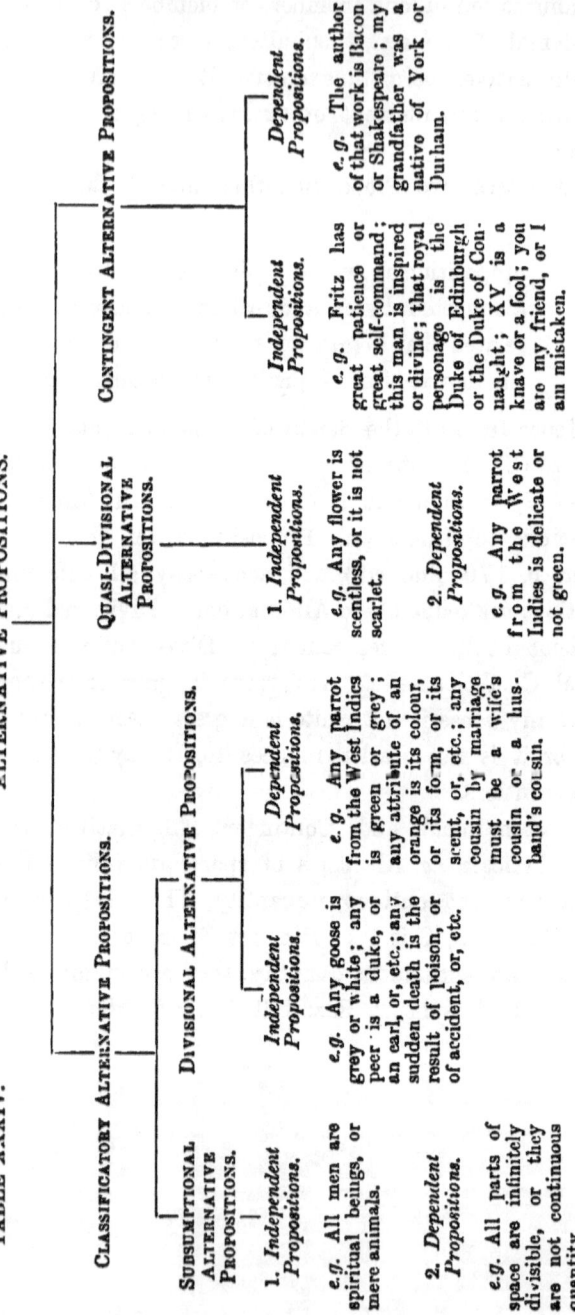

- **CLASSIFICATORY ALTERNATIVE PROPOSITIONS.**
  - **SUBSUMPTIONAL ALTERNATIVE PROPOSITIONS.**
    - **1. *Independent Propositions.***
      - *e.g.* All men are spiritual beings, or mere animals.
    - **2. *Dependent Propositions.***
      - *e.g.* All parts of space are infinitely divisible, or they are not continuous quantity.
  - **DIVISIONAL ALTERNATIVE PROPOSITIONS.**
    - ***Independent Propositions.***
      - *e.g.* Any goose is grey or white; any peer is a duke, or an earl, or, etc.; any sudden death is the result of poison, or of accident, or, etc.
    - ***Dependent Propositions.***
      - *e.g.* Any parrot from the West Indies is green or grey; any attribute of an orange is its colour, or its form, or its scent, or, etc.; any cousin by marriage must be a wife's cousin or a husband's cousin.
- **QUASI-DIVISIONAL ALTERNATIVE PROPOSITIONS.**
  - **1. *Independent Propositions.***
    - *e.g.* Any flower is scentless, or it is not scarlet.
  - **2. *Dependent Propositions.***
    - *e.g.* Any parrot from the West Indies is delicate or not green.
- **CONTINGENT ALTERNATIVE PROPOSITIONS.**
  - ***Independent Propositions.***
    - *e.g.* Fritz has great patience or great self-command; this man is inspired or divine; that royal personage is the Duke of Edinburgh or the Duke of Connaught; XY is a knave or a fool; you are my friend, or I am mistaken.
  - ***Dependent Propositions.***
    - *e.g.* The author of that work is Bacon or Shakespeare; my grandfather was a native of York or Durham.

SECTION XIV.

NOTE ON CLASSIFICATION AND DIVISION.

A convenient way of expressing a Classification or Division briefly and clearly in words is by a combination of Divisional Propositions (Inferential or Alternative) and Quantified Enumerative Propositions; *e.g.* If any triangle is not equiangular, it is isosceles or scalene (or, Any triangle is isosceles or scalene, or not equiangular); and, Equiangular triangles, isosceles triangles, and scalene triangles are all triangles. The Enumerative Propositions would hardly be sufficient taken alone, because of a possible confusion between Distributive and Collective Propositions; and Divisional Propositions, though they often are used alone to express Division or Classification, are not of themselves formally sufficient, because they are not distinguishable in form from Quasi-Divisionals.

Division and Classification are the same thing looked at from different points of view; any table presenting a Division presents also a Classification. A Division starts with unity and differentiates it; a Classification starts with multiplicity, and reduces it to unity, or at least to system. If the Classification stops short of unity, it presents not one Division, but a plurality of Divisions. A Table is generally most convenient which starts from unity, that is, which is primarily a Division. Some Tables in Whewell's *Novum Organon Renovatum* are an example of the reverse arrangement, which is that which naturally occurs in a synthetic procedure; while Division is as naturally the appropriate form in cases where the procedure is analytical.

From a Division or Classification, a Definition of any Constituent class (not, of course, the *Summum Genus*) may be framed. It is not the business of a Definition to indicate the place of the thing defined in any except a very simple Classification; to do so where the Classification is at all complex, would make the Definition intolerably cumbersome. It is desirable, I think, to distinguish (1) the collection into a group, of things which are quantitively different but qualitively similar; (2) the arrangement of such groups in their relations to one another;[1] (3) the arrangement of differing parts, which do not consist of groups of homogeneous members, in their relations to each other and to the whole which they constitute. (1) might be conveniently distinguished from (2) as *Classification* from *Classing*; (3) might be perhaps distinguished from the other two as *Systematization*. This term seems more applicable than Classification to the arrangement of the Sciences in relation to one another, or the arrangement of the parts of an organic whole, *e.g.* the human body, etc.

SECTION XV.

QUANTIFICATION AND CONVERSION.

Quantification of the Predicate in Categorical Propositions seems to me to occupy an impregnable position in Logic, a position, however, very different from that assigned to it by Sir William Hamilton, Dr. Thomson, Professor Baynes, and others. My opinion is that while the traditional form of A, E, I, O Propositions is to be retained, Quantification is an indispensable instrument of Conversion, and therefore of Reduction. The place of Quantification in Logic is very curious, its function being often as completely hidden from those whose processes of Conversion, etc., involve it, as the subterranean course of a train in one of the loop-tunnels of the Swiss Alps would be to an observer who only saw it rush into one opening, and emerge again in a few minutes from another, just above or just below. My meaning will be best elucidated by taking an ordinary proposition and tracing the

---

[1] Cf. *The Logic of Classification*, by Rev. W. L. Davidson, *Mind*, vol. xii. p. 233.

changes which it undergoes in Conversion. Let the proposition be—

All human beings are rational (1).

The ordinary converse of this is—

Some rational creatures are human beings (2),

or—

Some rational creatures are human (3).

(3) is perhaps the more perfect converse, because (1) and (3) resemble each other in having an Adjectival Term for P, while (2) has a Substantive Term for P. (1) and (3) are Adjectival Propositions, (2) a Coincidental Proposition. Adjectival Propositions cannot be converted. If I alter the relative position of S and P in (1) as it stands, and say—

Rational are all human beings,

it is clear that Conversion in the logical sense has not taken place; for *Rational* is still the Predicate, and *all human beings* is still the Subject. The proposition has been merely turned round. No Conversion of (1) while it is (1), that is, while it retains the Adjectival form, is possible. But it may be transformed to the equivalent Coincidental Proposition—

All human beings are rational creatures (4);

and with this we can deal. *It* is not, however, any more than the Adjectival (1), simply convertible. If altered into

Rational creatures are all human beings,

the proposition thus obtained, besides being awkward, is ambiguous—it is by no means clear which term is to be taken as Subject, and the *all* might even be understood to qualify (or quantify) *Rational creatures.*

The first step towards real Conversion is taken when we pass from the unquantificated Coincidental (4) to the quantificated proposition—

All human beings are some rational creatures (5);

from this we go on to the quantificated converse—

Some rational creatures are all human beings (6);

and from (6) to the unquantificated converse of (5)—

Some rational creatures are human beings (7).

From (7) we can pass to the equivalent Adjectival Proposition—

Some rational creatures are human (8).

It is to be observed that in going from (4) to (7), we have not only inserted a sign of quantity before the new Subject-name (rational creatures) which, as the old Predicate, had not any to start with; we have also dropped the sign of quantity which the new Predicate (human beings) had when it was the old Subject-name. Thus, as we began with an unquantificated proposition, so we end with an unquantificated proposition. The propositions which logicians (on the whole) have recognised and dealt with are unquantificated propositions; it is for enabling us to pass (by an elliptical procedure) *from* unquantificated *to* un-quantificated propositions that the ordinary rules of Conversion and Reduction are framed; it is of unquantificated propositions that the "nineteen valid moods" of the traditional Categorical Syllogism are composed. And it is hardly necessary to remark that in ordinary speech it is almost always unquantificated propositions that are used (that is, when we are dealing with Unrestricted Names; cf. Table III.).

In converting an E proposition, we should, I think, proceed as follows: Let the proposition to be converted be, No R is Q (1). (1) = (2) Any R is not Q (by mere equivalence). Quantificating (2) we get, Any R is not any Q (3). (3) Converts to, Any Q is not any R (4). By disquantificating (4) we reach (5), Any Q is not R. And (5) = No Q is R (by equivalence).

The usage of Logic and of ordinary speech can be justified,[1]

---

[1] It is this usage of both Logic and ordinary speech, I think, which explains the common failure to distinguish between terms and term-names. Taking, *e.g.*, the proposition *All R's are Q's* (1), our terms, so far as expressed, are—(a) All

and also the validity and necessity (in a subordinate office) of Quantification can be shown, I think, by reference to the Import of Categorical Propositions. What a significant Categorical Proposition affirms or denies is, it seems, *identity of denomination* of the S and the P in *diversity of determination.* Denomination (and application) of S and of P in an affirmative Categorical Proposition are the same; determination of the S and P being, of course, always diverse, unless we admit propositions of the form *A is A*, and being in any case diverse in all propositions of the form *A is B.* And denomination is sufficiently indicated by the S; *identity* or *non-identity* is indicated by the copula; while *diversity of determination* comes into view only when the Predicate is enunciated. In regard to any assertion, we want to know in the first place *what it is* of which something is affirmed or denied; this knowledge is given with the enunciation of the Subject, which indicates the thing or things spoken of. We want, in the second place, to know *what it is that is affirmed or denied of the thing or things* indicated by the Subject. This information is supplied by the Predicate—that is, by its determination—since it is evident that in affirmative propositions the denomination of the Predicate is identical with, in negative propositions is altogether distinct from, that of the Subject. Hence it seems clear that in the *Predicate* of any proposition, it is naturally and inevitably *determination* and not *denomination* which is prominent.[1] This is confirmed by the

R's, (*b*) Q's. Converting (1) we get (2), Some Q's are R's, and here our expressed terms are (*a*) Some Q's, (*b*) R's—hence All R's and R's, Some Q's and Q's, are indiscriminately called *terms*. And a further point which throws light upon this, and also upon the appropriateness of the Canon and Rules of Categorical Syllogism to *classes* rather than to *terms*, is that we have a practical interest in the relations of classes (which are indicated by term-names), and we are continually comparing propositions which have the same *term-names* but not the same *terms*.

[1] This interpretation seems to me to be very forcibly illustrated by Mill in chap. xxii. of his *Examination of Hamilton*. *E.g.* "when, for example, I say, The sky is blue, my meaning, and my whole meaning, is that *the sky* has *that particular colour*. I am not thinking of the class blue, as regards extension, at all. I am not caring, nor necessarily knowing, what blue things there are, or if there is any blue thing except the sky. I am thinking only of the *sensation of blue*, and am judging that *the sky* produces this sensation in my sensitive

consideration that we commonly use Adjectival rather than Coincidental Propositions, if appropriate Adjectival Terms are available; and that such terms in English cannot take the sign of the plural (cf. *ante*, p. 13), though the Substantive Terms which they qualify can, and though no one doubts that the denomination of an Adjectival Term *is* the same as that of the Substantive Term which it qualifies. It is also to be remembered that an Adjectival Term cannot be Subject in a proposition. Now if it is the primary function of the S in any Categorical Proposition to indicate denomination, while it is the primary function of the P to indicate determination,[1] it seems obvious that quantification is appropriate, and may be necessary in the case of S, but not in the case of P, under ordinary circumstances. And a further reason against admitting Quantification of the Predicate (except as a transformation-stage) in most propositions, is deducible from the consideration that what propositions assert or wholly deny is the identity of denomination (in diversity of determination) of S and P; for in a quantificated affirmative, though indeed denominational identity of the terms is still *asserted* (as it is bound to be), the fact that the denomination of *both* terms is made prominent tends to obscure this—especially where *difference* of denomina-

---

faculty; or (to express the meaning in technical language), that *the quality answering to the sensation of blue*, or *the power of exciting the sensation of blue*, is *an attribute* of *the sky*. When again I say, All oxen ruminate, I have *nothing to do with the predicate, considered in extension*. . . . The *Comprehension of the predicate*—the *attribute* or *set of attributes signified by it*—are all that I have in my mind; and the relation of *this attribute or these attributes* to *the subject* is the entire matter of the judgment" (pp. 497, 498, 4th ed.).

" . . . When we say, Philip is a man, or a herring is a fish, do the words man and fish signify anything to us but the *bundles of attributes connoted* by them ? Do the propositions mean anything except that *Philip* has the *human attributes*, and *a herring* the *piscine ones?* Assuredly not. Any notion of a multitude of other men, among whom Philip is ranked, or a variety of fishes besides herrings, is foreign to the proposition" (p. 498).

Cf. also Dr. Venn (*Empirical Logic*, p. 219): "I have little doubt that, speaking generally, *the subject* is by comparison contemplated as a class, *i.e. in its extension*, and *the predicate* as *an attribute*, *i.e. in its intension*." (The italics in both quotations are mine.) Cf. also Keynes, *Formal Logic*, p. 92.

[1] If *both* terms are taken in denomination, S is P=S is S, since S and P have *identical* denomination, and hence apply to the very same objects. If *both* terms are taken in determination, again all propositions must be of the form S is S, since of any determination *S*, we cannot affirm a different determination *P*.

tion of the *classes* referred to is suggested. And, moreover, quantificated affirmatives are all collective. It might indeed be asserted that where *both* terms of our propositions are taken in denomination, quantificated propositions are most appropriate, and are the form of proposition which makes the denomination of both S and P most prominent. But I should maintain that both Terms *cannot* be taken *purely* in denomination. If, *e.g.*, in *S is P*, both S and P are taken in denomination only, then to say *S is P* is exactly equivalent to saying *S is S*, for the denomination of P is the very same as that of S. But *S is S* is not entitled to be called a significant assertion (cf. *ante*, p. 52, also *note* 1, p. 128). On the other hand, the view here advocated of the Import of Categorical Propositions justifies the recognition of Quantification as a phase of propositions. For the Predicates of propositions *have* denomination as well as the Subjects,[1] and (in affirmative propositions) a denomination which is identical with that of the Subjects. It is therefore (in a Coincidental proposition) possible, and under certain conditions allowable and necessary, to make this prominent by quantification. And the Subjects of propositions *have* determination; and this may be allowed to come into prominence by dropping the sign of quantity (Term-Indicator) which inevitably fixes attention rather upon the denominational than the determinational aspect of a term.

The above view of Quantification is, I think, confirmed and illustrated by a consideration of the traditional logical treatment of O propositions. Of the four categorical propositions, A—E—I—O, the first three have always been regarded as capable, the fourth as incapable, of Conversion.

We have seen that propositions on their way to Conversion have to undergo the process of Quantification. But the reason why O is pronounced inconvertible is not because there is any more difficulty in quantificating it than in quantificating the other propositions, but because, *when the quantificated*

---

[1] Cf. that in many languages (Greek, Latin, French, Italian, etc.) adjectives that qualify a plural term *always take the sign of the plural*.

converse of O has been reached, the quantification of its predicate cannot be dropped without an illegitimate alteration of signification. For the commonly accepted signification of the dis-quantificated converse of O *involves* a quantification *different from that which has been dropped* — the *dropped* P-indicator being *some*, the P-indicator understood as involved in the unquantificated proposition reached by dropping it being *any*. And as, at the same time, ordinary thought and speech will not admit the *explicitly* quantificated form, it is inevitable that a Logic which deals with the forms of ordinary thought and speech should regard O as inconvertible. To take an instance—The proposition, Some blackbirds are not black birds (1), becomes by quantification (2) Some blackbirds are not any black birds. This converts to (3) Any black birds are not some blackbirds. Dropping the quantification of (3) we get (4) Any black birds are not blackbirds, and this would be understood to mean (5) Any black birds are not any blackbirds (= No black birds are blackbirds).

SECTION XVI.

THE MEANING OF *SOME*.

If Quantification of ordinary propositions is recognised as being admissible and necessary in processes of Conversion, but to be discarded as soon as the process has been gone through, it seems desirable to inquire a little more particularly into the force and meaning of propositions while in the quantified stage. This depends principally upon the signification given to *Some*. *Some*, it is said, may mean—(1) "Some but not all;" (2) "Some at least, it may be all" (cf. *c.g.* Jevons, *Elementary Lessons in Logic*, 7th ed. p. 67). But when the above are offered as interpretations or explanations of Some, the question obviously arises, What exactly does the Some in Some at least, Some at most, mean? Must not the meaning which it has *as constituent of these expressions* be its real minimum of meaning?

Again, *Some* has been defined to mean *not none* (cf. *e.g.* Bain, *Logic*, i. p. 81, 2nd ed.; Venn, *Empirical Logic*, p. 223). This definition is more satisfactory than (1) or (2), since it is wide enough to cover the meaning intended by each (while (1) excludes (2), and is evidently not applicable in all cases), and also it does not present a direct and explicit *circulus in definiendo*. But I am afraid it is still open to the reproach of being circular; for how is *none* to be defined except as *not some*? And if *Some* means merely *not none*, and *none* means merely *not some*, what do we know about either except that it is the negative of the other? *Some is not-none* contraposits (contraverts) to *None is not-some*, and if we have nothing else to say about the meaning of None and Some, we are simply revolving in a circle which is closed against all connection with other meanings.

If we ask, What is intended by, *e.g.*, *Some R*, in common speech, it must be admitted (and is recognised by logicians) that the almost invariable intention of the speaker, in any particular case, is to indicate some modification of R quantitively different from All R (this must be the case, for instance, whenever it is got by Sub-alternation—Subversion—from *All R*); or some modification of R qualitively diverse from mere R. Therefore it may be said that what is intended is *part (not all) of R, or certain (somehow distinguished) R*. If *All R* were intended, then in order that the *intended* meaning might be unequivocally conveyed, *All R* would be used. Similarly, if R unmodified were intended, R unmodified would be used.

But it must be admitted that *Some R* may *happen* to have the same extension (application) as All R; *e.g.* I may *say*, *Some* scarlet flowers are scentless; and it may *be true*, though I did not know it, that *All* scarlet flowers are scentless.

Or I may say, *Some* (= certain somehow distinguished) cloven-hoofed animals are ruminants; and it may turn out that I might with equal truth (whether or not I was aware of it) have asserted simply that Cloven-hoofed animals are ruminants.

The recognition of such cases as these, and of other cases where one is fully conscious that one's knowledge is indeterminate, makes it clear that any definition of *Some* which restricts it to (1) Less-than-all, or (2) Certain-somehow-dis-distinguished (and (1) and (2) involve each other), cannot be valid.

I should propose to define *Some R* as meaning *An indefinite quantity or number of R*. Such a definition, it is clear, involves no implication either (*a*) of there being or not being *other* R, or (*b*) of what may be asserted concerning those other R, if there are any. And the definition will be found to give all the meaning that is common to Some in all cases, and that justifies its use—that is, it gives the whole determination of the word.

This account of the meaning of Some makes the question (which is sometimes asked), Does *Some* mean One at least, or Two at least? appear irrelevant.

If Some means merely an indefinite quantity, Quantification by Some makes our *terms* explicitly indeterminate; for it excludes (1) explicit universality, and (2) definite limitation. And it affords no definite determination of the *relations of the classes involved*.

The reason why it can be used where All cannot (as in the Conversion per Accidens (Intraversion) of an A proposition), is that it does not explicitly claim Universality.

The results of quantifying with *Some* when *Some* means *not-all, and what is asserted of part is denied of the rest*, are fully discussed in Mr. Keynes' *Formal Logic*, Part iii. ch. ix. 2nd ed.

The function of Quantification on the whole seems to be simply to *bring into prominence the quantitive aspect* of the Predicate.

PART II.

RELATIONS OF PROPOSITIONS.

SECTION XVII.

GENERAL REMARKS ON THE RELATIONS OF PROPOSITIONS.

UNDER the head *Relations of Propositions*, we may consider—
I. Relations of two Propositions to each other; II. Relations of two Propositions taken together to a third.

I. subdivides into Relations between

(i.) Incompatible
(ii.) Compatible $\begin{cases} (1) \text{ Unattached} \\ (2) \text{ Attached} \end{cases} \begin{cases} (a) \text{ Correlative} \\ (b) \text{ Premissal} \end{cases}$ Propositions.

(i.) are propositions which are inconsistent, *i.e.* cannot both be true.

E.g. $\begin{cases} \text{S is P} \\ \text{S is not P} \end{cases}$ $\begin{cases} \text{All Q is R} \\ \text{Some Q is not R} \end{cases}$ $\begin{cases} \text{All Q is R} \\ \text{No Q is R} \end{cases}$
$\begin{cases} \text{A is B or C} \\ \text{A is neither B nor C.} \end{cases}$

The Propositions under this head may be distinguished into

(*a*) Those which can $\Big\}$ both be false.
(*b*) Those which cannot

E.g. (*a*) $\begin{cases} \text{All men are trustworthy} \\ \text{No men are trustworthy.} \end{cases}$

(*b*) $\begin{cases} \text{No scarlet flowers are fragrant} \\ \text{Some scarlet flowers are fragrant} \end{cases}$ $\begin{cases} \text{S is P} \\ \text{S is not P} \end{cases}$

In categoricals, this distinction depends upon the distinction between Term and Term-name—any Proposition expressed as *S is P* has only one negative, namely, *S is not P*. Any one of a pair of Incompatibles and *the negative of the other* are either Correlative or Identical.

(ii.) (1) are propositions which are consistent with each other, but neither of them is inferrible from the other, and the two, when taken together, do not constitute the premisses of an argument.

$$\left.\begin{matrix} S \text{ is } P \\ Q \text{ is } R \end{matrix}\right\} \qquad \left.\begin{matrix} \text{Some } Q \text{ is } R \\ \text{Some } Q \text{ is not } R \end{matrix}\right\} \qquad \left.\begin{matrix} \text{Some } N \text{ is } R \\ \text{Some } N \text{ is } Q \end{matrix}\right\}$$

A relation of consistency between one proposition and another is reciprocal. A relation of independence need not be so—*e.g.* Some Q is R (1) may be independent of All Q is R (2)—*i.e.* in the case where (1) is not got by Sub-alternation from (2); for (2) is not inferrible from (1), and (1) may be true while (2) is false. But (2) can never be independent of (1), for it cannot be true unless (1) is true, and (1) is always inferrible from it. No doubt any proposition of the form Some R is Q might be expressed as an Universal—*e.g.* All *XQ* is R,—but the relation of All XQ is R to (2) is the same as that of (1) to (2).[1] The relation between Unattached Propositions is altogether undetermined. They must of course be, really, Incompatible or Attached, but the relation is not apparent.

(ii.) (2) subdivides into (*a*) Correlative Propositions (propositions related as inference and inferend), *e.g.*,

$$\left.\begin{matrix} \text{All } Q \text{ is } R \\ \text{[Therefore] Some } Q \text{ is } R \end{matrix}\right\} \qquad \left.\begin{matrix} \text{No } Q \text{ is } R \\ \text{[Therefore] No } R \text{ is } Q \end{matrix}\right\}$$

$$\left.\begin{matrix} \text{If } E \text{ is } F, K \text{ is } H \\ \text{[Therefore] If } K \text{ is not } H, E \text{ is not } F. \end{matrix}\right\}$$

---

[1] It may be remarked also that any Universal Proposition, *All R is Q* (1) may be expressed as a Particular (if the R is definable, that is, is not a Genus Generalissimum). For R is resolvable into [the determination of] Genus + Difference—*e.g.* into X and Y ; and when thus resolved, (1) may be expressed as
Some X (*i.e.* the X that is Y) is Q.
Where we take a strictly formal view, and consider the *terms* of propositions and not the *term-names*, the logical difference between (1) Universal or General, and (2) Particular Categoricals, disappears.

GENERAL REMARKS ON THE RELATIONS OF PROPOSITIONS. 135

Under this head come the relations betweeen all pairs of propositions of which either one is immediately inferrible (educible) from the other.

(*b*) Premissal Propositions are two propositions having some element in common, and from which, taken together, a third proposition may be inferred. These are interesting and important only when we come to II., but they are mentioned here for the sake of formal completeness. Examples of (*b*) are—

    All M is P ⎱   If E is F, K is H ⎱
    All S is M ⎰   If K is H, L is M. ⎰

II. Here we consider the relation of any two Premissal Propositions to a third proposition. This relation may be one of

    (i.) Inferribility
    (ii.) Non-Inferribility;

(i.) gives us valid syllogisms (or what, by some Immediate Inference, may be reduced to valid syllogisms). (ii.) gives us invalid syllogisms. Examples are—

    (i.) M is P   (ii.) All M is P
         S is M   Some R is M
         ――――   ――――
         S is P.   All R is P.

         If E is F, K is H   All M is P
         E is F   No S is M
         ――――   ―――
         K is H.   All S is P.

         A is B or C
         A is not B
         ――――
         A is C.

Under this head we are principally concerned with (i.), and it is of (i.) only that I have given examples in the Table of Inferences. But we may, of course, consider the relation (of Compatibility, etc.) between any two (or more) propositions, and another which is not an inference from them.

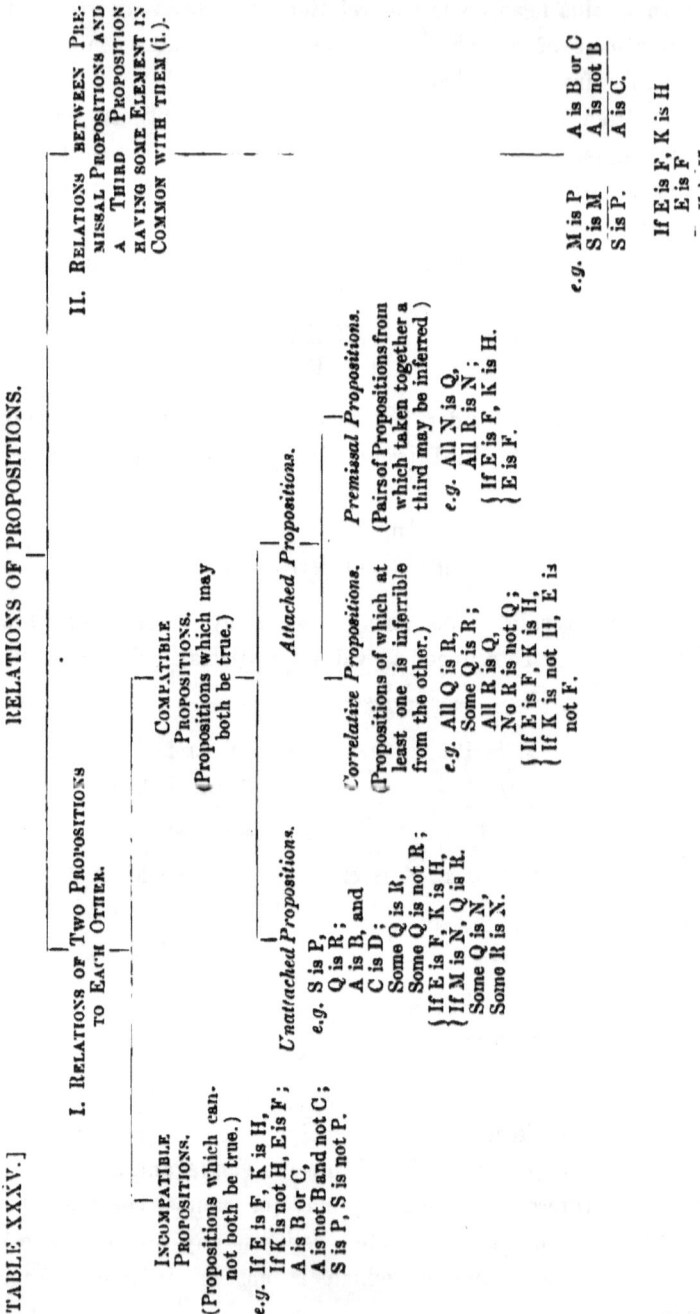

SECTION XVIII.

INFERENCE.

Before going on to consider briefly Categorical, Inferential and Alternative Syllogisms, I desire to offer a few remarks on what are commonly called Induction and Deduction, and Immediate and Mediate Inference.

An Induction, unless it is formal, does not seem to be logical at all. There is, of course, a broad and important difference between (1) arguing from two universal statements, or applying an universal to a particular case; and (2) arguing from *one* universal in conjunction with some fact or facts, and reaching therefrom a fresh universal. But if a deductive inference means simply an argument (or Mediate Inference), the conclusion of which is justified by the premisses, (2) is a deductive inference as much as (1); and the conclusion of (2) is as much " contained " in the premisses as (1) is.[1] If we pass from

	These X's are Y's	(a)
to	All X's are Y's	(b)
or to	Those X's are Y's.	(c)

there is nothing cogent in the process—it is wholly unlogical. (b) or (c) cannot follow from, or be justified by, or contained in, (a) taken alone. If we take any case of the application of one of Mill's " Four Methods of Experimental Inquiry " (*Inductive Methods*),[2] and set out at length the reasoning

---

[1] On the other hand, if *deductive* is taken in a narrower sense and restricted to (1), we cannot describe an "inductive" Inference as *deductive*. It seems convenient to use *deductive* in the narrower sense, as contrasted with *inductive* and *traductive*, using *Syllogism* instead of Deduction in the wider sense.

The employment of the name *Eduction* instead of Immediate Inference would make the terminology here more symmetrical and convenient, I think.

[2] Mill's "Methods" seem to be methods for determining in what cases we are justified in assuming *connection* (not mere *conjunction*) between phenomena.

involved, what we get is a plurality of Syllogisms.[1] No doubt we often do think that All X's are Y's, *because* we have met with *some X's* that are Y's; but our thought here is not logical thought, and the premiss merely suggests, it does not really justify, the conclusion. It can only justify it in so far as this, that the actual occurrence, in some cases, of X's that are Y's proves that the attributes connoted by X and Y respectively are not incompatible; so that the experience of some X's that are Y's is ground for asserting that *possibly all* X's *may be* Y's (as long, that is, as we have no experience of X's that are not Y's).

If we could conclude directly from (1) *Some X's are Y's* to (2) *All X's are Y's*, or (3) *Some other X's are Y's*, (2) and (3) must be called Immediate Inferences from (1) (according to the usual definition of an Immediate Inference). But we never find that Inductions are treated under the head of Immediate Inferences; if they were, it would be apparent at once that such "Immediate Inferences" are not illative. The qualification *immediate* indicates, of course, that we know directly or intuitively, that, *e.g.*, if *S is P*, then *P is S*. But do we not know just as intuitively or directly that if *M is P and S is M*, then *S is P?* And is not any argument, however long and complex, reducible to just a *series* of intuitions?

---

[1] *E.g.* an "Induction" by the Method of Difference might be obtained thus:—

(i.) (Anything, the introduction of which has on one occasion been followed by Y), is (on one occasion the cause of Y).
(X) is (a thing, the introduction of which, etc.)
(X) is (on one occasion the cause of Y).
(Deductive Syllogism.)

(ii.) (Anything that has on one occasion been cause of Y) is (always cause of Y).
(X) is (a thing that has on one occasion, etc.)
(X) is (always cause of Y). (= All X is cause of Y.)
(Inductive Syllogism.)

For the answer which I should suggest to the question, What justification can be given for the assertion of such a proposition as the Major Premiss of (ii.)? cf. *post*, Section on the Ground of Induction. I call (ii.) an *Inductive* Syllogism on account of the *content* of its Major Premiss, which makes it possible to pass, with the help of a single instance, to a new law or generalization.

And when we have fully grasped all the connections, and have the whole argument before the mind at once, must it not be regarded as really only one highly complex intuition? It one takes the proof of some theorem in Euclid, *e.g.* the 47th Proposition of the 1st Book, and goes through it step by step, one sees (or may see) the connection between every two contiguous steps before grasping the whole reasoning, and therefore one cannot avoid believing, even at this stage, that the Q.E.D. follows from the data. Here one has, strictly speaking, just a series of intuitions. But when the proposition has been so grasped that the whole reasoning is before the mind simultaneously, then I think that it must be said that one has not a series of intuitions, but just one complex intuition, and one *sees* that the final conclusion follows from the data. It seems to me, therefore, that an "Inductive" Inference must be allowed to be formal, as well as the Inferences commonly distinguished as "Deductive" (cf. Table XXXVI.), and that a "Mediate" Inference only differs from an Immediate Inference in being more complex.

I would suggest the following definitions—I. of Inference in general; II. Of Immediate Inference; III. Of Mediate Inference:—

> I. One proposition is an inference from another, or others, when the assertion of the former is justified by the latter, and the latter is, in some respect, different from the former.
>
> II. An Immediate Inference is a proposition inferred from *one* other proposition (the Inferend).
>
> III. A Mediate Inference is a proposition (the Conclusion) inferred from *two* other propositions (the Premisses).

I should like to define *Equivalent* as follows:—

> Any two Categorematic words (or phrases) are equivalent when they have identical denomination and diverse determination; and any two Syncategore-

matic words are equivalent when they have the same meaning;[1]

and to suggest the following as Canons of

(1) { Conversion.
      Conversion per Accidens (Intraversion).

(2) Obversion.

(3) { Complex Conception }
      { Added Determinants } (Extraversion).

(4) Substitution generally. (This seems to me to include a brief Canon of Syllogism, and might perhaps be offered as an amended form of Jevons' "Substitution of Similars.")

Taking any two equivalent terms, of either one the other (1) may be affirmed, and (2) its negative denied: and taking any two terms which are non-coincident, of either one the other (1) may be denied, and (2) its negative affirmed—provided, in each case, that the change does not result in tautology.

(3) If any qualification or determination is attached to a name, *the same* qualification or determination may be attached to its equivalent; and

(4) Any equivalent of a word can be substituted for it, provided the substitution does not produce tautology.

The *Dictum de omni et nullo* supplies a Canon of Subalternation (Subversion).

As regards terminology, I think the following restrictions and additions would be convenient:—

(1) Inference (in narrow sense) = proposition inferred to (cf. above).

(2) Inferend = proposition or propositions inferred from.

---

[1] *E.g. also, likewise* are equivalent Syncategorematic words. Any two differing *propositions* are equivalent which are reciprocally inferrible.

(3) Inference (in wider sense) = (1) and (2) taken together.
(4) To infer = to pass from (2) to (1), (2) being the justification for (1), and (1) and (2) being in some respect different from one another.
(5) Educt = An inference (1) from *one* proposition.
(6) Educend = The one proposition inferred from.
(7) Eduction = (5) together with (6).
(8) Educe = to pass from (6) to (5).
(9) Conclusion = An inference (1) from *two* (or more) propositions taken together.
(10) Premisses = The two (or more) propositions from which a conclusion is drawn.

142 RELATIONS OF PROPOSITIONS.

TABLE XXXVI.]

INFERENCES.

- **FROM ONE PROPOSITION TO ANOTHER = *Immediate Inferences* (*Eductions*).** Cf. Table XXXVII.

- **FROM TWO PROPOSITIONS TO A THIRD = *Mediate Inferences* (*Syllogisms*).**
  - CATEGORICAL SYLLOGISMS.
    - *Traductive Syllogisms.*
      - e.g. Snowdon is the highest mountain in Wales.
      - Snowdon has the most extensive views of any hill in Wales.
      - The highest mountain in Wales has the most extensive views.

      - These men are statesmen.
      - These men are authors.
      - Some statesmen are authors.
      - (Cf. *ante*, p. 60.)
    - *Deductive Syllogisms.*
      - *Limited Syllogisms* (having a General Proposition for major premiss), commonly called "Perfect Induction," etc.
        - e.g. Sunday, Monday, etc., are all the days of the week.
        - All the days of the week are seven periods, which are each 24 hours long.
        - ∴ Sunday, Monday, etc., are seven periods, which are each 24 hours long.
      - *Unlimited Syllogisms* (Deductive Categorical Syllogisms, having an Universal Proposition for major premiss).
        - e.g. All matter gravitates.
        - Comets are matter.
        - Comets gravitate.
  - INFERENTIAL SYLLOGISMS. Cf. Table XXXVIII.
    - *Inductive Syllogisms.*
      - e.g. What has been once the cause of Y will be always the cause of Y.
      - X has been once the cause of Y.
      - X will be always the cause of Y.

      - What has been once *coherent* (not merely conjoined) with Y will be always coherent with Y.
      - X has been once coherent with Y.
      - X will be always coherent with Y.
  - ALTERNATIVE SYLLOGISMS. Cf. Tables XXXIX., XL.

SECTION XIX.

IMMEDIATE INFERENCES (EDUCTIONS).

WHEN we pass from one proposition to another, and the latter is justified by the former, and differs from it in some respect, the latter is an Immediate Inference (Eduction) from the former.

Eductions may have—I. Categoricals (*a*), or Inferentials (*b*), or Alternatives (*c*) for both educt and educend; these may be called *Pure Eductions or Eversions*. Or II. they may have a Categorical with an Inferential (*a*), or a Categorical with an Alternative (*b*), or an Inferential with an Alternative (*c*). These may be called *Mixed Eductions*, or *Transversions*.

Five principal subdivisions of Categorical Eversions are recognised, to which the names Subalternation, Obversion, Simple Conversion, Conversion per Accidens (the two latter being frequently included under the one name of Conversion or Ordinary Conversion), and Contraposition have been given. It would be convenient, I think, to make the terminology here more uniform, using *Subversion* for Subalternation, *Reversion* for Simple Conversion, *Intraversion* for Conversion per Accidens, and *Contraversion* for Contraposition. This terminology, besides its uniformity, would have the further advantage of allowing of convenient distinctive terms (framed on the model of the current *Converse* and *Convertend*) for the educt and educend in each of these particular cases. Perhaps to these five Eductions there may be added the Inverse and the Obverted Converse, both of which have been recognised by some recent writers. The latter seems to stand on precisely the same footing as the Converted Obverse, to which, however, a distinctive name has been already appropriated. For the sake of symmetry and convenience I would propose to assign one to the Obverted Converse also, and to call it the *Retroverse*.

Two other kinds of Eversion are mentioned by some

logicians, called respectively Inference by Added Determinants and Inference by Complex Conception[1] (they might, I think, be conveniently classed together as *Extraversions*). However, where significant terms are used, the force of words becomes so variously and subtilely altered by combination with others, that in inferences of this kind (constant and indispensable as they are) there is a liability to Fallacies of Accident which can only be guarded against by reference to the *special* circumstances of each case.

In Subversion we pass from a Complete or Total Proposition to a Partial Proposition, having the same Subject-name, the same Predicate, and the same Quality. *E.g.*, from

>Every wind is ill to a broken ship

to

>Some winds are ill to a broken ship.

In Obversion, the passage is from an affirmative (or negative) proposition (1) Total, or (2) Partial, to a negative (or affirmative), (1) Total, or (2) Partial. The obverse has the same Subject-name and the same Quantity as the obvertend, but different Quality; and the Predicate-name of the obverse is the negative of the Predicate-name of the obvertend. *E.g.*,

>All is fine that is fit

obverts to

>Nothing is not fine that is fit.

The principle of obverting is, that the affirmation (or denial) of any Predicate justifies the denial (or affirmation) of its negative (cf. Law of Contradiction, *note*, p. 177). Every categorical proposition can be obverted.

In a Reversion, the educt has the P-name of the educend for its S-name, and the S-name of the educend for its P-name. Reverse and revertend do not differ in Quantity or Quality. Of the four propositions, A, E, I, O, it is only E and I that can be reverted; for if A and O propositions are treated in this way, the propositions which result are not justified by

[1] Cf. *ante*, Section XVIII. p. 140.

those from which we started. All affirmative Partial Propositions can be reverted (cf. Tables XXVII.–XXXI.).

To take two simple examples—
>Those plants are biennials

reverts to
>Some biennials are those plants.

No man is a free agent who cannot command himself
reverts to
>No free agent is a man who cannot command himself.

In what I have called Intraversion, we infer from an Affirmative Proposition which is Complete or Total to a Partial Proposition of the same Quality, and having the P-name of the educend for its S-name, and the S-name of the educend for its P-name. *E.g.*,
>An honest miller has a black thumb

intraverts to
>Some persons having a black thumb are honest millers.

In Contraversion the educt differs from the educend in the following respects:—

(1) The Subject-name of the educt is the negative of the Predicate-name of the educend.

(2) The Predicate-name of the educt is the Subject-name of the educend.

(3) Educt and educend differ in Quality.

(4) Every Contraverse but that of E has the same Quantity as the Contravertend; the contraverse of E has different Quantity. *E.g.*,
>IF is stiff

contraverts to
>Not-stiff is-not IF.

There is no contraverse of I, because its obverse is O, which cannot be converted; and to reach the contraverse of any proposition, it has to be obverted, and then the obverse thus obtained has to be converted.[1] Hence every proposition of which the obverse can be converted is capable of being contraverted.

---

[1] Cf. Keynes, *Formal Logic*, 2nd ed. p. 100.

In Retroversion (which applies to all Categorical Propositions except O) the educt differs from the educend in Quality, the Predicate-name of the educend is the Subject-name of the educt, and the negative of the Subject-name of the educend is the Predicate-name of the educt. In the case of A, educt and educend differ in Quantity; in other cases the Quantity is the same.

To take examples—

    All who love me keep my commandments

retroverts to

    Some who keep my commandments are not those who do not love me.

    Some true doctrines are universally accepted

retroverts to

    Some things universally accepted are not doctrines which are not true.

Some believers in Spiritualism are these well-known writers

retroverts to

    These well-known writers are not disbelievers in Spiritualism.

    These R's are Q's

retroverts to

    Some Q's are-not not-these R's.

In an Inversion "we obtain from a given proposition a new proposition having the contradictory of the original subject [name] for its subject [name], and the original predicate for its predicate" (Keynes, *Formal Logic*, 2nd ed. p. 107).[1]

Also the Inverse of any proposition differs from the invertend in both Quantity and Quality. A and E are the only propositions which can be inverted.

---

[1] The whole subject of Categorical Immediate Inferences has been admirably worked out and systematized by Mr. Keynes in Part ii. of the second edition of his *Formal Logic*.

The following are examples:—
>No sunshine is without shadow

inverts to
>Some things that are not sunshine are without shadow.

>A friend in need is a friend indeed

inverts to
>Some who are not friends in need are not friends indeed.

Only Coincidental propositions can be converted, contraverted, retroverted, or inverted. Only A Propositions can be intraverted. Adjectivals as well as Coincidentals may be subverted, obverted, and extraverted.

With Inferentials there seems to be only one kind of Eversion, which corresponds pretty nearly to Contraversion. *E.g.* from any Hypothetical—
>If A, then C,

another Hypothetical—
>If not C, then not A,

may be educed. The reason why this is the only kind of Eduction in which the Inferential form is retained is that from its very form an Inferential must be affirmative and Whole (cf. Table XXXVIII.).

Apparently the only Alternative Eversion is the unimportant one (which may perhaps be called a Converse) in which from *A or B* we pass to *B or A*.

It is, in my opinion, only Complex Categoricals (cf. Jevons, *Elementary Lessons in Logic*, 7th ed., p. 91) which are Universals or Generals, that are formally reducible to an Inferential or an Alternative (cf. *ante*, Section XII.). A Categorical of the form—
>Any D that is not E is F (1)

is reducible to the Conditional—
>If any D is not E, that D is F (2),

and to the Alternative—
>Any D is F or E.

(This latter proposition is reducible indifferently to (1) or its contraverse, and to (2) or its contraverse.)

Again (2) is equivalent to—

If all D's are not E, all D's are F.

This proposition is Hypothetical (cf. the distinction between Hypotheticals and Conditionals referred to above, Section XII.), and it is reducible to Conditional and to Categorical form if we know that the Subject of A and C is to be taken distributively. Of an Inferential which is in the form—

If D is E, F is G,

or—

If A, then C,

it is impossible to say, on inspection, whether it is Hypothetical or Conditional. If we know that it is Hypothetical, then, without still further information, we cannot say whether or not it is equivalent to a Conditional of the form—

If *any* K is E, *that* K is G,

just as it is impossible to say, from mere inspection, whether a Categorical expressed as

All R is Q

is an Adjectival or a Coincidental Proposition.

Table XXXVII. contains illustrations in symbols of all the above-mentioned kinds of Eversions.

In Transversion, the most interesting points are that all Inferentials and Alternatives may (as I think) be fully and accurately expressed in Categorical form; that Conditionals and Categoricals, of which S and P in the one correspond to A and C in the other, are reciprocally educible; that Inferentials are educible from Alternatives and Alternatives from Inferentials, and thus the Alternative answering to any Inferential has a corresponding Categorical, educible from the Categorical which answers to the Inferential.

For instance, the Conditional

> If any flower is a Datura, that flower is fragrant (1)

is equivalent to the Categorical

> (2) Any flower that is a Datura is fragrant (is a flower that is fragrant);

(1) is also equivalent to the Categorical

> That any flower is fragrant is an inference from its being a Datura (3);

but (2) is the most natural and characteristic Categorical equivalent of (1).

The Hypothetical

> If Honesty is not the best policy, life is not worth living,

may be expressed as—

> *Life is not worth living* is an inference from *Honesty is not the best policy* (4).

The meaning of (4) is expressed in the Alternative,

> Life is not worth living or Honesty is the best policy;

and this has its meaning conveyed by the Categorical

> *Life is not worth living* is alternative with *Honesty is the best policy* (5).

We feel the Categorical expression here (as the Inferential form in (3)) to be somewhat awkward and inappropriate; but this being admitted, it appears to me to be adequate. And (5) is equivalent to (4), not formally, but in virtue of a knowledge of what is involved in the relations of inference and alternation between propositions, (4) and (5) being Systemic or Dependent Propositions. (Cf. *ante*, Section IX.)

[TABLE.

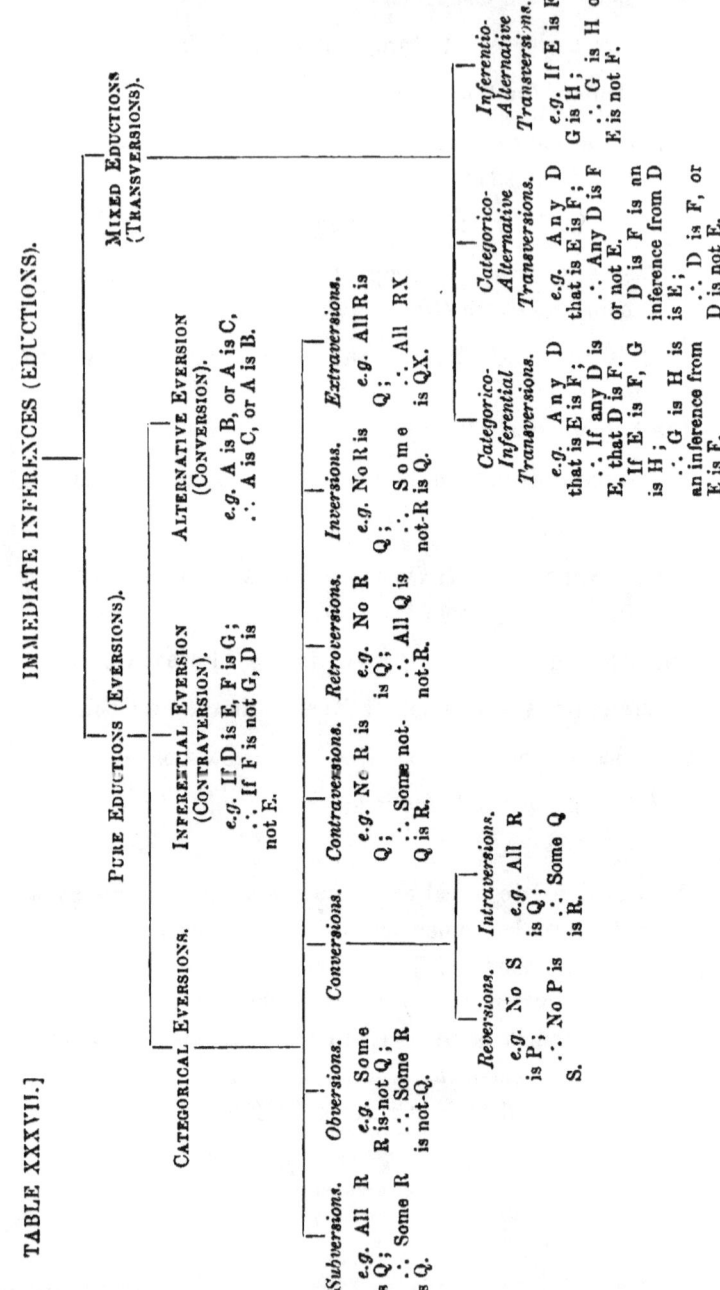

SECTION XX.

INCOMPATIBLE PROPOSITIONS.

Propositions are Incompatible when they cannot both be true; and while of Propositions related as educt and educend, the first is true if the second is true, of propositions related as Incompatibles, either is false if the other is true.

Propositions are generally said to be *contrarily* opposed when they cannot both be true but may both be false—*e.g.* All R is Q, No R is Q; *contradictorily* opposed when they cannot both be true and cannot both be false—*e.g.* All R is Q, Some R is not Q. With simple Categoricals, it is only where we are concerned with class-names that Propositions can be contrarily opposed. All R is Q and No R is Q are, I think, the only contraries ordinarily recognised. We may indeed have opposition between such propositions as

$$\begin{cases} \text{These R's are Q (1)} \\ \text{Some of these R's are not Q (3).} \end{cases}$$

$$\begin{cases} \text{These R's are not Q (2)} \\ \text{One of these R's is Q (4);} \end{cases}$$

but the relation between (1) and (2), (1) and (3), (2) and (4) respectively, exactly corresponds to that between A and E, A and O, E and I. For *These R's* as contrasted with *Some of these R's* is equivalent to *All these R's*.

In all other cases, each Categorical that is not compound (cf. Jevons, *Elementary Lessons in Logic*, p. 90) has but one formal categorical Incompatible, and that one is its Contradictory.

E.g.
$$\begin{cases} \text{S is P} \\ \text{S is not P.} \end{cases}$$

$$\begin{cases} \text{Charles I. was a saint} \\ \text{Charles I. was not a saint.} \end{cases}$$

$$\begin{cases} \text{His set are to be trusted} \\ \text{His set are not to be trusted.} \end{cases}$$

{ X's children are my cousins.
{ X's children are not my cousins.

In such a proposition as

Billy and Colin are at school,

we have what Jevons calls a Compound proposition, which is really an abbreviated expression of a plurality of single propositions. And here, as in the case of A and E, we may have two Categorical Incompatibles—but here both of them are contrary—*e.g.*

Neither Billy nor Colin is at school (1)
One only of the two is not at school (2).

The contradictory is obtained by a combination of (1) and (2). It must be true either that—

(*a*) Billy and Colin are at school,

or that

(*b*) One only is at school, or neither is.

Billy is at school and in the first class,

may be treated in the same way.

A Conditional Proposition—

If any D is E, that D is F (1)

is certainly incompatible with

If any D is E, that D is not F (2).

But if the import of (1) can be expressed by saying—

That any D is F *is an inference from* its being an E (3),

then (1) and (2) do not exhaust all possibilities; for it may be that neither *D is F* nor *D is not F* is an inference from *D's being E*; it may be that no connection is known between *D's being E* and *D's being F*. No doubt between *any* two identifications there must *be* a connection if we only knew it; but unless we do know it, we cannot make any inference from the one to the other. Just in the same way, Any A must be B or not B; but we may not be in a position to affirm either the one Predicate or the other.

Again—

> This D is E and this D is not F,

though it is certainly incompatible with (1), does not seem to me to be properly called its contradictory. For if I take such a proposition as the following:—

> If any figure has 1000 equal sides, it has 1001 equal angles,

am I not to be allowed to deny it, unless I can say, indicating some figure,

> This figure has 1000 equal sides, and it has not 1001 equal angles?

But taking what seems to be the more natural and characteristic interpretation of (1), namely,

> Any D that is E is F,

we get a perfectly simple and satisfactory contradictory in

> Some D's that are E are not F.

The contrary of (1) as thus interpreted would be

> No D that is E is F
> (= If any D is E, that D is not F).

(3) can, however, be simply and fully negatived by

> That any D is F *is not an inference from* its being an E.

And all Hypotheticals without exception may, I think, be contradicted in the same way—*e.g.*,

> (1) If S is P, P is S
> (2) If M is P, S is P,

are contradicted by

> (1′) *P is S* is not an inference from *S is P*.
> (2′) *S is P* is not an inference from *M is P*.

If we take such propositions as—

> If black is white, he is a person to be trusted;
> If I pain you, I pain myself more;
> If this bill becomes law, it will be to the advantage of tenant-farmers;
> If the earth were only 6000 miles in diameter, it would be less than 24,000 miles in circumference;
> If ye love me, ye will keep my commandments;
> If it is six o'clock, Mary will soon be here—

in each case the full import can, I think, be expressed in a Categorical of the form

> C is an inference from A.

(Perhaps the exact form, in the case of the proposition about the earth's diameter, would be

> C *would be* an inference from A.)

And
> C is an inference from A

is contradictorily opposed by

> C is not an inference from A.

Neither
> If A, not C

nor
> A and not C

seem possible contradictories in the concrete cases given above.

And this seems strikingly the case too, if we take such an absurd Inferential as

> If Middlemarch is a fine book, Sarah Battle was devoted to whist.

An Alternation of the form

> (1) A is B or C is D (or, A is B or A is D)

is said to be contradicted by

> (2) A is not B and C is not D (or, and A is not D).

But here again, as in the case of Inferentials, I think a third possibility remains. The import of (1) is that the elements of the alternation are so related as that the denial of either justifies the affirmation of the other. The import of (2) is that the denial of either member is bound up with the denial of the other. But it may be that not only is there *not* the relation between A is B, C is D, which is indicated by (1), but also that in addition there is not the (incompatible) relation indicated by (2); and since (1) and (2) exhaust the possible relations of inference between A is B, C is D, and their negatives, the only possibility that remains is, that A is B, C is D, are entirely unconnected.

To take an example :—
The " Alternative "

> Sarah Battle was devoted to whist, or Middlemarch is not a fine book,

does not seem to be effectively denied by

> Sarah Battle was not devoted to whist, and Middlemarch is a fine book.

> *Sarah Battle was devoted to whist* is not alternative with *Middlemarch is not a fine book*,

appears to me a more satisfactory contradictory. And this form of denial (C is not alternative with not-A) seems to be applicable in every case.

In Inferentials where A cannot be simply affirmed, nor C simply denied—as in, *e.g.*,

> If Charles I. had not deserted Strafford, he would have been more deserving of sympathy;
> If this bill passes, the dock labourers will benefit;
> If any violet were scarlet, it would be scentless;
> If I finish my paper this morning, I shall be at liberty this afternoon—

we cannot use the Inferential as it stands as the Major Premiss of an Inferentio-Categorical Syllogism. We can, of course, affirm that a negation of the identity indicated by A, and an affirmation of the identity indicated by C, cannot be asserted together; but this will not enable us to go on to any syllogistic Inference as long as we are unable in each case to affirm the identity indicated by A because of its falsity or uncertainty—this falsity or uncertainty being shown by the peculiar phrasing of the proposition.

Inferentials like some of the above are exceedingly frequent. They express forecasts of consequences which we are continually making and acting upon. How often one thinks, If I buy those books, I shall be inconveniently short of money; If I undertook this work, it would interfere with more important business; If I go to Switzerland for July and August, I must put off these visits in England—and so on. Prevision or estimation of the probable effects of action must constantly be expressed, or expressible, in such propositions as these.

MEDIATE INFERENCES (SYLLOGISMS).

SECTION XXI.

(A.) CATEGORICAL SYLLOGISMS.

It seems to me that Mill's criticism of the *Dictum de omni et nullo* is well founded, and that that Canon merely amounts to saying that what is predicated of every member or every portion of a class, may be predicated of any member or any portion of that class. For when we say, "Whatever is predicated of a *term distributed* may be predicated in like manner of everything contained under it," it seems clear that by *term* is meant the *term-name*—for in, *e.g.*, *Some men are mortals*, the *S* (*i.e. Some men*) is as much (or as little) "distributed" as in *All men are mortals*—*i.e.* some class-name; and what is predicated of a class-name distributed is, *ex vi termini*, predicated of each member of the class—the Dictum is not a Canon of Syllogism (if Syllogism means Formal Mediate Inference), nor even a statement of relations between different classes, but merely a formulation of the truth that if any object or objects belong to a class, what can be said about the class (distributively) can be said about it or them. It seems to apply only in cases in which we are dealing with A, E, I, or O propositions.[1] But a Canon of Syllogism ought to apply, whatever terms and term-names we are dealing with, and whatever admissible arrangement of these we are considering. It ought to apply to Syllogisms in the 2nd, 3rd, and 4th figures, and to arguments in which all the terms are Partial or Single, as well as to Syllogisms in Fig. 1, which have a class-name "distributed" for the S-name in the major premiss. When Jevons says (*Principles of Science*, p. 9, 3rd ed.) that "the great rule of inference" is that "so far as there exists sameness, identity, or likeness, what is true of one thing will be true of another," I do not think he helps us much. For in any purely formal (affirmative) inference by Categorical Syllogism, it is not "two things" that are *named* by the terms in each proposition, but *one* thing (or group); and in a whole syllogism, not *two* things, or *three* things, or *six* things, but *one* thing, or *one* thing and *part* of that same "thing." The denomination (and the application) of the two *terms* in any affirmative proposition must be absolutely identical, and where there are more than three *terms* in an affirmative syllogism, the extra ones must be identical in

---

[1] Somewhat similar remarks seem to be applicable to the ordinary rules of Conversion and the traditional rules of the Categorical Syllogism. They are all framed for application to certain *class* propositions—propositions of the A, E, I, O type. Indeed the rules of the Syllogism seem to be just a kind of rule of thumb for facilitating the application of the Dictum to propositions of this kind. The traditional Formal Logic is rather a Logic of Classes than a Logic of Propositions.

denomination with part of the denomination of some one of the three. *E.g.* in

> All N's are Q's,
> Some R's are N's,
> ─────────────
> Some R's are Q's,

we have four terms, viz. :—(1) *all N's*, (2) *some Q's*, (3) *some N's*, (4) *some R's;* but we have not three (or more) *things*, but *one group of things*, viz. :—*the Q's that are N's*, and a group that is *all* or *a part* of this, *the R's that are N's*. And in negative propositions and syllogisms we have only two "things," or two things and a part of one of them. Jevons' rule has the further fault of being reducible to tautology, for "So far as there exists sameness, identity, or likeness, what is true of one thing will be true also of another," can only mean, "two things are like in as far as they are like" (*two things cannot be identical or the same*). In this "rule" some of the important terms are in themselves ambiguous, and they are very loosely used. In employing *likeness, identity, sameness, what is true*, as he does in this Canon, Jevons errs, it seems to me, in two ways—(1) he confuses things that differ (qualitive likeness and quantitive identity—this confusion runs through his whole account of inference); (2) his phraseology implies a distinction where there is no difference, and thus a real tautology wears the guise of significant assertion. When (*op. cit.* p. 10) he says, in speaking of measuring extended objects, that "we obviously employ the axiom that whatever is true of a thing as regards its length is true of its equal" [in length], the absolute uselessness of the "axiom" seems clear—it amounts to no more than this, "What is true of a given length in one case, is true of that length in another case;" but this is only equivalent to saying that a given length *is* a given length—a form of words which has no predicative force. The matter is not mended by the further discussion (*op. cit.* p. 17, and following pages) of logical inference, which appears to me to be spoiled all through by the ever-recurring confusion—(1) between quantitive identity (what Jevons would perhaps call numerical sameness or identity) and qualitive likeness; (2) between what I have called Independent and Dependent Propositions (to which latter class all Mathematical Equations belong). There is perhaps also some confusion between *terms* and *application* (Denotation) *of terms*.—The implication that two things can be so similar, point for point, as to be capable of being logically substituted one for another (cf. p. 20, etc.), seems due to (1). It appears to me that Jevons was constantly on the very verge of escaping from the first of the confusions indicated above, but that somehow he always just missed doing so.

I should propose to define Categorical Syllogism as follows:—

A *Categorical Syllogism* is a combination of three categorical propositions, one of which (the Conclusion) is inferred from the other two taken together—these two being called the Premisses, and having in common one term-name which does not occur in the conclusion. The conclusion has its S-name in common with one premiss, and its P-name in common with the other premiss.

Taking *Term* as meaning Term-name + indicator, it is clear that in a Syllogism as thus defined, though there can be only *three* term-names there may be *five* terms (when we are dealing with class-names).

E.g. in

$$\frac{\text{All N is Q,}}{\text{All R is N,}}$$
Some R is Q;

the *Terms* are, All N, [Some] N, All R, Some R, [some] Q.

If I may still use the names *Middle Term, Major Term*, and *Minor Term*, All N and [some] N are Middle Terms, All R and Some R are Minors, and [some] Q is Major both in premisses and conclusion. [Some] N of course coincides, *ex vi termini*, with part of All N, and it is this part of All N that is the real medium of connection between Major and Minor—just as when we call N the Middle Term in the above Syllogism, it *is that part of N which is coincident with both R and Q* that is the real medium between them.

The *Middle Term* in either premiss of a Syllogism is that which has the Term-name common to both premisses.

The *Major Term* in the premisses of a Syllogism is that which has its term-name in common with the P of the conclusion.

The *Minor Term* in the premisses of a Syllogism is that which has its term-name in common with the S of the conclusion.

The *Major Premiss* is that which contains the Major Term.

The *Minor Premiss* is that which contains the Minor Term.

I think the Canon of Categorical Syllogism may be amended as follows:—

If the denomination of two terms is identical (or non-identical), any third term which has a different term-name and is denominationally identical with the whole (or part) of one of those two, is also identical (or non-identical), in whole or part, with the denomination of the other.

To take examples of application, in

No N is Q,
All R is N,
———
No R is Q;

the denomination of (1) All N is non-identical (absolutely uncoincident) with the denomination of (2) [all] Q; and the denomination of (3) All R is identical with some of the denomination of All N; hence All R is non-identical with [all] Q.

In

All Q is N,
No R is N,
———
No R is Q;

the denomination of (1) All R is non-identical with that of (2) [all] N; the denomination of (3) All Q is identical with some of the denomination of [all] N; hence the denomination of All R is non-identical with the denomination of [all] Q.

In
>
All N is Q,
All N is R,
―――――――
Some R is Q;

denomination of (1) All N is identical with that of (2) [some] Q; denomination of (3) [some] R is identical with that of All N; therefore the denomination of Some R is identical with that of [some] Q.

In
>
All Q is N,
All N is R,
―――――――
Some R is Q;

(1) All N is identical in denomination with (2) [some] R; the denomination of (3) All Q is identical with some of the denomination of All N; hence the denomination of Some R is identical with some of the denomination of All Q (namely [some] Q).

In considering the ordinarily accepted rules of Syllogism, the distinction between *term* and *term-name* again becomes important.[1] For if, in, *e.g.*, the syllogism

>
All N's are Q's,
Some R's are N's,
―――――――――
Some R's are Q's,

we call (1) *all N's*, (2) *some Q's*, (3) *some R's*, (4) *some N's*, *Terms*, then the rule that in a valid syllogism we must have only three terms, excludes all syllogisms except those in Fig. 3, which have the middle "term" distributed twice. In the instance above taken we have four terms.

But if we call R, Q, and N "Terms," then, if Syllogism is defined as having only three Terms, *to have three Terms* is no differentia of *valid* (no rule for *valid*) Syllogism. (In any case the rule is superfluous, the condition which it lays

―――――――
[1] Cf. *ante*, pp. 4, 5.

down being secured by the other ordinarily received rules of Syllogism.)

Again, if Syllogism is *not* defined as having only three Terms, then the other rules of Syllogism exclude valid arguments admitted by the definition, such as—

$$\frac{\begin{array}{l}\text{A is greater than B,}\\ \text{B is greater than C,}\end{array}}{\text{C is not less than A,}}$$

and (still taking *Term* to mean *Term-name*) Rule 3 excludes such an argument as—

$$\frac{\begin{array}{l}\text{These men are my brothers,}\\ \text{These men are under 7 foot,}\end{array}}{\text{My brothers are under 7 foot,}}$$

and Rule 4 does not exclude Illicit process of the Major and Minor Terms, *e.g.*,

$$\frac{\begin{array}{l}\text{All N's are Q's,}\\ \text{Four R's are N's,}\end{array}}{\text{Five R's are Q's;}}$$

$$\frac{\begin{array}{l}\text{All N's are some Q's,}\\ \text{All R's are some N's,}\end{array}}{\text{Some R's are most Q's.}}$$

I would suggest the following as substitutes for the old syllogistic rules:—

(1) In every syllogism the denomination of the middle term in one premiss must be identical with the whole, or a part, of the denomination of the middle term in the other premiss;[1] and the denomination of the major term and minor term in the conclusion must be identical with the whole, or a part, of the denomination of the major and minor terms respectively in the premisses.[2]

[1] By Obversion of either premiss, these corresponding terms in the two premisses may, of course, be made absolutely non-identical.

[2] By Obversion of the conclusion, the denomination of the major and minor terms in the conclusion may be made absolutely non-identical with the denomination of the corresponding terms in the premisses.

This Rule (or Rules) will replace Rules 1, 2, 3, 4, 7, 8, and it provides against Tautological Fallacy, which they do not.

(2) Identity of denomination of the terms in the conclusion requires identity of terms in both premisses; and non-identity of terms in the conclusion requires non-identity of terms in one, and only one, premiss.

This will replace Rules 5 and 6.

Breach of (2) involves breach of (1)—cf. Section XXVI.; hence any invalid Categorical Syllogism involves the Fallacy of more or less than three Terms, directly or indirectly. There are many valid arguments which are not expressed in strict syllogistic form; but every such argument is, I think, *reducible* to *formally* valid inferences—Syllogisms (Categorical, Inferential, or Alternative), and Eductions. Such a syllogism as—

$$\frac{\text{A is greater than B,}}{\text{B is greater than C,}}$$
$$\text{A is greater than C,}$$

I do not consider *formal* in the strictest sense, though its cogency would be immediately evident to most persons.

$$\frac{\text{A is not-B,}}{\text{C is B,}}$$
$$\text{C is not A,}$$

is a cogent form of argument to which, by means of Obversion of one premiss, valid *syllogisms* may be reduced, and a form which itself, by Obversion of one premiss, reduces to valid *syllogism*. (Cf. *post*, Section XXVI.)

SECTION XXII.

(B.) INFERENTIAL SYLLOGISMS.

I would define Inferential Syllogism as

A Syllogism having an Inferential premiss;

Pure Inferential Syllogism as
>A Syllogism of which the conclusion and both the premisses are Inferential Propositions;

Mixed Inferential Syllogism as
>A Syllogism of which the major premiss is an Inferential Proposition, the minor premiss and the conclusion being Categorical Propositions.

I propose to classify Inferential Syllogisms as follows:—
What Mr. Keynes calls (1) Conditional and (2) Hypothetical Syllogisms (cf. *Formal Logic*, 2nd ed. pp. 264, 265). I would propose to group together as "Pure Inferentials," subdividing into
>(1) Pure Hypotheticals,
>(2) Pure Conditionals;

(1) are what Mr. Keynes calls Hypothetical Syllogisms;
(2) are what he calls Conditional Syllogisms.

The other two kinds of Inferentials I would call "Mixed Inferentials," and what Mr. Keynes calls Hypothetico-Categorical, *e.g.*,

$$\frac{\text{If E is F, G is H}}{\text{G is not H}} \quad (1)$$
$$\text{E is not F,}$$

I would call by the same name—giving the name Conditio-Categorical Syllogisms to Syllogisms of the form—

$$\frac{\text{If }any\text{ }D\text{ is E, }that\text{ }D\text{ is F}}{XD\text{ is E}} \quad (2)$$
$$XD\text{ is F.}$$

(1) is Modus Tollend, (2) is Modus Ponend.

The only further subdivision of Inferential Syllogisms which seems to me to be of consequence on a formal view, is that into Dependent and Independent, which may be carried out under each head. By a Dependent Syllogism, I mean a Syllogism that contains at least one Dependent Term.

I would suggest the following as Canons of (1) Hypothetico-

Categorical, (2) Conditio-Categorical, (3) Hypothetical, (4) Conditional Syllogisms.

(1) If one Categorical Proposition, C, is inferrible from another Categorical Proposition, A; then the assertion of A justifies the assertion of C, and the denial of C justifies the denial of A.

(2) If from some distinguishing mark, D, in any member of a given class, K, some further mark, M, is to be inferred; then the assertion that any K is D, justifies the assertion that that K is also M; and the assertion that any K is not M, justifies the further assertion that that K is also not D.

(3) If from one Categorical Proposition, A, another proposition, C, is inferrible, and from C there is inferrible a third proposition, D; then D is inferrible from A.[1]

(4) If from the presence in any member of a class, K, of a distinctive mark, D, a second mark, M, may be inferred; and if from the presence of M in any K, the presence (or absence) of a further mark, M^2, may be inferred; then from the presence of D in any K, the presence (or absence) of M^2 may be inferred.[1]

[1] A valid Inferential reasoning may need to have some of its propositions obverted before this Canon will apply directly.

[TABLE.

[TABLE XXXVIII.]

INFERENTIAL SYLLOGISMS.

PURE INFERENTIAL SYLLOGISMS.

Hypothetical Syllogisms.

e.g. If A is B, C is D;
If E is F, A is B;
If E is F, C is D.

Conditional Syllogisms.

e.g. If any D is E, that D is F;
If any D is H, that D is E;
If any D is H, that D is F.

MIXED INFERENTIAL SYLLOGISMS.

Hypothetico-Categorical Syllogisms.
(*Ponend and Tollend.*)

e.g. If S is P, P is S;
S is P (or P is not S);
P is S (or S is not P).

If all R's are Q's, some R's are Q's;
All R's are Q's (or No R's are Q's);
Some R's are Q's (or some R's are not Q's).

If M is P, S is P;
M is P (or S is not P);
S is P (or M is not P).

If A is equal to B, B is equal to A;
A is equal to R (or B is not equal to A);
B is equal to A (or A is not equal to B).

Conditio-Categorical Syllogisms.
(*Ponend and Tollend.*)

e.g. If any D is E, that D is F;
XD is E (or XD is not F);
XD is F (or XD is not E).

If X has been once the cause of Y,
X will be always the cause of Y;
X has been once the cause of Y;
X will be always the cause of Y.
(*Inductive Syllogism.*)

If you are pleased, I am contented;
You are pleased,
I am contented.

SECTION XXIII.

(C.) ALTERNATIVE SYLLOGISMS.

An Alternative Syllogism may be defined as—

   A syllogism of which *one* premiss is an Alternative Proposition or a combination of Alternative Propositions, and of which one premiss and the conclusion, or both premisses, or both premisses and the conclusion, *may be* alternative.

Alternative Syllogisms may be divided into — I. Pure Alternative Syllogisms ; II. Mixed Alternative Syllogisms.

I. In a Pure Alternative Syllogism, both of the premisses and the conclusion are alternative, *e.g.*,

$$\frac{\begin{array}{l}\text{C is D, or A is not B;}\\ \text{E is F, or C is not D;}\end{array}}{\text{E is F, or A is not B.}}$$

II. Mixed Alternative Syllogisms may be distinguished as (1) Categorico-Alternative Syllogisms, in which either constituent (major or minor premiss, or conclusion) of the syllogism that is not alternative is categorical; and (2) Inferentio-Alternative Syllogisms, in which the major premiss is always inferential in form, and the other premiss and the conclusion are either (*a*) one alternative and the other categorical, or (*b*) both alternative.

Inferentio - Alternative Syllogisms, which include what are commonly called Disjunctive Syllogisms and Dilemmas, may be divided into (i.) Hypothetico - Alternative, and (ii.) Conditio - Alternative ; and each of these again into Ponend Syllogisms and Tollend Syllogisms (corresponding to the two ordinarily recognised forms of Inferential Syllogisms).

The following may be suggested as Canons of

(1) Pure Alternative
(2) Categorico-Alternative
(3) Hypothetico-Alternative
(4) Conditio-Alternative

} Syllogisms.

(1) From two alternative propositions, of which one has an alternative that is the negative of an alternative in the other, a third alternative proposition may be inferred, having for its members the remaining alternatives of the premisses.

(2) The denial of one member (or more) of any alternation (or combination of alternations) justifies the affirmation of the other member or members.

(3) Of two Hypothetical Propositions determinately combined, if (Modus Ponend) A be alternatively affirmed, then C may be alternatively affirmed (when not diverse, categorically affirmed); and if (Modus Tollend) C be alternatively denied, then A may be categorically denied (when diverse, alternatively denied).

(4) Modus Ponend.

Of any two Conditional Propositions determinately combined, if the P's of the A's are alternatively affirmed of any member (or members) of the class (or classes) indicated by the S-name (or S-names) of the A's; then of that member (or those members) the P of C may be affirmed—categorically if the C's are indistinguishable, alternatively if the C's are diverse.

Modus Tollend.

Of any two Conditional Propositions determinately combined, if the P's of the C's are alternatively denied of any member (or members) of the class (or classes) indicated by the S-name (or S-names) of the A's; then of that member (or those members) the P of A may be denied—categorically if the A's are indistinguishable, alternatively if the A's are diverse.

[TABLE XXXIX.] ALTERNATIVE SYLLOGISMS. 169

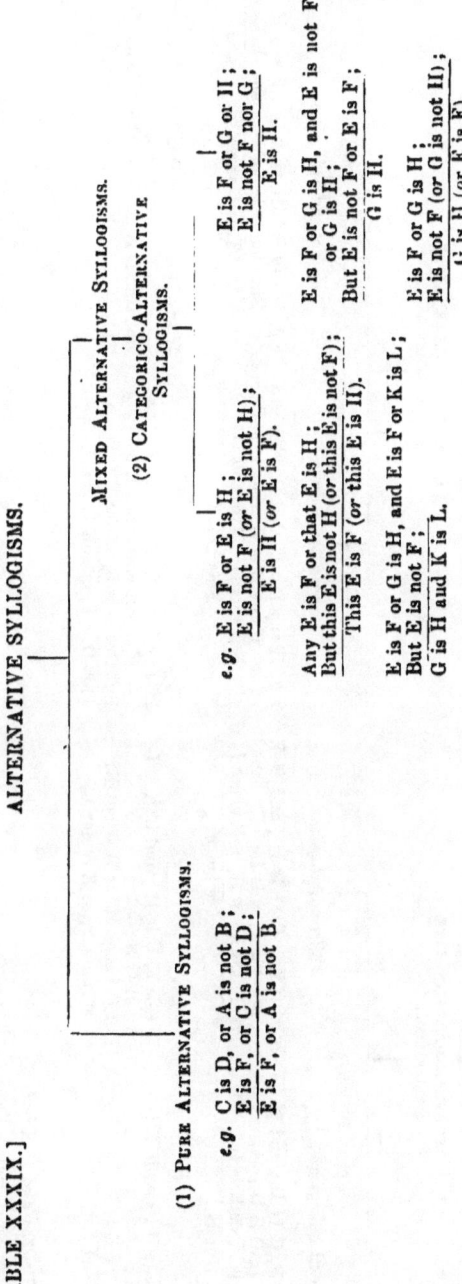

ALTERNATIVE SYLLOGISMS.

(1) PURE ALTERNATIVE SYLLOGISMS.

e.g. C is D, or A is not B;
E is F, or C is not D;
_____
E is F, or A is not B.

MIXED ALTERNATIVE SYLLOGISMS.

(2) CATEGORICO-ALTERNATIVE SYLLOGISMS.

e.g. E is F or E is H;
E is not F (*or* E is not H);
_____
E is H (*or* E is F).

Any E is F or that E is H;
But this E is not H (*or* this E is not F);
_____
This E is F (*or* this E is H).

E is F or G is H, and E is F or K is L;
But E is not F;
_____
G is H and K is L.

E is F or G or H;
E is not F nor G;
_____
E is H.

E is F or G is H, and E is not F
or G is H;
_____
But E is not F or E is F;
G is H.

E is F or G is H;
E is not F (*or* G is not H);
_____
G is H (*or* E is F).

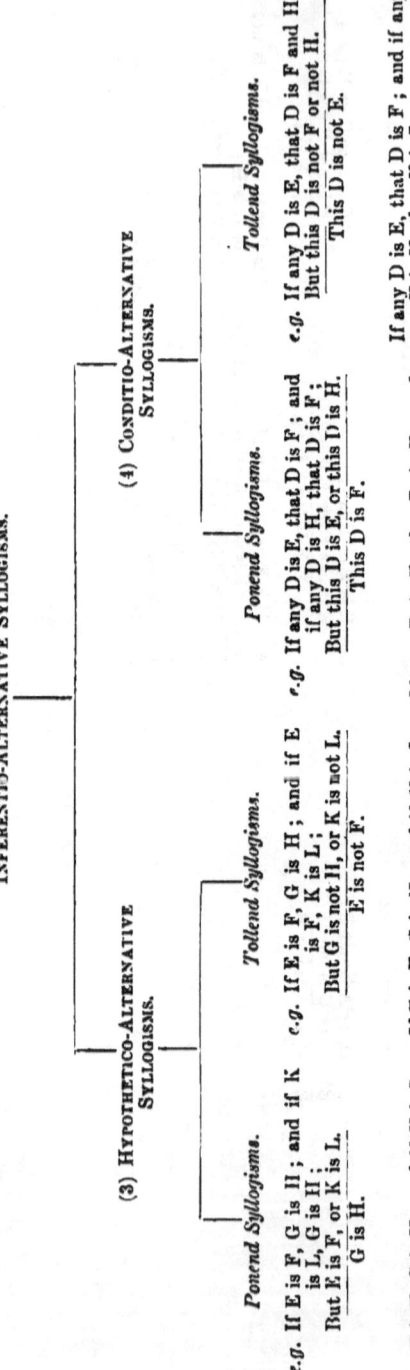

SECTION XXIV.

NOTE ON THE GROUND OF INDUCTION.

Mill tells us (*Logic*, Bk. iii. ch. iii.) that the fundamental axiom or ground of Induction is the axiom which asserts " that the course of nature is uniform ; that the universe is governed by general laws." This axiom or principle is itself a generalization from particulars, " an instance of induction, and induction by no means of the most obvious kind." It seems, when we inquire closely, to reduce itself to the Law of Causation, for Mill (Bk. iii. ch. iii. § 1, p. 358 of vol. i. in the 9th ed.) refers to ch. xxi., " Of the evidence of the Law of Universal Causation," as concerned with the "fundamental axiom of induction ; " and in ch. v. of the same book—" Of the Law of Universal Causation "—he says that " the notion of Cause " is " the root of the whole theory of Induction " (vol. ii. p. 376); that " of all truths relating to phenomena, the most valuable to us are those which relate to the order of their succession " (vol. i. p. 374); that " there is no general axiom standing in the same relation to the uniformities of co-existence as the law of causation does to those of succession " (vol. ii. p. 117); and that this " great deficiency . . . precludes the application to the ultimate uniformities of coexistence, of a system of rigorous scientific induction, such as the uniformities in the succession of phenomena have been found to admit of " (vol. ii. p. 117); that Bacon's great error lay in thinking (vol. ii. p. 118) " that as every event has a cause, or invariable antecedent, so every property of an object has an invariable coexistent, which he called its Form,"—Mill holding, on the contrary, that objects which are, *e.g.*, soft or moist, etc., " agree in the one point inquired into, and in nothing else " (vol. ii. p. 118), so that when dealing with coexistences we are thrown back upon Induction by Simple Enumeration. What the Law of Causation asserts is that every event has a cause (" change can only be produced by change," vol. i. 407), and that [unconditional] "invariability of succession is found by observation to obtain between every fact in nature and some other fact which has preceded it" (cf. pp. 377 and 392 of vol. i.)—the cause of anything is "the antecedent which it invariably [and unconditionally] follows" (vol. i. p. 390).

Cause as thus defined seems a contradictory notion; for let ABC be any antecedent, and let DEF be its consequent, that which unconditionally and invariably follows—If ABC be the *sole* antecedent, it cannot be *followed* by DEF; because, since ABC *alone* is sufficient cause, the moment ABC, the all-sufficient cause, is present, that same moment the effect of which it *is* the sufficient cause must be there too; therefore DEF must be *simultaneous* with ABC. The Law of Causation as formulated by Mill is not workable. And if for *Antecedent* we put *Concomitant* we get a law, not of succession, but of coexistence.[1]

If we consider that *event* means *change in subjects of attributes*, it would seem that our power of predicting that one event A, will be followed by another event B, must depend wholly upon coexistence of attributes in the subjects concerned. If we have seen one animal dosed with arsenic and subsequently die, and hence conclude that another animal, called by the same name, and dosed with an equal amount of arsenic, will die, is not our inference based upon the assumption of a certain constant coinherence of attributes, both in the animal and in the poison—a coinherence of such a kind that when the two subjects are so collocated as to act upon each other, a result similar to that produced in the first case will be produced in the second also? If the properties of this arsenic are different from the other, or if the second animal, though looking like the first, has a different internal constitution, there is no reason why death should result. This sort of uniformity—an uniformity primarily of coexistence—is the only sort that we look for or find in terrestrial

[1] The difficulty raised here does not seem to me to be met by what Mill says at the end of § 7 of the chapter on the Law of Causation (*Logic*, i. 397); especially when this is taken in connection with what he says elsewhere in that chapter, and in various other places.

nature. What subjects of attributes will be collocated, and when and where, we cannot say beforehand; all that we can say is, that if subjects having certain attributes are collocated, certain changes in them will take place. Hence laws of succession in events seem to depend upon laws of coexistence of attributes in subjects, and proof of Causation (in another sense than that which Mill professedly adopts) is perhaps chiefly valuable as an indirect proof of connection of attributes. And I think not only that every attribute is invariably accompanied by some other attribute, as Bacon surmised, but also that every kind of attribute is one of an unique group with which it is invariably and inseparably connected. We certainly act as if we believed this; from the perception of a mere odour, we infer unhesitatingly the neighbourhood of roses or jessamine or lavender, of coffee or tea, hay, ripening corn, freshly fallen snow, or a bean-field; from a mere vocal sound, we infer the neighbourhood of a man, or woman, or child, or bird or dog—or even of a particular individual in a particular mood. A mere touch or taste will enable us fully to describe objects of a familiar kind; the mere view of a thing will enable us to say what it is called, how it will act on various sense-organs, what effect it will have under a great variety of circumstances. Perhaps the principle which we proceed on in these cases might be formulated as follows:—

> Any subject of attributes that is like another in one respect, is like it in a plurality of respects.

And where *mere* coexistence is in question, the same thing holds. If I see an object looking like what I am accustomed to call a squirrel, sitting on the top bar of a stile, or on a branch, I infer unhesitatingly that if I startle it, it will escape with the kind of movement common to squirrels; that if I shoot it and examine its structure, I shall find it to have a backbone, a brain, etc. No two things are alike only in visual appearance, or only in smell, or only in taste, etc. From one bone a whole skeleton may be made out; from one specially modified symptom the whole diagnosis of a disease. We may, I think, say that any intensive attribute can occur only with special modifications of all the other intensive attributes of its subject — and similarly of extensive and adventitious (temporal, circumstantial, etc.) attributes respectively. (I believe this is substantially Lotze's view.) What particular modifications of attributes are connected, can, of course, be known only from special experience—one kind of experience establishes the connection in the case of classes, and a different kind in the case of individuals. If we believe that in any case certain attributes are really *connected* as coexistent, and not merely collocated, as stones may be in a heap, we infer at once (as in the case of cause and effect) that they are invariably connected. Why should they be connected in that one case, unless there were ground for formulating a *law* of their connection? We need the Universal to justify the Particular.

The principle above suggested may perhaps be called the Principle of Similarity.

We may add to it as a kind of converse the rule that, No subject of attributes is unlike another (or its former self) in one respect only. This may be called the Principle of Dissimilarity. If we observe two objects unlike in one respect, we always infer further unlikeness; if we observe a person or thing to be changed in one point, we always infer some further change. In such inferences we proceed upon this Principle of Dis-similarity. We see here the close connection there is between Induction (so called) and Analogy— both may proceed upon the principles here suggested. There seem to be two other principles which are complementary to these—one (similar to Leibnitz's " Identity of Indiscernibles ") that, No two objects are alike in all respects (two classes alike in all respects would be the same)—this may be called the Principle of Differentiation; the other that, No two objects or classes are unlike in all respects — this may perhaps be called the Principle of Community.

The maxim by which we are guided in practice might

perhaps be said to be this, *Apparent* likeness, unlikeness, or alteration is accompanied by *non-apparent* likeness, unlikeness, or alteration.

SECTION XXV.

NOTE ON THE LAWS OF THOUGHT.

Logic has frequently been defined as the Science of the Laws of Thought, and the Laws of Thought as commonly enumerated are the laws—
    (1) Of Identity.
    (2) Of Contradiction.
    (3) Of Excluded Middle.
(1) and (2) are generally represented by the formulæ
    A is A, A is-not not-A
respectively; (3) is expressed as
    A is B or not B.

What I wish to do in this Section is to inquire what the force and meaning of these Laws is, and what seems the most appropriate expression for them.

If (1) and (2) have meaning, that meaning cannot, I think, be adequately conveyed by *A is A, A is-not not-A*, because (for reasons which I have already given at length, cf. *ante*, p. 52) those forms of words appear to me to have absolutely no predicative force whatever—that is, if they are taken literally as they stand. They are, however, as Mr. Bosanquet says (*Mind*, vol. xiii. p. 356), "susceptible of many interpretations"—*interpretation* meaning that they are understood to carry implications which go beyond the strict signification of the terms used. We have instances of this sort of implication in such phrases as "Cards are Cards" (Sarah Battle), "A man's a man (for a' that)," "Man is man (and master of his fate)," "Love is love (in the humblest cottage)" (cf. also "There are books and books," etc.). In such "propositions,"

I think that, as a matter of fact, we generally take the Subject-term in its Denomination, and the Predicate-term in Determination; and probably the currency of such formally tautological locutions, into which we thus read a real meaning, helps to make the form *A is A* seem plausible.

If *A is A* and *A is-not not-A* mean that *every A* is *nothing whatever besides A*, i.e. if they entirely exclude difference (cf. *op. cit.* p. 357), all propositions of the form *A is B* are prohibited. But we can and do constantly use propositions of the form *A is B*; no one disputes their propriety and value. Therefore, propositions of this form being admitted, the above interpretation must be rejected.

Again, *A is A* may be explained to signify that terms have an uniform meaning—that A, wherever occurring, has the same Determination (hence also the same Denomination), i.e. that This A is (*e.g.*) X, That A is X, etc.; *i.e. All A's are X*. We regard the various A's—the actually recurring words or symbols—*as members of a class*, and of them, as such, we assert exact similarity of Determination. But it seems hardly fair to express this Universal as *A is A*; and its expression as *All A's are X* presupposes a general uniformity in reference and significance of symbols. The presupposition is, of course, capable of expression in language, but only in language every word of which itself *involves* the presupposition. This law of the use of language is indeed a law of Identity in Diversity; for it affirms that the reference of A, under whatever diversity of occurrence, is to some thing or things quantitively identical and qualitively similar. But it is a rule of language made possible and necessary by a Law of Identity in things, rather than the Law of Identity itself. What I regard as this Law, is a necessary condition of there being anything at all which can be named, much more therefore of there being *names* of those things. But I cannot regard it as meaning, as even Lotze says that it does (*Logic*, p. 60, English translation), "What is contradictory is contradictory, What is, is," etc., and this for the reasons which I have given for holding that *A is A* has not really any predicative force. The Law of Identity seems to me to be an expression of the principle of the *permanence* of things—their existence in time. Whatever exists in time at all has some permanence; whatever has permanence at all has existence in time; and since time is infinitely divisible, what exists *in time* is necessarily an identity in diversity, the diversity, namely, of *change* (succession) *in time*. This seems to me to be the root of identity. One cannot conceive *anything* which does not to some extent perdure, and thus exist as a unity in diversity. If this is so, it must be possible to assert of the simplest thing A that it is B (or not B). And I should agree with Mr. Bosanquet (*op. cit.* p. 357) that "Every A is B, would be much better than Every A is A" as a schematic expression of the Law of Identity. I should differ from him, however, in being disposed to accept this formula, which he is not.

A is-not non-A, as an expression of the Law of Contradiction, is open to objections similar to those brought against the answering form *A is A* as representative of the Law of Identity.

If A is B, A is-not non-B,[1]

or—

Two contradictory propositions cannot both be affirmed,

seem preferable; and in this form the Law of Contradiction precisely corresponds to the Law of Excluded Middle, which is seen to be complementary to it, and may be thus expressed—

A is either B or not B,

or—

Two contradictory propositions cannot both be denied.

---

[1] There is a distinction of the last importance between

If A is B, A is not not-B (1),

and

If A is B, A is B (2);

for in (1) the Consequent and Antecedent are obverses of each other, either is inferrible from the other; while in (2) the Consequent is simply a repetition of the Antecedent; there is no relation of inference between them, and the whole Hypothetical has no assertive force.

If this formulation is adopted, it appears that the Law of Identity is the principle of the possibility of significant assertion, while the Law of Contradiction is the principle of consistency, and the Law of Excluded Middle may be regarded as a principle of inter-relation or reciprocity.[1] The three might, I think, be appropriately called the Axioms of Logic.

SECTION XXVI.

FALLACIES.

I should prefer not to speak of Fallacies of Confusion, but to reckon Confusion as a *source* of Fallacy. Any Fallacy itself, however caused, will be reducible to one of the heads which follow (cf. pp. 182–193).

Where there is confusion, we cannot say what our propositions really are or mean. This may be (*a*) because of the ambiguity of some Term or Term-Constituent (Term-name or Term-indicator). Fallacy produced by the use of Question-begging Epithets seems to come under this head. Or (*b*)

---

[1] As I have referred to Mr. Bosanquet's interesting article on "The Importance of a True Theory of Identity," in *Mind*, vol. xiii., I ought perhaps to mention that I cannot accept the sense which he sometimes seems to give to *Identity, identical*. *E.g.* when he says, "The element of identity between two outlines can be accurately pointed out and limited, but the moment they cease to be two, it ceases to be an identity" (p. 359). "If Identity is atomic or abstract, *i.e.* excludes difference, then you cannot speak of your present impression as being identical, or having identical elements with a former impression which, *quâ* former, is by the hypothesis different" (p. 360). "If there is no identity, we cannot *revive a former impression*, but only one like it" (p. 361). In these passages *identity* seems to mean *exact similarity*, not *sameness of individuality* (cf. *ante*, Section VI. *note*, p. 46). The meaning to which I should wish to restrict *Identity*, and the meaning which the whole theory of Identity seems to me to require, is what I should call *quantitive* (not qualitive) *sameness* — what Jevons would perhaps call *numerical sameness* — the sameness that I mean when I say, This pencil is the *identical* pencil which I lost last week.

because of the ambiguity of construction. Or (*c*) because of the ambiguity of context or implication. I think it is allowable to take (*c*) as a third head here. What is called the Fallacy of Continuous Questioning may be referrible to confusion of this sort. (In this case, however, it seems to me that the confusion is of a kind which rather brings one to a standstill altogether than gives rise to Fallacy.) *E.g.* if I ask, " Is what you are thinking of, over 1 lb. in weight ?" the difficulty to the person questioned of framing an answer, if his "object" is without weight, is due to what may be called ambiguity of implication or reference, for there is no ambiguity in the *terms* or *construction* of my question. "Why does a dead fish weigh more than a living one?" is another and familiar instance of a fallacious question. In these cases it is assumed that the conditions exist which are necessary in order to make the question such as is capable of receiving a truthful answer, without necessarily referring to some other question, when, as a matter of fact, this may not be the case. Fallacy of Accent (as explained in recent Text-books of Logic) seems to come also under the head (*c*).

In other instances of Fallacious Questioning, the fallacy, in as far as there is fallacy, may be due to ambiguity of construction; *e.g.* Are you ready and willing ? Have you read *Robert Elsmere* and *John Ward, Preacher?* Are Billy and Colin at school ?

What are called Fallacies of Equivocation (*a*), Amphibology (*b*), and Figure of Speech, are due to confusion. Composition, Division, Accident (arguing from a general rule to a special case), Converse Fallacy of Accident (arguing from a special case to a general rule), and arguing from one special case to another special case, are instances of Equivocation. When the confusion to which such fallacies are due has been pointed out, they generally appear at once as Eductive Fallacies of three or more Terms, or as Syllogistic Fallacies of more than three distinct Terms. The Fallacy of the Consequent (or Non-Sequitur) reduces to a Syllogistic Fallacy of more than three distinct terms—

E.g.

> The sea was the place where the incidents of my story occurred;
> There is the sea;
> ———
> Therefore my story is true.[1]

The Fallacy of the False Cause (Non Causa pro Causa, Post hoc ergo propter hoc) reduces to an Eductive Fallacy of three Terms ("Simple Conversion of an A Proposition"). *E.g.*

> Whatever is cause of X precedes X;
> ∴ Whatever precedes X is cause of X.

The Fallacy of Irrelevant Conclusion is reducible to an Eductive Fallacy of four, or of three Terms. (A perfectly valid Eductive Inference may, of course, have *three* Terms, taking *Term* in the sense indicated at the beginning of Section II. (cf. *ante*, pp. 4, 5), as distinct from *Term-name*. *E.g.*

> All R is Q,
> ∴ Some R is Q;

or *four* terms—*e.g.*

> All R is Q,
> ∴ All not-Q is not-R.

To all such cases the rules of Immediate Inference (Eduction) in Section XIX. are applicable, and the proposition educed must contain no Term-names except those occurring in the *original proposition*, or the precise negatives of these.) A person who, *wishing to prove that S is Q*, argues as follows:—

> M is P,
> S is M,
> ———
> S is P,

and offers this argument in support of the assertion *S is Q*, commits the fallacy of Irrelevant Conclusion (Ignoratio Elenchi). He proves a conclusion other than that required

[1] This "argument" was actually used by a beggar in my hearing.

to be proved. What is implied in this procedure is, that *because* S is P, *therefore S is Q*. When thus barely stated, the illicit nature of the inference is at once apparent. To such a case the rules of Eduction referred to above will not apply.

Since all Fallacy consists in identifying what is different or differencing what is identical, we get a primary subdivision of Fallacies into (*a*) those of *professed Difference*, which may be called Fallacies of Tautology; (*b*) those of *professed Identification*, which may be called Fallacies of Discontinuity.

(*a*) Embrace all such Fallacies as Circulus in Definiendo, Petitio Principii, Arguing in a Circle.

Fallacy in the broadest sense may perhaps be defined as, The assertion or assumption of some relation between (i.) Terms, or (ii.) Propositions which does not hold between them. (i.) are not generally treated among logical Fallacies, though they are included by Mansel (Mansel's *Aldrich*, Note M) as Fallacies of Judgment. It would, I think, be convenient to call them Elemental Fallacies. All combinations of words having the form of a proposition, which either (*a*) cannot be significant, or (*β*) cannot be true, would come under this head. *A is A* would be a case of (*a*)—the case where compatibility between the terms merges into complete tautology; *A is not-A* would be a case of (*β*)—the case where diversity merges into absolute incompatibility (or discontinuity).

If Fallacy is understood in a narrower sense, as being concerned only with relations between Propositions, it may be defined as follows:—

There is Fallacy whenever we conclude from one or more propositions to another, the conclusion not being justified by the premiss or premisses.

This must be understood to include the cases (Tautological) in which a proposition which professes to be a conclusion simply repeats the datum or a part of it, or claims to be proved by the help of an assertion which the professed conclusion has itself contributed to prove—for clearly a proposition can be no justification for itself.

Where fallacious Inference is from *one* proposition to another, there is a Fallacy of Immediate Inference (or Eduction); where it is from two propositions taken together to a third, there is a Fallacy of Mediate Inference (or Syllogism). There are, besides, certain Tautologous Fallacies which involve relations between a plurality of Syllogisms.

FALLACIES OF IMMEDIATE INFERENCE OR EDUCTION.

These may be divided into *Eversive* and *Transversive* Fallacies. Eversive Fallacies may be—I. Categorical; II. Inferential; III. Alternative.

I. Here we may (1) pass from one proposition to another when the two propositions have no Term or Term-name in common—*e.g.* from M *is* N to Q *is* R. This is not a common form of Fallacy. It may be called an Eductive Fallacy of Four Terms.

(2) Or we may pass from one proposition to a second proposition which contains one Term or Term-name not contained in the first proposition. Here there are two cases—(*a*) when the second proposition contains a Term-name not contained in the first, nor formally equivalent to any contained in it; *e.g.* when from *All* R *is* Q it is inferred that *Some* X *is* Q; or from *Some* R *is not-Q* that *Some* Q *is* R.

This, again, is not perhaps a common Fallacy.

(*b*) When one of the terms of the second proposition has a wider Term-indicator than the corresponding Term in the first proposition, *e.g.* when from

Some R is Q

it is inferred that

All R is Q, or All Q is R,

(2) may be called Eductive Fallacies of Three Terms.

(3) Or we may profess to educe a Proposition from itself —to infer S *is* P from S *is* P.

II. Inferential Fallacies of Eduction. Here, beside Tautologous Fallacies, in which it is professed to educe a proposition from itself, there are two Fallacies which, from their correspondence with the Syllogistic Inferential Fallacies, it seems best to call the Fallacy (*a*) of the Antecedent, (*b*) of the Consequent.

E.g. (*a*) If E is F, G is H ;
∴ If E is not F, G is not H.

(*b*) If E is F, G is H ;
∴ If G is H, E is F.

III. Alternative Fallacies of Eduction. Here, besides Tautologous Fallacies, we may enumerate the four following Fallacies of Discontinuity :—

(1) Fallacy of Denial.

E.g. All R is Q or T ;
∴ No R is Q and T.

(2) Fallacy of Conversion.

E.g. Any R is Q or T ;
∴ Any Q or T is R.

(3) Fallacy of Enlargement.

E.g. Some R is Q or T ;
∴ Any R is Q or T.

(4) Fallacy of Analogy.

E.g. R^1 is Q or T ;
∴ R^2 is Q or T.

or

R^1 is Q^1 or T^1 ;
∴ R^2 is Q^2 or T^2.

Transversive Fallacies occur in passing from Categorical to Inferential or Alternative Propositions, from Inferentials to Categoricals or Alternatives, and from Alternatives to Categoricals or Inferentials. All Transversive Fallacies are Fallacies of Discontinuity.

SYLLOGISTIC FALLACIES.

Syllogistic Fallacies likewise fall into the three subdivisions of—I. Categorical; II. Inferential; III. Alternative.

I. In I. we have either (i.) the case where *no* conclusion is inferrible; or (ii.) the case where the proposition, which is professedly inferred, is not inferrible, though *some* conclusion is inferrible—including the cases (tautological) where the proposition professedly *inferred* is simply a repetition of one of the premisses, or asserts *part* of what is asserted by one of the premisses.

(i.) All cases here are reducible to cases (1) of Tautology, or (2) of four terms and two non-identities in the premisses.

In (1), one premiss repeats the other, (*a*) wholly, or (*b*) partly. *E.g.*

(*a*) M is P,   (*b*) All R is Q,
M is P.   Some R is Q.

In (2) there is (*a*) the case of four Term-names. Then (*b*) if the Term-name of the Middle Term is a class-name and not distributed, the *Some N* of one premiss is, for all we know, quite different in Denomination from the *Some N* of the other premiss.

(*Some N* is ambiguous on account of the indeterminateness of *Some*.)

(*c*) If the Term-name of the Middle Term is ambiguous, again, for all we know, it is a different term in both premisses. And the only case where from two negative premisses it is impossible to infer some conclusion, is the case where these premisses cannot be reduced to *affirmative premisses* having three terms; or four terms, one of which is included in one of the others, so that though there are *apparently* four Terms, there are not *really* four distinct Terms.

E.g.   No N is Q,
             No R is N,

reduces to
>All N is not-Q,
>All N is not-R,

formally justifying the conclusion—
>Some not-R is not-Q.

But from
>Some N is not Q, (1)
>Some R is not N,

which will not reduce to less than four distinct Terms, no conclusion can be obtained.

Again, from
>Some N is not Q, (2)
>Some N is not R,

from
>Some N is not Q, (3)
>Some N is R,

and from
>Some N is Q, (4)
>Some N is not-R,

we can draw no conclusion—because *Some N* is ambiguous, and thus we have what is equivalent to four distinct Terms.

From two particular affirmative premisses, for the same reason, we can draw no conclusion.

From a particular major and a negative minor we can get a conclusion—*e.g.*

>Some N is Q,
>No R is N,

reduces to
>Some N is Q,
>All N is not-R,

which gives the formally valid conclusion—
>Some not-R is Q.

And with a negative minor in Fig. 1 we can get a conclusion, by reducing to Fig. 3—*e.g.*

> All N is Q,
> No R is N,

reduces to

> All N is Q,
> All N is not-R,

and gives the formally valid conclusion—

> Some not-R is Q.

(ii.) Where the third proposition which is inferred is not inferrible, though *some* conclusion is inferrible.

Under this head come the fallacies of

(*a*) Tautology—*e.g.*

> M is P,   (5)
> S is M,
> ―――
> M is P.

(*b*) The Consequent (or Non-Sequitur)—*e.g.*,

> All N is Q,   (6)
> Some R is N,
> ―――
> No R is Q
> (or, All X is Y, etc.).

(In all cases of (ii.), except (*a*), the whole syllogism contains more than three distinct Terms—by which I mean that it contains more than three term-names, or that some term in the conclusion is wider than the corresponding term in the premisses.)

(*c*) Illicit major and minor, (*d*) negative conclusion from affirmative premisses, and (*e*) affirmative conclusion from a negative premiss. *E.g.*

(*c*)   All N is Q,   (7)
         Some R is N,
         ―――
         All R is Q.

Some Q is not N,   (8)
All R is N,
───────────
All R is not Q.

(The conclusion *Some Q is not R* is valid.)

In these two cases we conclude to a fourth Term not coincident with the whole or a part of any term in the premisses.

(*d*)   All N is Q,
All R is N,
───────────
No R is Q.

(A fourth Term (Q *minus* some-Q), not known to be coincident with any term in the premisses, is inferred to in the conclusion.)

(*e*)   No N is Q,
All R is N,
───────────
All R is Q.

This reduces to

All N is not-Q,
All R is N,
───────────
All R is Q (four distinct Terms).

All the Categorical Fallacies of Syllogism pointed out above are excluded by the Canon of Syllogism suggested in Section XXI. ("If the denomination of two terms is identical (or non-identical), any third term which has a different term-name and is denominationally *identical with the whole (or a part) of one of those two*, is also identical (or non-identical), in whole or part, with the denomination of the other."[1] Cf. *ante*, p. 160.) For instance, (1) and (2) are incompatible with that part of it which indicates that there must be identity of denomination between two of the terms.

───────

[1] I take *identical* to mean *completely coincident*, and *non-identical* to mean *altogether uncoincident*.

For in (1)

> Some N is-not Q,
> Some R is-not N,

if we take either Q or Some R as a third term, we cannot say that it is denominationally identical with the whole (or a part) of any other term in the two premisses.

Similar objections apply to (2)—

> Some N is-not Q,
> Some N is-not R.

And again, in (3), of neither of the premisses can it be said that one of its terms is identical (in whole or part) with either term of the other premiss, since *Some N* is ambiguous. And the same holds of (4).

(5) is not in accordance with the condition indicated by the last clause of the Canon (and referring to the conclusion), that "the denomination of any *third* term . . . is also identical (or non-identical) in whole (or part) with the denomination of *the other*" (*i.e.* with that other which is not a Middle Term).

In (6), (7), (8), etc., a term is introduced in the conclusion, of which it cannot be said that its whole denomination is either identical with, or a part of, the denomination of any term in the premisses.

II. *Fallacies of Inferential Syllogism.* These fall under four heads, corresponding to the division of Inferential Syllogisms, into—

(i.) Pure Hypothetical
(ii.) Pure Conditional
(iii.) Hypothetico-Categorical
(iv.) Conditio-Categorical
} Syllogisms.

Besides Tautological Fallacy, which occurs under each head, the Fallacies incident to (i.) appear to be of two kinds. (1) Where the premisses are such that *no* conclusion can be drawn. When this is the case, there is no such connection between the two premisses that a third proposition (having elements in common with both the premisses) can be inferred from them. This may arise from the fact either (*a*) that the elements of the propositions consist of four distinct Categoricals, or (*b*) that the element which is common occurs as Antecedent in both premisses, or as Consequent in both premisses.

The following are examples :—

(*a*) If K is L, F is G;
If D is E, M is N.

(*b*) If F is G, K is L;
If F is G, D is E.

If K is L, F is G;
If D is E, F is G.

If K is L, F is G;
If F is not G, D is E.

If F is G, K is L;
If D is E, F is not G.

(2) Where the conclusion drawn is not deducible from the premisses, though some conclusion is deducible. Here, unless the Fallacy consists (*a*) in asserting as Conclusion an entirely fresh Inferential, it consists either (*b*) in denying the Antecedent, or (*c*) in affirming the Consequent.

E.g.

(*b*) If K is L, F is G;
If D is E, F is not G;
If K is not L, D is E.

(If K is L, D is not E may be deduced.)

(*c*) If K is L, F is G;
If F is G, D is E;
If D is E, K is L.

(The consequence, If D is not E, K is not L, *is* deducible.)

(ii.) *Fallacies of Pure Conditional Syllogism.*

In as far as Conditional Propositions are similar to Hypotheticals, the Fallacies under this head correspond precisely with those under the preceding head. In as far as they are similar to Categoricals, Conditional Fallacies are the same as Categorical; but Conditional Propositions on my view differ in some respects from Categoricals.

(iii.) and (iv.) Fallacies of Hypothetico-Categorical Syllogism, and of Conditio-Categorical Syllogism have corresponding subdivisions. They include Tautological Fallacies and Fallacies of Discontinuity. The chief Fallacies of Discontinuity are two—namely (1) the Fallacy of the Antecedent, (2) the Fallacy of the Consequent. *E.g.*

(1) If D is E, F is G; If any D is E, that D is F;
    D is not E;   This D is not E;
    ―――――――   ―――――――――
    F is not G.   This D is not F.

(2) If D is E, F is G; If any D is E, that D is F;
    F is G;   This D is F;
    ―――――   ―――――――
    D is E.   This D is E.

Fallacy here may be due also (3) to the presence in the Minor Premiss of a constituent not contained in the Major Premiss, thus rendering it impossible to draw any conclusion. (4) to the presence in the Conclusion of a constituent not contained in the Premisses — the Conclusion thus being invalid.

III. *Fallacies of Alternative Syllogism.* In Pure Alternative Syllogisms we have Fallacies of Tautology (1) in the premisses alone (*a*) when one premiss repeats the other; (*b*) when an alternative in one premiss is wholly the same as one in the other; (*c*) when an alternative in one premiss is partly the same as one in the other.

E.g.   (*a*) A is B or C is D,
                C is D or A is B.

FALLACIES. 191

(b) All A is B or C is D,
All A is B or E is F.

(c) All A is B or C is D,
Some A is B or K is L, etc.

(2) In concluding from valid premisses when (a) the Conclusion is the same as a premiss.

E.g.   (a) A is B or C is D,
E is F or A is not B,
A is B or C is D.

(b) The Conclusion asserts part of a premiss.

E.g.   (b) C is not D or E is F,
Any A is B or C is D,
Some A is B or C is D.

We may have Fallacies of Discontinuity (1) in the premisses, when the premisses are not connected by means of an alternative of which the affirmative occurs in one premiss and the negative in the other.

E.g.   A is B or C is D,
E is F or G is H.

A is B or C is D,
C is D or G is H.

(2) In passing from premisses to conclusion, where the alternatives of the conclusion are not the extremes of the premisses.

E.g.   C is D or A is not B,
E is F or C is not D,
K is H or L is M.

The Fallacies of Discontinuity which are most obviously possible in what I have called Categorico-Alternative Syllogisms are, (1) the introduction into the Minor Premiss of an element distinct from those contained in the Major Premiss—in which case no inference is possible. (2) The introduction into the Conclusion of an element not contained in the Premisses—in which case the Conclusion is unjustifiable. (3) The Fallacy of Denial, corresponding to the Inferential Fallacies of Antecedent and Consequent.

Again, in Fallacies of Inferentio-Alternative Syllogism there may be Fallacy due to the unwarrantable introduction of a fresh element (*a*) into the Minor Premiss, (*b*) into the conclusion, but the chief Fallacies are those of the Antecedent and Consequent (as in the case of Inferentio - Categorical Fallacies). With both kinds of Alternative Syllogism, Tautological Fallacies may occur.

CIRCULAR FALLACIES.

Besides Elemental, Eductive, and Syllogistic Fallacies, there are the Fallacies that occur when, in the attempt to prove an assertion, recourse is had to some proposition which that assertion itself has contributed to prove—which Fallacies involve relations between a plurality of Syllogisms.

The name *Circular Fallacies* may, I think, be conveniently appropriated to these. They occur in the simplest form when there are only two Syllogisms concerned, but may (and often do) involve relations between *several* Syllogisms.

The following are examples. Taking the Syllogism

$$\frac{\begin{array}{c} Q \text{ is } P, \\ M \text{ is } Q, \end{array}}{M \text{ is } P,}$$

it may be required to *prove* M is Q. If this is done by means of the Syllogism

$$\frac{\begin{array}{c} P \text{ is } Q, \\ M \text{ is } P, \end{array}}{M \text{ is } Q.}$$

we have a case of circular reasoning.

Or if we have the Hypothetical Syllogism

$$\frac{\text{If } G \text{ is } H, K \text{ is } L,}{\text{If } E \text{ is } F, G \text{ is } H,}$$
$$\text{If } E \text{ is } F, K \text{ is } L,$$

and proceed to prove the Minor Premiss by the following argument:—

$$\frac{\text{If } K \text{ is } L, G \text{ is } H,}{\text{If } E \text{ is } F, K \text{ is } L,}$$
$$\text{If } E \text{ is } F, G \text{ is } H,$$

we have again a case of arguing in a circle.

Again, taking the Syllogism

If Jack is a good boy, he will do what he is told;
He is a good boy;
He will do what he is told—

if we go on to prove the Minor Premiss by the following Syllogism:—

If Jack will do what he is told, he is a good boy;
Jack will do what he is told;
He is a good boy,

we have committed a Circular Fallacy.

194 RELATIONS OF PROPOSITIONS.

[TABLE XLI.]

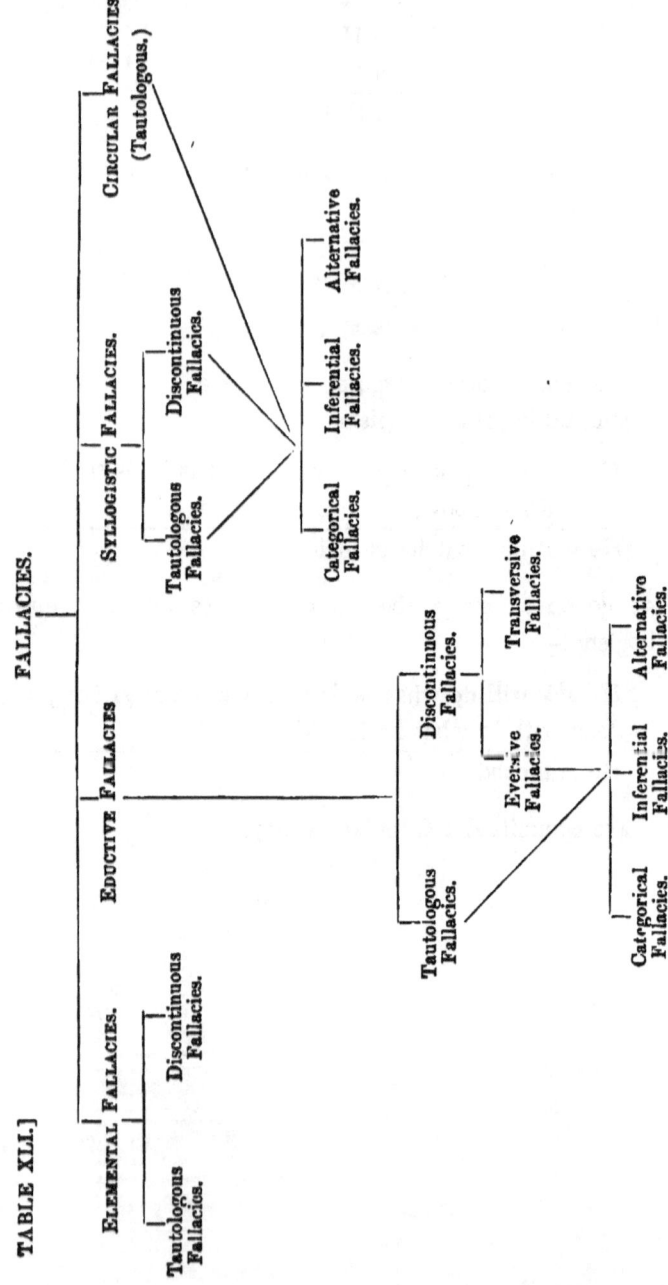

FALLACIES. 195

TABLE XLII.] **FALLACIES WITH CATEGORICAL PROPOSITIONS.**
(Eductive and Syllogistic.)

Eductive Fallacies.

- **Fallacies of Tautology.**
  e.g. R is Q;
  ∴ R is Q.

- **Fallacies of Discontinuity.**
  - *Fallacy of Four Terms.*
    e.g. M is N;
    ∴ Q is R.
  - *Fallacy of Three Terms.*
    e.g. (a) All R is Q;
    ∴ Some S is Q;
    Some S is not-P;
    ∴ Some P is S.
    (b) Some R is Q;
    ∴ All R is Q
    (or ∴ All Q is R).

  No Conclusion inferrible.
  (Four distinct Terms in Premisses.)

  - *Four Term-names.*
    e.g. All Q is N;
    All R is T.
  - *Undistributed Middle (a particular case of Ambiguous Middle).*
    e.g. Some N is Q;
    Some N is R.
  - *Term-name of Middle Term ambiguous.*
    e.g. All angels are good spirits;
    All angels are worth ten shillings;
    Some good spirits are worth ten shillings

Syllogistic Fallacies.

- **Fallacies of Tautology.**
  (a) In Premisses.
  e.g. All R is Q;
  Some R is Q.
  (b) In Conclusion.
  e.g. All R is N;
  All N is Q;
  All R is N
  (or, Some N is R, etc.).

- **Fallacies of Discontinuity.**

  Some Conclusion inferrible, but not the one inferred. (More than three distinct Terms in Premisses + Conclusion.)

  - *Illicit Major.*
    e.g. All N is Q;
    Some R is not N;
    Some R is not-Q.
  - *Illicit Minor.*
    e.g. No Q is N;
    Some R is N;
    No R is Q.
  - *Negative Conclusion from Affirmative Premisses.*
    e.g. All N is Q;
    All R is N;
    No R is Q.
  - *Affirmative Conclusion with a Negative Premiss.*
    e.g. No N is Q;
    All R is N;
    All R is Q.
    Reduces to
    All N is not-Q;
    All R is N;
    All R is Q.

SUPPLEMENT.

SECTION XXVII.

RECAPITULATORY.

WHAT I wish to do in this concluding Section is to recapitulate some points which seem to me specially important, and to repair as far as I can any omission or want of clearness in previous Sections of which I have become aware.

In what precedes I have, I hope, been working towards a unification and generalization of Logic. On my view, there can be no chasm between "Formal" and "Material" Logic. All Logic is (more or less strictly) Formal, and Material Logic almost a contradiction in terms. Logic may be defined as The Science of Propositions—a definition which is obviously all-embracing as far as knowledge is concerned, and which will be found to apply with great appropriateness to the actual treatment of logicians who set out by defining Logic as a psychological or semi-psychological science—as the Science of Reasoning, of The Laws of Thought, or of Inference. It may be observed that the "mental processes" of Reasoning and Inference are not expressly treated by all Psychologists. And it is evident that however Logic may be defined, our only means of arriving at truth or exhibiting inconsistency is by a consideration of *propositions* and their relations to one another. This being so, the question which first arises is, What do propositions mean? And as a preliminary to answering this question, it is necessary to inquire into the character of *Terms*, which are the constituents of categorical propositions. Terms have a reference beyond themselves, and the reference is, I think, always to some thing or things which, besides being *existent* in some fashion (as seems to be implied in the word *thing*), have characteristics. In every term, therefore, two *momenta* may be distinguished—(1) Denomination, corresponding to the *existence* of the thing named; (2) Determination, corresponding to the *character* of the thing named. Whether in any case Denomination or Determination is most prominent depends upon two considerations—(i.) the character of the term itself, considered as a *name*, and not with reference to its place in the proposition in which it occurs; and (ii.) the position which it has as actually used in predication. Taking (i.), it appears that names may be primarily divided into (*a*) Substantival Names; (*b*) Attribute Names; and (*c*) Adjectival names—(*a*) being Names of Subjects of Attributes, (*b*) Names of Attributes, and (*c*) Names which are added (adjected) to (*a*) or (*b*), and help to characterize further the Subjects of Attributes, or Attributes, to which (*a*) and (*b*) apply. This being their essential character and office, it is clear that Determination is naturally prominent in adjectives. And since they are never used by themselves as Subjects of propositions, but only as Predicates, this prominence is never obscured. At least this is my view, for I hold that it is inevitably Denomination which is prominent in the Subject of a categorical proposition, while, as inevitably, Determination is felt to be the most important aspect in the Predicate of a proposition. And the use which we make of adjectives in modern English justifies this view (cf. *ante*, pp. 13, 128); for where we have an adjective for Predicate, qualifying a *plural* Subject, the Predicate does *not* take the sign of the plural, whereas a Substantive Term in the same position *does*. It may be said that this is no proof, for that we *never* inflect adjectives. This latter fact, however, seems to me in itself a very strong proof that characterization, involving, of course, prominence of Determination, has been felt to be the essential function of adjectives. In German this feeling has so far operated, that an adjective occurring by itself as Predicate is not inflected.

In Substantive Names, Denomination appears naturally prominent; in Attribute Names, Determination.

But in predication, if an Attribute Name is Subject, this prominence becomes relatively subordinate; and if a Substantive Name is Predicate, we inevitably become most interested in its Determination. For the Denomination of what we are talking about is settled by the Subject; and what we say of it must in affirmative propositions *have* precisely the same Denomination (though it may not be prominent), and in negative propositions a totally different Denomination. This Denomination which the Predicate *has*, may be *made* prominent; and this is done to some extent when the Predicate is inflected, so that a plural Subject has a plural Predicate (cf. *ante*, pp. 128, 129). It is done more decidedly when the Predicate is quantified. And the Determination, which the Subject always *has*, is *made prominent* when in conversion it becomes Predicate, and drops any sign of quantity which it had as Subject.

Any categorical proposition may, I think, be analysed into three parts—namely, two Terms (Subject and Predicate) and the Copula. I take the copula to be always *is* or *is not*, *are* or *are not*. The whole of the rest of the proposition goes to make up the Subject and the Predicate. This use of *Term* necessitates a distinction between Term and Term-name (cf. *ante*, pp. 3–5, and pp. 161, 162), and the admission of *all* categorical propositions, and not merely the class propositions, A—E—I—O, to logical treatment.

What a categorical proposition imports is complete Identity, or complete Difference (Non-Identity) of Denomination in Diversity of Determination — that is, what the Predicate applies to in affirmative propositions is the same thing as what the Subject applies to, but the Attributes by which the Subject refers to it are diverse from the Attributes by which the Predicate refers to it. The affirmative copula imports identity, and identity can only be identity of *existence*. This identity can only be expressed or apprehended in diversity— that is, in difference of attributes or characteristics. The pencil with which I am now writing may be the identical pencil with which I wrote yesterday, but if I could refer to it for only one indivisible moment, it would be absurd to talk of its *identity*. I am the identical person I was twenty years ago, or last week. If I say, That pretty child is my cousin's heir, S and P apply to one identical thing, a being having continued existence throughout some appreciable extent of time; but it is referred to by diverse attributes, by Subject and Predicate respectively; if it were not, there could be no statement or apprehension of identity. Identity (which is quantitive) can only be apprehended or expressed as an *identity in qualitive diversity* (cf. *ante,* pp. 46–49, 51, 52, 127, 128 (note 1), 129, 176, 177). And exact similarity (which is qualitive) can only be apprehended as *qualitive oneness in a quantitive manifold*—*i.e.* in a variety of manifestations, whether of *the same identical one* or of *different identicals* (cf. *ante,* p. 46, *note*).

In negative categorical propositions what is asserted is, that the Denomination of the Subject is *absolutely different from (non-identical with)* the Denomination of the Predicate—the identity of the things denoted by the Subject is *different from* the identity of the things denoted by the Predicate. In other words, the things to which the Subject applies are *not* the things to which the Predicate applies. And the *determination* of Subject and Predicate is diverse—otherwise all negative propositions would be of the form, *A is-not A.*

I have in Section VI. tried to test and illustrate the above account of the import of categoricals by applying it to various propositions; but as I have reason to think that the illustrations which I gave in that Section were insufficient, I will add a few more here.

In

Some violets are white,

certain objects are indicated by the Subject (Some violets), and the Denomination (and hence the application) of the term *Some violets* is identical with that of the Predicate. For if it is not, the application of the Predicate is *different from* that of the Subject, and we are declaring *Some violets* to *be* something different from themselves. But while Denomination, and hence application, of Subject and Predicate are identical the Determination of the two terms is diverse. Certain objects having more or less continued existence and distinctive characteristics are referred to by the term, *Some violets*, and it is the very same objects that are referred to by the term *white*. The quantitiveness of the things referred to by the two terms, and hence the Denomination of those terms, is identical—the Denomination of the Predicate necessarily follows that of the Subject. But the *characteristics* indicated by *Some violets* are diverse from the characteristic indicated by *white*.

In

Kemeys is my cousin,

the Denomination (and hence the application) of *Kemeys* is identical with that of *my cousin*—only one existent being is referred to—but the Determination of *Kemeys* would not be the Determination of *my cousin*.

In

240 pennies are equal to £1,

the Subject (240 pennies) has the same Denomination, and hence the same application, as the Predicate (equal to £1). An object is indicated, and to that object the term *Equal to £1* applies, just as much as the term *240 pennies* applies. If not, *Equal to £1* applies to something different from *240 pennies*, and there is no positive connection between Subject and Predicate, for the *characteristics* signified by *240 pennies* are diverse from those signified by *equal to £1*.

This proposition may also be written

240 pennies = £1,   (1)
i.e. (Any 240 pennies) is (some equal to £1).

But the last two propositions differ from the first example given in this, that they are what I have called Dependent or Systemic Propositions (cf. *ante*, Section III. p. 20, and Section IX.), and from them, besides the eductions common to all categoricals, a large number of other eductions may be derived by any one who knows the systems to which in the different cases reference is made. *E.g.* from (1) it may be inferred that

$$£1 = 240 \text{ pennies}$$

(*i.e.* £1 is equal to 240 pennies)

(cf. *ante*, Section X.). But taking any proposition which has numbers for the terms, and = for the copula, what Indicator is to be given to the terms? *E.g.* does

$$2 + 2 = 4$$

mean

All $(2+2)$'s = all 4's?

And if so, are the terms to be taken collectively? Mr. Monck (*Introduction to Logic*, p. 19) says, "In Algebra the terms are always used collectively. . . . All armies = all soldiers, is a perfectly correct algebraic equation; but as no army is a soldier, it is inadmissible in Logic, except, indeed, as a singular proposition of the same kind as, Hyde was Clarendon."

If in the example

All armies = all soldiers,

we replace *armies* by (*e.g.*) $2 + 2$, and soldiers by 4, it appears that this is not a satisfactory account of mathematical propositions, whether the 2's and the 4 are understood as having the most abstract possible application—*i.e.* as applying to numbers merely—or as having a more concrete application—as applying to *some assigned unit*. And if we took *1, 2,* etc., *collectively,* to mean *all 1's, all 2's,* etc. (cf. *ante,* p. 85), we might have

$$1 + 1 + 1 + \text{etc.} = 1,$$
$$1 + 1 + 1 + \text{etc.} = 1 + 2 + 3 + \text{etc.},$$

and so on. For if we have taken *all* 1's, whether of an assigned unit or of abstract numbers, we have taken the whole sum and there is no way of increasing it; and it includes, of course, all groups composed of and analyzable into units. We must then, it would seem, quantify either with a distributive *all*, or with a Partial Term-indicator (This, These, Some, etc.). But

$$2 + 2 = 4$$

assuredly means more than

$$\text{This } 2 + 2 = \text{that } 4,$$

or than

$$\text{Some } (2 + 2)\text{'s} = \text{Some } 4\text{'s}.$$

It must therefore mean

$$\text{Any } 2 + 2 = \text{Any } 4.$$

And the numbers used must be understood in the most abstract sense (cf. *ante*, Section X. p. 86).

In the concrete example

$$\pounds 1 = 240 \text{ pennies},$$

we can also quantify with *all* (distributive) or *any*, because the *pounds* and the *pence* referred to are, *ex vi terminorum*, different objects.

But in, *e.g.*—

$$(24 \times 10) \text{ pence} = 240 \text{ pence}, \qquad (2)$$

we cannot do so, because a thing cannot be equal to *itself* (cf. *ante*, pp. 85, 86).

We must say that (2) means

$$\text{Any } (24 \times 10) \text{ pence} = \text{Some } 240 \text{ pence},$$

i.e. Any (24×10) pence is something equal to some 240 pence.

I have said in the Section on Quantification (p. 129) that all quantificated affirmative propositions are collective, but it appears to me now that that statement requires qualification. For a proposition of the form

$$(3) \text{ Any R is some Q},$$

which is quantificated, is by the very force of the S-indicator a Distributive Proposition. (3) is equivalent to

An R is a Q,

and this may have its import analysed in the same way as the Singular Proposition, Kemeys is my cousin, given on p. 100 (cf. also pp. 47, 48). The difference between these two propositions is, that (3) having a Subject determined only as *being an R*, has the force of an Universal (cf. *ante*, p. 61).

Substituting *different from* for *identical with*, the same analysis applies to the Universal Negative E (Any R is-not any Q; An R is-not a Q).

I think, however, that a plural affirmative categorical that is quantificated, may always be put in a form in which it may be understood as Collective; and I do not see how a quantificated Indefinite Particular or Indefinite Plurative Proposition (cf. Tables XXVII.–XXXI.) is to be taken otherwise than as Collective.

It is, I think, only the recognition of Existence and Character (Quantitiveness and Qualitiveness) in the Things to which Terms refer, and of Denomination and Determination of Terms (corresponding to these *momenta* in the Things), together with the possibility of making either aspect of the Term prominent, which enables us to frame and manipulate significant assertions. And it seems to me to be some statement concerning the possibility of significant assertion that is needed, in place of the unmeaning formula *A is A*, which is offered to us under the name of the Law of Identity (cf. *ante*, Section XXV.).

All Inferential Propositions may, as I think, be reduced, more or less naturally and more or less immediately, to Categoricals related as Inference and Inferend (cf. Sections XII., XIX., XX., and Tables XXXII., XXXIII., XXXVII.). And Alternatives are likewise reducible to Categoricals, either directly or through Inferentials (cf. Sections XIX., XX., and

Table XXXVII.). But it is obvious that the meanings of Inferentials and Alternatives are likely to be best and most naturally expressed in Inferentials and Alternatives respectively.

Unless *A is C or B* is an Eduction from *A is B or C*—and I think that it is one, and the only one absolutely formal (cf. pp. 121, 147, 148)—the Alternative got by Transversion from an Inferential states more than the Transvertend; while similarly in the Inferential got by Transversion from an Alternative, the Transverse states less than the Transvertend. To take an example—

$$\text{If A is B, A is-not not-B,} \quad (1)$$

transverts to

$$\text{A is-not not-B, or A is-not B,} \quad (2)$$

and the meaning of (2) would be explicitly stated in Hypothetical form only by giving both (1) and its Contrapositive, thus—

$$\begin{cases} \text{If A is B, A is-not not-B,} \\ \text{If A is not-B, A is-not B—} \end{cases}$$

just as, for instance, *S is P and P is S* would state more than *S is P*.

My treatment of Alternatives perhaps requires some explanation, possibly some apology also. The question whether alternatives are to be regarded as exclusive or unexclusive has been one of extreme difficulty to me. And the fact that the most distinguished names in Logic are about equally divided on this matter, and that neither side, as far as I know, seems to see any reason in the view of the other, and neither attempts to give any explanation of the divergence, makes one feel that, in the first place, there must be some reason on both sides, and that it is very desirable to get at it if possible; and, in the second place, that the reason, though sure to be there, is probably somewhat difficult to find. My own experience has been, that after having long believed in the exclusiveness of *or*, I became converted to the view that it is *unexclusive;* but eventually found that also unsatisfactory, and have now reached the opinion that Alternatives may have some element of unexclusiveness, but must also have *some element* of exclusiveness, that otherwise there is no true alternation; that so far as alternatives are absolutely unexclusive, our "alternation" is of the form A or A, which means neither more nor less than A simply. Where the alternatives are propositions, there must be *some difference of meaning* in the propositions or there is no alternation, and so far there is exclusiveness; but alternatives may be *true together*, and so far there is unexclusiveness. *E.g.* in

XY is a knave or XY is a fool,

there is the element of exclusiveness which seems to me indispensable—there is also an undoubted *possibility* of unexclusiveness (in the sense above assigned). Where the alternatives are (or appear to be) terms, there may be unexclusiveness of *denomination*, but there must be some exclusiveness of *determination*. *E.g.* in

Any voter is a householder or a ratepayer,

the denomination (and therefore the application) of *householders* and *ratepayers* is to some extent coincident; but in *determination* the two terms are exclusive—that is, they would be differently defined. Perhaps it may be said that all this is so obvious that it is superfluous to state it; but I do not remember to have seen it either expressed or implied, and it appears to me to provide some solution of what many have felt to be a serious difficulty.

My treatment of Categorical Syllogisms (Section XXI.) results entirely from the view which I take of the import and analysis of Categorical Propositions.

The Relations of Propositions with which Logic is preeminently concerned are relations of Inference. This may be inference from the *truth* of some propositions to the *truth* of others, as in Eductions, Syllogisms, and Hypothetical

Propositions. Or it may be inference from the truth of some propositions to the falsehood of others, or from the falsehood of some to the truth of others—as with Incompatible Propositions. Or from the falseness of some we may conclude to the falseness of others. *E.g.* from the falseness of an I proposition we may conclude to the falseness of the corresponding A, or from the denial of the Consequent of any Hypothetical to the denial of its Antecedent.

The validity of these inferences in particular instances, and of the Canons of the different kinds of inference is, in most cases, self-evident; and the infringement of any of the Canons involves breach of the Laws of Contradiction and Excluded Middle (which I have proposed, in Section XXV., to regard as the axioms of Consistency and Reciprocity).

What the Law of Identity conveys is, that since any name applies to something which is an identity in diversity, of that name, as Subject of a proposition, some Predicate other than itself may be asserted. It also involves, I think, that no term can be predicated of itself or denied of itself. What the Law of Excluded Middle conveys is, that if of any term, A, some other term, B, is denied, then of A, not-B is to be affirmed; and if of that term A, not-B is denied, then of A, B is to be affirmed. What the Law of Contradiction conveys is, that if of any term, A, some other term, B, is affirmed, then of that term A, B cannot be denied.

In an Induction there is a characteristic element which essentially differentiates it from all the other relations of propositions with which Logic deals, namely, an element of discovery. In an Induction the starting-point is perception or recognition of the Universal in the Particular. Of this there seem to be two aspects or stages. First, a perception of some connection between things (whether Subjects of Attributes or Attributes) in some particular case or cases. Second, an extension from this known case to unknown cases—a recognition that the particular connection involves a connection holding universally. In Mill's and Whewell's treatment of Induction, Mill lays most stress upon the second point, Whewell upon the first; and Mill is concerned chiefly with the connections of attributes in some given subject. The first stage is the sphere of Hypothesis; and here the business of Logic is to require the fulfilment of certain conditions on the part of any Hypothesis before it is regarded as admissible. These conditions seem to me to be two: (1) that the Hypothesis should be in harmony with accepted knowledge, (2) that it should explain and connect the facts to which it is applied. (1) involves an application of the Laws of Contradiction and Excluded Middle to the relation between the facts under consideration and other facts; (2) applies the same laws to the inter-relation of those facts themselves.

In the second stage the business of Logic is to *justify* the extension from the known to the unknown.

In Section XXIV. (cf. also pp. 137, 138, and Table XXXVI.) I have indicated what seem to me to be the assumptions, and the connections of propositions, required for such justification.

The way in which I should justify the *assumptions* which I propose in Section XXIV. is as follows. These assumptions seem to be necessarily involved in all inductions—inductions which we constantly make, and on the trustworthiness of which we unhesitatingly depend. If we accept the inductions, we must, in consistency, accept the principles which they involve. And if we do not accept the inductions, we are entangled in a web of hopeless inconsistencies.

I have referred (p. 174) to Analogy as explicable on the same principles as Induction. One further point I should like to notice, the case of Mathematical and Geometrical Induction. Here the principles suggested in Section XXIV. apply just as much as to the other species of Inductions, and the absolutely unquestioned certainty which we have in these cases, and the fact that we argue unhesitatingly from a single instance to the universal, seem explicable from the consideration that we here *see* at once the connection, which in other cases we *believe* on grounds very different from a perception of self-evident interdependence of attributes. When the equality of the interior angles of any one triangle to two right angles has been demonstrated to us, we infer without a moment's doubt that the same relation of equality may be asserted of the interior angles of *every* triangle, and this because we have *seen* that with the attributes signified by "the interior angles of a triangle" there is bound up the attribute of "being equal to two right angles." We *believe* that if a certain amount of arsenic has on some occasions produced death, it will always produce death, on the ground that the apparent likenesses are connected with unapparent likenesses; but we have not *seen* in this case that there is a self-evident interdependence between them. This is why, in the case of Mathematical Inductions, we do not need to use Mill's Inductive Methods (cf. *ante*, p. 137, *note* 2).

T. and T. Clark's Publications.

LOTZE'S MICROCOSMUS.

Just published, in Two Vols., 8vo (1450 pages), SECOND EDITION, *price 36s.,*

MICROCOSMUS:
Concerning Man and his relation to the World.
By HERMANN LOTZE.

Translated from the German
By ELIZABETH HAMILTON AND E. E. CONSTANCE JONES.

'The English public have now before them the greatest philosophic work produced in Germany by the generation just past. The translation comes at an opportune time, for the circumstances of English thought, just at the present moment, are peculiarly those with which Lotze attempted to deal when he wrote his "Microcosmus," a quarter of a century ago. . . . Few philosophic books of the century are so attractive both in style and matter.'—*Athenæum.*

'These are indeed two masterly volumes, vigorous in intellectual power, and translated with rare ability. . . . This work will doubtless find a place on the shelves of all the foremost thinkers and students of modern times.'—*Evangelical Magazine.*

'Lotze is the ablest, the most brilliant, and most renowned of the German philosophers of to-day. . . . He has rendered invaluable and splendid service to Christian thinkers, and has given them a work which cannot fail to equip them for the sturdiest intellectual conflicts and to ensure their victory.'—*Baptist Magazine.*

'The reputation of Lotze both as a scientist and a philosopher, no less than the merits of the work itself, will not fail to secure the attention of thoughtful readers.'—*Scotsman.*

'The translation of Lotze's Microcosmus is the most important of recent events in our philosophical literature. . . . The discussion is carried on on the basis of an almost encyclopædic knowledge, and with the profoundest and subtlest critical insight. We know of no other work containing so much of speculative suggestion, of keen criticism, and of sober judgment on these topics.'—*Andover Review.*

In Two Vols., 8vo, price 21s.,

NATURE AND THE BIBLE:
LECTURES ON THE MOSAIC HISTORY OF CREATION IN ITS RELATION TO NATURAL SCIENCE.

By Dr. FR. H. REUSCH.

REVISED AND CORRECTED BY THE AUTHOR.
TRANSLATED FROM THE FOURTH EDITION BY KATHLEEN LYTTELTON.

'Other champions much more competent and learned than myself might have been placed in the field; I will only name one of the most recent, Dr. Reusch, author of "Nature and the Bible."'—The Right Hon. W. E. GLADSTONE.

'The work, we need hardly say, is of profound and perennial interest, and it can scarcely be too highly commended as, in many respects, a very successful attempt to settle one of the most perplexing questions of the day. It is impossible to read it without obtaining larger views of theology, and more accurate opinions respecting its relations to science, and no one will rise from its perusal without feeling a deep sense of gratitude to its author.'—*Scottish Review.*

'This graceful and accurate translation of Dr. Reusch's well-known treatise on the identity of the doctrines of the Bible and the revelations of Nature is a valuable addition to English literature.'—*Whitehall Review.*

'We owe to Dr. Reusch, a Catholic theologian, one of the most valuable treatises on the relation of Religion and Natural Science that has appeared for many years. Its fine impartial tone, its absolute freedom from passion, its glow of sympathy with all sound science, and its liberality of religious views, are likely to surprise all readers who are unacquainted with the fact that, whatever may be the errors of the Romish Church, its more enlightened members are, as a rule, free from that idolatry of the letter of Scripture which is one of the most dangerous faults of ultra-Protestantism.'—*Literary World.*

T. and T. Clark's Publications.

Just published, in post 8vo, price 7s. 6d.,

THE PREACHERS OF SCOTLAND FROM THE SIXTH TO THE NINETEENTH CENTURY.

TWELFTH SERIES OF CUNNINGHAM LECTURES

By W. G. BLAIKIE, D.D.,

PROFESSOR OF APOLOGETICS AND PASTORAL THEOLOGY, THE NEW COLLEGE, EDINBURGH.

'Exceedingly interesting and well worth reading both for information and pleasure. . . . A better review of Scottish preaching from an evangelical standpoint could not be desired.'—*Scotsman.*

Just published, in crown 8vo, price 3s. 6d.,

SECOND EDITION, REVISED

THE THEOLOGY

AND

THEOLOGIANS OF SCOTLAND,

CHIEFLY OF THE

Seventeenth and Eighteenth Centuries.

Being one of the 'Cunningham Lectures.'

By JAMES WALKER, D.D., CARNWATH.

'These pages glow with fervent and eloquent rejoinder to the cheap scorn and scurrilous satire poured out upon evangelical theology as it has been developed north of the Tweed.'—*British Quarterly Review.*

'We do not wonder that in their delivery Dr. Walker's lectures excited great interest; we should have wondered far more if they had not done so.'—Mr. SPURGEON in *Sword and Trowel.*

In Two Vols., 8vo, price 21s.,

A SYSTEM OF BIBLICAL THEOLOGY.

BY THE LATE

W. LINDSAY ALEXANDER, D.D., LL.D.,

PRINCIPAL OF THE THEOLOGICAL HALL OF THE CONGREGATIONAL CHURCHES IN SCOTLAND.

'A work like this is of priceless advantage. It is the testimony of a powerful and accomplished mind to the supreme authority of the Scriptures, a lucid and orderly exhibition of their contents, and a vindication, at once logical, scholarly, and conclusive, of their absolute sufficiency and abiding truthfulness. It is a pleasure to read lectures so vigorous and comprehensive in their grasp, so subtle in their dialect, so reverent in spirit, and so severely chaste in their style. There are scores of men who would suffer no loss if for the next couple of years they read no other book than this. To master it thoroughly would be an incalculable gain.'—*Baptist Magazine.*

'This is probably the most interesting and scholarly system of theology on the lines of orthodoxy which has seen the light.'—*Literary World.*

'This has been characterised as probably the most valuable contribution which our country has made to theology during the present century, and we do not think this an exaggerated estimate.'—*Scottish Congregationalist.*

'Oh, that Scotland and Congregationalism had many worthies like Dr. Lindsay Alexander! . . . The ripe man, full of rich experience and heavenly knowledge, will prize each leaf, and give himself a glorious drilling as he masters chapter by chapter.'—Mr. SPURGEON in *The Sword and Trowel.*

T. and T. Clark's Publications.

WORKS BY PROFESSOR I. A. DORNER.

Just published, in demy 8vo, price 14s.,

SYSTEM OF CHRISTIAN ETHICS.

BY DR. I. A. DORNER,
PROFESSOR OF THEOLOGY, BERLIN.

EDITED BY DR. A. DORNER.

'TRANSLATED BY

PROFESSOR C. M. MEAD, D.D., AND REV. R. T. CUNNINGHAM, M.A.

'This noble Book is the crown of the Systematic Theology of the author. . . . It is a masterpiece. It is the fruit of a lifetime of profound investigation in the philosophical, biblical, and historical sources of theology. The system of Dorner is comprehensive, profound, evangelical, and catholic. It rises into the clear heaven of Christian thought above the strifes of Scholasticism, Rationalism, and Mysticism. It is, indeed, comprehensive of all that is valuable in these three types of human thought.'—Professor C. A. BRIGGS, D.D.

'There rested on his whole being a consecration such as is lent only by the nobility of a thorough sanctification of the inmost nature, and by the dignity of a matured wisdom.'—Professor WEISS.

'This is the last work we shall obtain from the able pen of the late Dr. Dorner, and it may be said that it fitly crowns the edifice of his manifold labours.'—*Spectator.*

In Four Volumes, 8vo, price £2, 2s.,

A SYSTEM OF CHRISTIAN DOCTRINE.

'In all investigations the author is fair, clear, and moderate; . . . he has shown that his work is one to be valued, for its real ability, as an important contribution to the literature of theology.'—*Scotsman.*

'Had it been the work of an entire lifetime, it would have been a monument of marvellous industry and rare scholarship. It is a tribute alike to the genius, the learning, and the untiring perseverance of its author.'—*Baptist Magazine.*

'The work has many and great excellences, and is really indispensable to all who would obtain a thorough acquaintance with the great problems of theology. It is a great benefit to English students that it should be made accessible to them in their own language, and in a form so elegant and convenient.'—*Literary Churchman.*

In Five Volumes, 8vo, price £2, 12s. 6d.,

HISTORY OF THE DEVELOPMENT OF THE DOCTRINE OF THE PERSON OF CHRIST.

'So great a mass of learning and thought so ably set forth has never before been presented to English readers, at least on this subject.'—*Journal of Sacred Literature.*

In crown 8vo, price 4s. 6d.,

THE BIBLE

AN OUTGROWTH OF THEOCRATIC LIFE.

BY D. W. SIMON,
PRINCIPAL OF THE CONGREGATIONAL COLLEGE, EDINBURGH.

'A more valuable and suggestive book has not recently come into our hands.'—*British Quarterly Review.*

'This book will well repay perusal. It contains a great deal of learning as well as ingenuity, and the style is clear.'—*Guardian.*

'A book of absorbing interest, and well worthy of study.'—*Methodist New Connexion Magazine.*

'Dr. Simon's little book is worthy of the most careful attention.'—*Baptist.*

'We have read the book with much appreciation, and heartily commend it to all interested in the subject with which it deals.'—*Scottish Congregationalist.*

T. and T. Clark's Publications.

HISTORY OF THE CHRISTIAN CHURCH.
By PHILIP SCHAFF, D.D., LL.D.
New Edition, Re-written and Enlarged.

APOSTOLIC CHRISTIANITY, A.D. 1–100. Two Vols. Ex. demy 8vo, price 21s.

ANTE-NICENE CHRISTIANITY, A.D. 100–325. Two Vols. Ex. demy 8vo, price 21s.

NICENE and POST-NICENE CHRISTIANITY, A.D. 325–600. Two Vols. Ex. demy 8vo, price 21s.

MEDIÆVAL CHRISTIANITY, A.D. 590–1073. Two Vols. Ex. demy 8vo, price 21s. (Completion of this Period, 1073–1517, in preparation.)

MODERN CHRISTIANITY. The German Reformation, A.D. 1517–1530. Two Vols. Ex. demy 8vo, price 21s.

'*Dr. Schaff's "History of the Christian Church" is the most valuable contribution to Ecclesiastical History that has ever been published in this country. When completed it will have no rival in point of comprehensiveness, and in presenting the results of the most advanced scholarship and the latest discoveries. Each division covers a separate and distinct epoch, and is complete in itself.*'

'No student, and indeed no critic, can with fairness overlook a work like the present, written with such evident candour, and, at the same time, with so thorough a knowledge of the sources of early Christian history.'—*Scotsman.*

'In no other work of its kind with which I am acquainted will students and general readers find so much to instruct and interest them.'—Rev. Prof. HITCHCOCK, D.D.

'A work of the freshest and most conscientious research.'—Dr. JOSEPH COOK, in *Boston Monday Lectures.*

'Dr. Schaff presents a connected history of all the great movements of thought and action in a pleasant and memorable style. His discrimination is keen, his courage undaunted, his candour transparent, and for general readers he has produced what we have no hesitation in pronouncing *the* History of the Church.'—*Freeman.*

Just published in ex. 8vo, Second Edition, price 9s.,

THE OLDEST CHURCH MANUAL
CALLED THE

Teaching of the Twelve Apostles.

The Didachè and Kindred Documents in the Original, with Translations and Discussions of Post-Apostolic Teaching, Baptism, Worship, and Discipline, and with Illustrations and Fac-Similes of the Jerusalem Manuscript.

By PHILIP SCHAFF, D.D., LL.D.,
PROFESSOR IN UNION THEOLOGICAL SEMINARY, NEW YORK.

'The best work on the Didachè which has yet appeared.'—*Churchman.*

'Dr. Schaff's "Oldest Church Manual" is by a long way the ablest, most complete, and in every way valuable edition of the recently-discovered "Teaching of the Apostles" which has been or is likely to be published. . . . Dr. Schaff's Prolegomena will henceforth be regarded as indispensable. . . . We have nothing but praise for this most scholarly and valuable edition of the Didachè. We ought to add that it is enriched by a striking portrait of Bryennios and many other useful illustrations.'—*Baptist Magazine.*

T. & T. CLARK,
38 GEORGE STREET, EDINBURGH.
LONDON: HAMILTON, ADAMS, & CO.

GRIMM'S LEXICON.

Just published, in demy 4to, price 36s.,

GREEK-ENGLISH LEXICON OF THE NEW TESTAMENT,

BEING

Grimm's Wilke's Clavis Novi Testamenti.

TRANSLATED, REVISED, AND ENLARGED

BY

JOSEPH HENRY THAYER, D.D.,

BUSSEY PROFESSOR OF NEW TESTAMENT CRITICISM AND INTERPRETATION IN THE DIVINITY SCHOOL OF HARVARD UNIVERSITY.

EXTRACT FROM PREFACE.

'TOWARDS the close of the year 1862, the "Arnoldische Buchhandlung" in Leipzig published the First Part of a Greek-Latin Lexicon of the New Testament, prepared, upon the basis of the "Clavis Novi Testamenti Philologica" of C. G. Wilke (second edition, 2 vols. 1851), by Professor C. L. WILIBALD GRIMM of Jena. In his Prospectus Professor Grimm announced it as his purpose not only (in accordance with the improvements in classical lexicography embodied in the Paris edition of Stephen's Thesaurus and in the fifth edition of Passow's Dictionary edited by Rost and his coadjutors) to exhibit the historical growth of a word's significations, and accordingly in selecting his vouchers for New Testament usage to show at what time and in what class of writers a given word became current, but also duly to notice the usage of the Septuagint and of the Old Testament Apocrypha, and especially to produce a Lexicon which should correspond to the present condition of textual criticism, of exegesis, and of biblical theology. He devoted more than seven years to his task. The successive Parts of his work received, as they appeared, the outspoken commendation of scholars diverging as widely in their views as Hupfeld and Hengstenberg; and since its completion in 1868 it has been generally acknowledged to be by far the best Lexicon of the New Testament extant.'

'I regard it as a work of the greatest importance. . . . It seems to me a work showing the most patient diligence, and the most carefully arranged collection of useful and helpful references.'—THE BISHOP OF GLOUCESTER AND BRISTOL.

'The use of Professor Grimm's book for years has convinced me that it is not only unquestionably the best among existing New Testament Lexicons, but that, apart from all comparisons, it is a work of the highest intrinsic merit, and one which is admirably adapted to initiate a learner into an acquaintance with the language of the New Testament. It ought to be regarded as one of the first and most necessary requisites for the study of the New Testament, and consequently for the study of theology in general.'—Professor EMIL SCHÜRER.

'This is indeed a noble volume, and satisfies in these days of advancing scholarship a very great want. It is certainly unequalled in its lexicography, and invaluable in its literary perfectness. . . . It should, will, must make for itself a place in the library of all those students who want to be thoroughly furnished for the work of understanding, expounding, and applying the Word of God.'—*Evangelical Magazine.*

'Undoubtedly the best of its kind. Beautifully printed and well translated, with some corrections and improvements of the original, it will be prized by students of the Christian Scriptures.'—*Athenæum.*

T. and T. Clark's Publications.

Just published, in demy 8vo, price 16s.,

HISTORY OF THE CHRISTIAN PHILOSOPHY OF RELIGION,
FROM THE REFORMATION TO KANT.

By BERNHARD PÜNJER.

TRANSLATED FROM THE GERMAN BY W. HASTIE, B.D.
WITH A PREFACE BY PROFESSOR FLINT, D.D., LL.D.

'The merits of Pünjer's history are not difficult to discover; on the contrary, they are of the kind which, as the French say, *sautent aux yeux*. The language is almost everywhere as plain and easy to apprehend as, considering the nature of the matter conveyed, it could be made. The style is simple, natural, and direct; the only sort of style appropriate to the subject. The amount of information imparted is most extensive, and strictly relevant. Nowhere else will a student get nearly so much knowledge as to what has been thought and written, within the area of Christendom, on the philosophy of religion. He must be an excessively learned man in that department who has nothing to learn from this book.'—*Extract from the Preface.*

'Pünjer's "History of the Philosophy of Religion" is fuller of information on its subject than any other book of the kind that I have either seen or heard of. The writing in it is, on the whole, clear, simple, and uninvolved. The Translation appears to me true to the German, and, at the same time, a piece of very satisfactory English. I should think the work would prove useful, or even indispensable, as well for clergymen as for professors and students.'—DR. HUTCHISON STIRLING.

'A book of wide and most detailed research, showing true philosophic grasp.'—Professor H. CALDERWOOD.

'We consider Dr. Pünjer's work the most valuable contribution to this subject which has yet appeared.'—*Church Bells.*

'Remarkable for the extent of ground covered, for systematic arrangement, lucidity of expression, and judicial impartiality.'—*London Quarterly Review.*

Just published, in Two Vols., in demy 8vo, price 21s.,

HANDBOOK OF BIBLICAL ARCHÆOLOGY.

By CARL FRIEDRICH KEIL,
DOCTOR AND PROFESSOR OF THEOLOGY.

Third Improved and Corrected Edition.

NOTE.—This third edition is virtually a new book, for the learned Author has made large additions and corrections, bringing it up to the present state of knowledge.

'This work is the standard scientific treatise on Biblical Archæology. It is a very mine of learning.'—*John Bull.*

'No mere dreary mass of details, but a very luminous, philosophical, and suggestive treatise. Many chapters are not simply invaluable to the student, but have also very direct homiletic usefulness.'—*Literary World.*

'A mine of biblical information, out of which the diligent student may dig precious treasures.'—*The Rock.*

'Keil's Biblical Archæology will be a standard work from the day of its appearance.' —*Presbyterian Review.*

Just published, in demy 8vo, price 10s. 6d.,

THE FORM OF THE CHRISTIAN TEMPLE.
Being a Treatise on the Constitution of the New Testament Church.

By THOMAS WITHEROW, D.D., LL.D.,
PROFESSOR OF CHURCH HISTORY IN MAGEE COLLEGE, LONDONDERRY.

'We welcome the appearance of another work from the scholarly pen of Dr. Witherow. . . . No such able discussion of the constitution of the New Testament Church has appeared for a long time.'—*The Witness.*

T. and T. Clark's Publications.

In Two Vols., demy 8vo.—Vol. I. now ready, price 10s. 6d.,

A NEW COMMENTARY
ON
THE BOOK OF GENESIS.
BY PROFESSOR FRANZ DELITZSCH, D.D.

MESSRS. CLARK have pleasure in intimating, that by special arrangement with the author they are publishing a translation of the Fifth Edition, thoroughly revised, and in large part re-written, of this standard Commentary. The learned author, who has for a generation been one of the foremost biblical scholars of Germany, and who is revered alike for his learning and his piety, has here stated with evident care his latest and most matured opinions.

'Thirty-five years have elapsed since Prof. Delitzsch's Commentary on Genesis first appeared; fifteen years since the fourth edition was published in 1872. Ever in the van of historical and philological research, the venerable author now comes forward with another fresh edition in which he incorporates what fifteen years have achieved for illustration and criticism of the text of Genesis. . . . We congratulate Prof. Delitzsch on this new edition, and trust that it may appear before long in an English dress. By it, not less than by his other commentaries, he has earned the gratitude of every lover of biblical science, and we shall be surprised if, in the future, many do not acknowledge that they have found in it a welcome help and guide.'—Professor S. R. DRIVER, in *The Academy.*

Just published, in post 8vo, price 9s.,

THE TEXT OF JEREMIAH:
OR,
A Critical Investigation of the Greek and Hebrew, with the Variations in the LXX. Retranslated into the Original and Explained.
BY PROFESSOR G. C. WORKMAN, M.A.,
VICTORIA UNIVERSITY, COBURG, CANADA.
WITH AN INTRODUCTION BY PROFESSOR F. DELITZSCH, D.D.

Besides discussing the relation between the texts, this book solves the difficult problem of the variations, and reveals important matter for the history, the interpretations, the correction, and the reconstruction of the present Massoretic text.

'A work of valuable and lasting service.'—Professor DELITZSCH.

Just published, in demy 8vo, price 7s. 6d.,

THE BOOK OF PSALMS.
The Structural Connection of the Book of Psalms both in single Psalms and in the Psalter as an organic whole.
BY JOHN FORBES, D.D.,
PROFESSOR OF ORIENTAL LANGUAGES, ABERDEEN.

'One cannot but admire the keenness of insight and deftness of handling with which thought is balanced against thought, line against line, stanza against stanza, poem against poem. Only long familiarity and loving research could have given such skill and ease of movement. . . . A more suggestive, able, and original biblical monograph has not appeared recently, the contents and purport of which commend themselves more powerfully to believers in the Christian revelation and the inspiration of the Scriptures.'—*British and Foreign Evangelical Review.*

T. and T. Clark's Publications.

Just published, in demy 8vo, price 10s. 6d.,

THE JEWISH
AND
THE CHRISTIAN MESSIAH.
A STUDY IN THE EARLIEST HISTORY OF CHRISTIANITY.

By VINCENT HENRY STANTON, M.A.,

FELLOW, TUTOR, AND DIVINITY LECTURER OF TRINITY COLLEGE, CAMBRIDGE;
LATE HULSEAN LECTURER.

'Mr. Stanton's book answers a real want, and will be indispensable to students of the origin of Christianity. We hope that Mr. Stanton will be able to continue his labours in that most obscure and most important period, of his competency to deal with which he has given such good proof in this book.'—*Guardian.*

'We welcome this book as a valuable addition to the literature of a most important subject. . . . The book is remarkable for the clearness of its style. Mr. Stanton is never obscure from beginning to end, and we think that no reader of average attainments will be able to put the book down without having learnt much from his lucid and scholarly exposition.'—*Ecclesiastical Gazette.*

Now ready, Second Division, in Three Vols., 8vo, price 10s. 6d. each,

HISTORY OF THE JEWISH PEOPLE IN THE TIME OF OUR LORD.

By Dr. EMIL SCHÜRER,
PROFESSOR OF THEOLOGY IN THE UNIVERSITY OF GIESSEN.

TRANSLATED FROM THE SECOND EDITION (REVISED THROUGHOUT, AND GREATLY ENLARGED) OF '*HISTORY OF THE NEW TESTAMENT TIME.*'

The First Division, which will probably be in a single volume, is undergoing revision by the Author. (The Second Division is complete in itself.)

'Under Professor Schürer's guidance, we are enabled to a large extent to construct a social and political framework for the Gospel History, and to set it in such a light as to see new evidences of the truthfulness of that history and of its contemporaneousness. . . . The length of our notice shows our estimate of the value of his work.'—*English Churchman.*

'We gladly welcome the publication of this most valuable work.'—*Dublin Review.*

'Most heartily do we commend this work as an invaluable aid in the intelligent study of the New Testament.'—*Nonconformist.*

'As a handbook for the study of the New Testament, the work is invaluable and unique.'—*British Quarterly Review.*

Just published, in demy 8vo, price 10s. 6d.,

AN EXPLANATORY COMMENTARY ON ESTHER.

With Four Appendices,
CONSISTING OF

THE SECOND TARGUM TRANSLATED FROM THE ARAMAIC WITH NOTES, MITHRA, THE WINGED BULLS OF PERSEPOLIS, AND ZOROASTER.

By Professor PAULUS CASSEL, D.D., BERLIN.

'A specially remarkable exposition, which will secure for itself a commanding position in Biblical literature. It has great charms from a literary and historical point of view.'—*Sword and Trowel.*

'A perfect mine of information.'—*Record.*

'It is manifestly the ready expression of a full and richly stored mind, dispensing the treasures accumulated by years of labour and research. . . . No one whose fortune it is to secure this commentary will rise from its study without a new and lively realization of the life, trials, and triumphs of Esther and Mordecai.'—*Ecclesiastical Gazette.*

www.ingramcontent.com/pod-product-compliance
Lightning Source LLC
Chambersburg PA
CBHW020811230426
43666CB00007B/961